D1733476

# THE HOUSE OF LORDS

# The House of Lords
## *Its Parliamentary and Judicial Roles*

Edited by

PAUL CARMICHAEL

and

BRICE DICKSON

·HART·
PUBLISHING

OXFORD
1999

Hart Publishing
Oxford
UK

Distributed in the United States by
International Specialized Book Services, Inc.
5804 N.E. Hassalo St., Portland
Oregon 97213-3644 USA

Distributed in Australia and New Zealand by
Federation Press Pty Ltd
PO Box 45, Annandale
NSW 203, Australia

Distributed in the Netherlands, Belgium and Luxembourg by
Intersentia, Churchillaan 108
B2900 Schoten, Antwerpen
Belgium

Hart Publishing is a specialist legal publisher based in Oxford, England.
To order further copies of this book or to request a list of other
publications please write to:

Hart Publishing, 19 Whitehouse Road, Oxford, OX1 4PA
Telephone: +44 (0)1865 434459 or Fax: +44 (0)1865 794882
e-mail: hartpub@janep.demon.co.uk

British Library Cataloguing in Publication Data
Data Available
ISBN 1 84113–020–6

Typeset in 10pt Sabon
by Hope Services (Abingdon) Ltd.
Printed in Great Britain on acid-free paper
by Biddles Ltd, Guildford and King's Lynn.

# *Contents*

# List of Tables

# List of Figures

# Notes on Contributors

Andrew Baker: Research Assistant in Public Policy, University of Ulster

Nicholas Baldwin: Director, Wroxton College, Oxford (Fairleigh Dickinson University)

Sir Louis Blom-Cooper Q.C.: Retired Deputy High Court Judge

Anthony Bradney: Senior Lecturer in Law, University of Leicester

Rodney Brazier: Professor of Law, University of Manchester

Paul Carmichael: Senior Lecturer in Public Administration, University of Ulster

Brice Dickson: Professor of Law, University of Ulster

Gavin Drewry: Professor of Social Policy, Royal Holloway, University of London

Barry Fitzpatrick: Jean Monnet Professor of European Law, University of Ulster

Simon Lee: Rector and Chief Executive, Liverpool Hope University College

Patricia Leopold: Senior Lecturer in Law, University of Reading

Patricia Maxwell: Lecturer in Law, University of Ulster

Kenny Mullan: Senior Lecturer in Law, University of Ulster

Michael Rush: Professor of Politics, University of Exeter

Robert Stevens: Master, Pembroke College, Oxford

PART ONE

# THE HOUSE AS A CHAMBER OF PARLIAMENT

# Introduction

PAUL CARMICHAEL

The House of Lords, first and foremost, is one of the two chambers of the United Kingdom's Parliament. In this capacity, although its powers are not as extensive as those of the House of Commons, it wields considerable legislative influence. Part One of this book is devoted to an examination of some of the issues arising in connection with that role. One special section of the House of Lords, comprising senior judges specifically appointed as peers for this purpose, constitutes the highest appeal court in the United Kingdom. This Appellate Committee, as it is called, forms the focus of inquiry in Part Two of the book.

The question is invariably posed, "why study the House of Lords at all?" Even in academia, the temptation to dismiss the House as largely irrelevant to the constitutional arrangements of the United Kingdom is great. After all, is it not an anachronistic institution, bereft of real power and mired in ceremony? How can it be worthy of serious scholarly investigation? In truth, of course, the House of Lords remains a key element within the complex array of institutions and processes which together make up the British Constitution. It would be misguided to dismiss its bearing on constitutional debate.

Moreover, given the current clamour for constitutional reform from across much of the political spectrum, a close examination of the role and work of the House of Lords is timeous. So tightly entwined is the intricate tapestry of Britain's constitution that changing the present arrangements would risk unravelling the threads, thereby raising other constitutional issues. Altering the *status quo* of the House of Lords would, for example, raise questions concerning: the role of the Westminster Parliament; relations generally between the country's executive and the legislature; the prospects for some form of electoral reform involving one or both parliamentary chambers; the devolution debate and the possibility of a second chamber reflecting a stronger regional dimension; the role of the Law Lords, and of the Lord Chancellor in particular, within the judiciary; and, given the importance of the hereditary principle in the Lords, the future of the Monarchy.

This book does not seek to offer a prescription for reform of the House of Lords. The range of contributors alone militates against that. Rather, it presents a diversity of viewpoints, thereby reflecting a wish to deepen and extend the analysis of the House's work which has so far been conducted. Our enterprise can best serve the unfolding debate by providing objective and reasoned argument based on carefully marshalled evidence. Although it is probably forlorn to expect that political expediency will defer to rational argument, we feel that, irrespective of the complexion of the government and the steps they propose to take, a bedrock of established facts and cogent reasoning is essential if wisdom is to prevail in this context. In many instances, the cases both for and against change carry an equal conviction, being argued with clarity and sincerity. Hence, to advocate no change is, in effect, to be far from neutral since it is a conscious statement about the merits of the *status quo*. Equally, "doing something" can take many forms.

The substantive chapters in Part One of the book begin with Michael Rush (Chapter 1) who provides an invaluable review of the historical and political background which needs to inform the current reform debate. Recalling the crisis of 1911, the resolution of which was supposed to involve the establishment of a second chamber constituted on a popular basis, Rush points out that there has been more modest reform: to quote Bernard Crick, a case of "nibbling at the ermine". For all that, Rush demonstrates that the House of Lords is a very active body and that much of what it does it does well. He singles out the Lords' Select Committees for special praise. Any assessment of proposals for change, of which there is currently no shortage, will need to be conducted alongside this helpful analysis of the House's present role.

Any review will also need to take account of the material presented here in Chapter 2 by Nicholas Baldwin, who examines in some detail the membership and work of the House of Lords, particularly from 1950 to 1998. As he reports, the Lords is an overwhelmingly male chamber, the composition of which, despite the introduction of Law Lords in 1876 and Life Peers in 1958, remains largely hereditary, and with a large bloc of Conservatives (though by no means providing a guaranteed majority for a Conservative government). Baldwin finds that there is some variance between potential and actual attendance. Almost a third of the members do not attend at all, whilst another third attend for fewer than forty-seven days. Whilst some of the functions discharged by the Lords are now "relics of the past", the Bryce Conference Report of 1918 still provides the clearest outline of what can be regarded as appropriate for a second chamber: examination and revision of bills from the first chamber, initiation of essentially uncontroversial bills, the delaying (but not the vetoing) of controversial bills and the provision of a forum for full and free discussion by an assembly of experts unimpeded by party discipline. Baldwin believes that the House of Lords has demonstrated "an inherent evolutionary adaptability", which alone is a measure of the importance that ought to be ascribed to it. However, profound though they may be, the changes in reality have not affected the outside perception of the body. The most visible manifestation of this change has been the willingness of peers to inflict defeat and embarrassment on governments. It was, of course, challenges to the will of the elected chamber which led to the Parliament Act of 1911. But, whilst the preamble to the 1911 Act envisaged an eventual shift in power to an elected chamber, this has not been forthcoming. Indeed, in the best traditions of the British constitution, subsequent legislation—the Parliament Act 1949 and the Life Peerages Act 1958—has been largely evolutionary in manner, though the Lords have acquired a "degree of professionalism previously unfamiliar to the House, an evolution" reflected in rising average attendance figures and a longer average working day. Baldwin concludes that the present arrangements of the House of Lords are its strength and that, were it not to exist, a body of comparable "purpose and utility" would be sought.

In Chapter 3, Rodney Brazier takes the reform debate a step further by considering the "paradoxes and plans" of the proposals for the future of the House of Lords. He notes that, since the Parliament Act 1911, there have been various additional proposals for change largely advanced by opposition parties which want to challenge and delay the government of the day but which then about-turn once in government themselves. For Brazier, the central critique of the Lords is that it is dominated by hereditary and mainly Conservative Peers. Yet, paradoxically, as complaints over this aspect of the Lords' complexion have gathered voice, he discerns that the introduction of Life Peers has heralded a reinvigoration of the institution by the infusion of "new blood", which has produced a strikingly greater even-handedness. Hence, in line with Baldwin's view, Brazier remarks that, whilst no-one starting from scratch would devise such an arrangement, the House of Lords "has become the only counterweight in the British constitution to elective dictatorship". The most radical proposals for change have emanated from the Liberal Democrats as part of their federal agenda. Following its 1997 General Election Manifesto, the Labour Party has signalled a two-stage reform process involving the removal of the voting rights of hereditary peers before consultation on a replacement and elected chamber. Brazier contends that since there might never be a politically appropriate time for a new chamber, the risk is that what emerges is an anaemic body in which, more than likely, prime ministerial patronage would be even greater than it is now. Instead, Brazier advocates incremental reform which would avoid an elected chamber, but use the party strengths in the Commons combined with share of the popular vote as a determinant of the composition of the Lords. In striving for a consensus, Brazier suggests that his proposals, though timid, would be more likely to succeed. He suggests that the aim should be to include more women, ethnic minorities, young people and the voice of the regions and nations of the United Kingdom.

The importance of understanding the comparative dimension to the reform debate is the rationale for Chapter 4, by Paul Carmichael and Andrew Baker. Simply, an awareness of the arrangements in other countries, with all their attendant advantages and disadvantages, can only yield important additional evidence with which to appraise the arguments for and against change at home. Essentially, if the case for bicameralism is virtually universally accepted within the United Kingdom, the form it should take poses more difficulties.

In Chapter 5, Patricia Leopold analyses a relatively neglected issue which bridges the gap between the realm of Parliamentary matters and that of legal concerns, *viz.* when should the House of Lords refrain from discussing an issue because it is currently pending before the courts, i.e. *sub judice*? She shows how the House's attitude to this question has shifted over time, culminating in a reform in 1995 which may leave the Lords in a better position than the Commons but still in a worse position than the media. Clearly, this is an issue which goes to the heart of democracy and which is likely to attract further attention if applications for judicial review continue to be made in respect of ministerial actions and decisions. Patricia Leopold's explanation of current law and practice will be a basic reference point for future commentaries.

# 1

# The House of Lords: The Political Context[1]

## MICHAEL RUSH

"Whereas it is expedient that provision should be made for regulating the relations between the two Houses of Parliament: And whereas it is intended to substitute for the House of Lords as it at present exists a Second Chamber constituted on a popular instead of hereditary basis, but such substitution cannot be immediately be brought into operation" (Preamble of the Parliament Act 1911).

### THE HOUSE OF LORDS AND THE CONSTITUTION: THE CRISIS OF 1911

The Parliament Act of 1911 was the culmination of the most serious constitutional crisis Britain had faced since at least 1832, when the Great Reform Act was passed. There has been no comparable constitutional upheaval since 1911.

To many of the politicians of the time the Reform Act of 1832 was the final settlement of the demand for electoral reform, but the Parliament Act of 1911, as its preamble ringingly declares, was intended to be the prelude to a more thoroughgoing reform of the House of Lords. It did not happen, but the 1911 Act marks the formal recognition of the constitutional superiority of the House of Commons over the House of Lords, although that superiority had long been proclaimed, especially through the primacy of the Commons over financial matters. It has also long been recognised that no government could be formed without securing the support of a majority of the members of the House of Commons and that, once secured, the government was dependent on retaining that confidence for its survival. This was massively reinforced by the Reform Act 1832, which, though it hardly made Britain a democratic society, placed the democratic principle firmly at the centre of the political system: elections became the normal means by which changes of government occurred.

Senior positions in the government, including that of Prime Minister, continued for some time to be held by members of the House of Lords, but increasingly the number of peers in the Cabinet declined, and no peer has held the office of

---

[1] An earlier version of this chapter was published as "The House of Lords: End it or Mend it?" in W. Wale (ed.), *Developments in Politics: An Annual Review* (Exeter, Causeway Press, 1994), v, at 21–38.

Prime Minister since Lord Salisbury retired in 1902, although the possibility of Lord Curzon becoming Prime Minister in 1923 and Lord Halifax in 1940 was not ruled out. By 1957, however, when Sir Anthony Eden was forced by ill-health to retire, there was no question of the Prime Minister coming from other than the House of Commons. Indeed, more recently the Labour Party has taken the view that no minister heading a government department should be in the Lords on the ground that the constitutional responsibility of ministers is to the Commons rather than the Lords, but this is not a view shared by the Conservatives. Lord Carrington served as Secretary of State for Defence from 1970 to 1973 and as Foreign Secretary from 1979 to 1982 and Lord Home as Foreign Secretary from 1960 to 1963 and 1970 to 1974, despite Labour protests.

What precipitated the crisis that led to the passage of the Parliament Act 1911? From time to time during the nineteenth century the House of Lords challenged the supremacy of the Commons, notably over the repeal of paper duties in 1861, over the Reform Bill of 1884, and over Home Rule for Ireland in 1893. Gladstone, who, as Chancellor of the Exchequer, had proposed the abolition of duties on paper, promptly included the same proposal in his Budget, which the Lords shrank from rejecting. In 1884 a compromise was reached by agreeing that the extension of the franchise should be offset in part by a major redistribution of seats, but on the rejection of Home Rule in 1893 the will of the House of Lords prevailed.

However, a more prolonged and systematic clash of wills between the Common and Lords was virtually inevitable with the election of a Liberal government in 1906. This was because the split in the Liberal Party over Home Rule in 1886 had resulted in the defection of a significant proportion of its less radical members, who as Liberal Unionists allied themselves with the Conservatives. The Liberal Party therefore became increasingly dominated by its radical wing, which favoured policies which were anathema to the Conservatives, especially many of those in the House of Lords.

With the election of the Liberals clashes could only be avoided by the government being willing to see its social legislation largely emasculated in the Lords or by the Upper House adopting a self-denying ordinance and passing legislation which most of its members bitterly opposed. Either was too much to expect and the House of Lords rejected a number of major bills, including the government's Education, Plural Voting, and Licensing Bills, and amended other legislation. All this paled before the rejection of the "People's Budget" of 1909, in which Lloyd George, the Chancellor of Exchequer, proposed a series of new taxes, including a land tax, to finance the government's social welfare legislation. All attempts at negotiating a settlement failed, and in January 1910 Asquith, the Prime Minister, called an election in which the Liberals lost their overall majority but continued in power with the support of the Irish Nationalists and the Labour Party. The House of Lords then passed the Budget, but the government was determined to curb the powers of the Upper House and introduced a Parliament Bill to abolish the Lords' veto. Negotiations with the opposition on the question of reform failed and a further election was held in December 1910. This produced little or no change in the party strengths in the Commons, but in the face of Asquith's advice to the King to create enough new Liberal peers to overwhelm the Conservative majority, the Lords gave way and allowed the Parliament Bill to pass.

After the Parliament Act the House of Lords could not reject any financial legislation passed by the Commons and could delay it for only a month. Other legislation could be delayed for up to two years, after which it could be passed without the assent of the Lords. To offset what amounted, potentially at least, to a significant increase in the power of the House of Commons, the maximum period between elections was reduced from seven to five years. What might have ensued after the passage of the Parliament Act, given the bitterness of the clashes between Lords and Commons and between the Conservative and Liberal Parties in particular, was a period of guerilla warfare between the two houses, but this did not happen and only three bills were subsequently passed under the terms of the 1911 Act. The first two were soon after the Act came into force: they were a Home Rule Bill in 1912 and a bill to disestablish the Church of Wales in 1913. Both became law in 1914, but the Home Rule Act was suspended on the outbreak of war in August 1914 and was overtaken by events after the end of the war, with the partition of Ireland in 1920. The third measure passed under the 1911 Act belongs to the next part of the story.

"NIBBLING AT THE ERMINE"

In spite of its declared intent, the Parliament Act of 1911 was not the first step towards the substantial reform of the House of Lords, nor to its abolition, nor to its replacement by a reconstituted second chamber. What has ensued can best be described by Bernard Crick's splendid phrase, "nibbling at the ermine", a process in which changes have taken place, but which cannot even be described as piecemeal reform.[2] The immediate reason for the failure to realise the intentions expressed in the preamble to the 1911 Act was, of course, the First World War, but in 1917 Lloyd George's wartime coalition government appointed a royal commission to draw up proposals for a reformed second chamber. The commission was chaired by Lord Bryce, an eminent academic lawyer and senior politician. The Bryce Commission[3] reported in 1918 and made detailed proposals on the functions, powers and composition of a reformed second chamber, but reform of the Lords did not have a high priority in the post-war reconstruction programme. However, it was assumed that reform would take place and there were debates in Parliament in 1922 and 1927 which gave general approval to the creation of an Upper House on lines similar to those proposed in the Bryce

[2] B. Crick, *The Reform of Parliament* (London, Weidenfeld & Nicolson, 1964).
[3] Bryce Commission, *Report of the Conference on the Reform of the Second Chamber* (London, HMSO, Cd. 9038, 1918).

Report, but the decline of the Liberals and rise of the Labour Party as the main opposition made the Conservatives wary of reforming the House of Lords. The Labour administrations of 1924 and 1929–31 were minority governments preoccupied with far more pressing matters, culminating in the collapse of the Labour government and the formation of a coalition government in 1931. Although there was talk in the 1930s of reforming Parliament, including the House of Lords, nothing further happened until after the Second World War and the election of the first majority Labour government in 1945.

There were suggestions that the Labour government might find itself in a situation similar to that which had confronted Asquith's Liberal government after the 1906 election. In both cases a radical, reforming party had come to power with a massive majority in the House of Commons, and in both cases the government feared that the Conservative Party would use its majority in the House of Lords to frustrate some of the more radical policies in the government's programme. In the period after 1906 these fears were fully justified. However, 1945 was different: Labour's real fear was less that of a full-scale repeat of the 1907–11 crisis and more that of the House of Lords being used as a means of delaying the introduction of some of its proposals, especially as the date of the next election drew closer.

In practice, the House of Lords adopted a basically conciliatory approach, accepting (on the advice of the Conservative Leader of the Opposition in the Lords, Lord Salisbury) the government's nationalisation and welfare state legislation on the ground that the Labour Party had secured a clear mandate for these proposals at the 1945 election. Even so, the Labour government introduced a Parliament Bill in 1947 to reduce the Lords' delaying power from two years to one. This was partly a precaution with the approach of the next general election, due in 1950 at the latest, and partly because of suspicions that the House of Lords would in particular delay the legislation nationalising the iron and steel industry. In the event, the Upper House did not oppose the second reading of the iron and steel bill, but the government agreed to delay implementation until after the election.

Meanwhile, the introduction of a new Parliament Bill led to inter-party talks, which, though they achieved widespread agreement on the need for reform of the Lords and the role it should play, failed to reach agreement over the powers it should have. The Parliament Bill was therefore opposed by the Conservative Opposition and by the House of Lords, eventually becoming the third bill to be passed under the terms of the Parliament Act 1911. However, only one piece of legislation, the War Crimes Act 1991, has been passed against the will of the Lords by invoking the Parliament Acts of 1911 and 1949.

The return of the Conservative Party to power in 1951 inevitably put further changes in the House of Lords low on the political agenda, but the unwillingness of a growing number of individuals, especially in the Labour Party, to accept hereditary peerages brought the Upper House back up the agenda. There was a particular problem of maintaining a credible Labour opposition in the Lords, all the more so after a further Conservative victory in 1955. More inter-party talks ensued, but without agreement, and Harold Macmillan's Conservative government acted unilaterally by introducing and securing the passage of the Life Peerages Act 1958. Life peerages had existed since 1875, but only for Lords of Appeal in Ordinary, who are principally concerned with fulfilling the Lords' judicial function as the highest court of appeal. The 1958 Act not only assisted the Labour Party by meeting its objections to hereditary peerages, but enabled more individuals with no partisan attachments to become members of the House of Lords and contribute to its work, almost certainly to an extent that was not fully anticipated. This led to the growth of a much larger crossbench or non-partisan element in the House, which later developed a significant degree of co-operation and organisation. Moreover, the introduction of life peers eventually deprived the Conservative Party of its absolute majority in the Upper House, leaving it as the largest single party. The Life Peerages Act thus was to have a profound affect on the House of Lords.

The next important development came with the passing of the Peerages Act 1963 which enabled hereditary peers to give up or disclaim their peerages. The significance of this politically was that politicians who were heirs to peerages were no longer forced to pursue what could only be a much more limited career in the Lords. The 1963 Act came about as a result of the strenuous efforts of Anthony Wedgwood Benn, as he was then known, to dispose of his status as Viscount Stansgate and resume his career as an MP and leading member of the Labour Party. Incidentally, the importance of accident in politics and the impact that the House of Lords can have are nicely illustrated by the Peerages Act. It had originally been proposed that the Act should come into force at the time of the next general election, but an amendment passed in the House of Lords changed this to the date of the Royal Assent. At that stage no one could have known that the Prime Minister, Harold Macmillan, would be forced to resign through ill-health and that the way would be open for senior Conservatives, such as Viscount Hailsham and the Earl of Home, to compete for the succession. The result was, of course, that Lord Home, now translated into Sir Alec Douglas-Home, became Prime Minister in November 1963.

Labour's return to power in 1964 might have precipitated further serious conflict between the two Houses, but following its experience between 1945 and 1951 the Labour government largely regarded the House of Lords as an anachronistic nuisance, whose impact was limited after Labour was re-elected with a substantial majority in 1966. Thus, although the government suffered defeats in the Upper House, most of these were reversed by the Commons and the Lords did not resist. However, the government instituted all-party talks on the reform of the House of Lords which resulted in considerable agreement between the party front benches. Unfortunately, the waters were muddied by the Lords' rejection of a statutory instrument renewing sanctions against Southern Rhodesia, and the government broke off the talks, but went ahead with proposals for reform by publishing a White Paper, which became the basis of the Parliament (No. 2) Bill introduced in the Commons in 1968.

The bill proposed the phasing out of hereditary membership of the House of Lords and its eventual replacement by an entirely nominated membership. It also proposed the reduction of the Lords' delaying power to six months. Most importantly, the bill envisaged that a system of voting and non-voting peers would ensure that the government of the day was guaranteed the position of being the largest single party, but without an overall majority in the Upper House. Although the White Paper was approved by majorities in both Houses, and passed its second reading in the Commons, during the committee stage opposition to the bill intensified, such that there would be difficulty in securing its passage. The bill was eventually withdrawn, ostensibly to provide parliamentary time for the government's controversial proposals on industrial relations (which ironically suffered a similar fate).

Governments of both major parties suffered defeats in the House of Lords, but it was, not surprisingly, the Labour Party which found them more frustrating and bitterly resented the actions of the unelected, "Conservative-dominated" upper chamber. This was especially so during the period of mostly minority Labour government between 1974 and 1979 and, combined with Labour's shift to the left in the early 1970s, resulted in the Labour Party Conference adopting a resolution in favour of abolishing the House of Lords. The proposal for abolition, however, was not included in the 1979 Labour Manifesto, but a further shift to the left resulted in an unequivocal commitment to abolition in the 1983 Manifesto. After 1983, Labour abandoned abolition in favour of an elected second chamber, probably representing the regions of the UK, a proposal essentially similar to that adopted by the Liberal Democrats. Meanwhile, in 1978 the Conservative Party produced a report recommending an upper house two-thirds of whose members would be elected and one-third nominated, but it was not received with any enthusiasm by the party leadership. Thus, before the 1997 general election the situation was one in which two of the three major parties supported an elected second chamber and the other favoured the *status quo* by default.

## THE HOUSE OF LORDS AND CONTEMPORARY POLITICS

*The House of Lords and Contemporary Politics* was the title of a book by Peter Bromhead and was the first major post-war academic study of the Upper House.[4] It was published in 1958, the same year in which the Life Peerages Act was passed, though too late to take account of that important development. It was also at a time when Parliament received little academic attention. This situation changed in the 1960s, when the House of Commons became the subject

[4] P. A. Bromhead, *The House of Lords and Contemporary Politics* (London, Routledge & Kegan Paul, 1958).

of a great deal of attention, not least through the activities of the Study of Parliament Group, founded in 1964, and consisting of academics and professional staffs of the two Houses of Parliament. Institutional reform was much in vogue, but, in spite of the 1968 White Paper and the Parliament (No. 2) Bill, the House of Lords was largely neglected by the academic community. It should be noted, however, that Crick's seminal and influential work, *The Reform of Parliament*, had two out of eleven chapters devoted to the Lords.

In the wider world too, there had long been a tendency for the House of Lords to be regarded as of little importance, even before the constitutional crisis in the early part of the century. W. S. Gilbert, in one of the Savoy operas, wittily gave the Upper House short shrift: " . . . the House of Peers . . . did nothing in particular and did it very well"! Much earlier, in 1766, on the occasion of the Elder Pitt's elevation to the Lords as Earl of Chatham, the Earl of Chesterfield observed:

> "To withdraw, in the fulness of his power, and in the utmost gratification of his ambition, from the House of Commons . . . and go into that Hospital of Incurables, the House of Lords, is a measure so unaccountable, that nothing but proof positive could have made me believe it."[5]

In 1962, Tony Benn called the Upper House "the British Outer Mongolia for retired politicians".[6] It has also been cited as being evidence of life after death and as an institution which no one could possibly have designed or, even if they had, would not dare to propose. It has survived because of a lack of agreement between the major parties and a lack of political will has thus far prevented substantial reform, replacement or abolition. In fact, the House of Lords can be cited as a prime example of the ability of the British political system and its institutions to adapt to changing circumstances, rather than engage in major constitutional reform.

More recently, the House of Lords has received significant academic attention, first with Janet Morgan's *The House of Lords and the Labour Government, 1964–70*[7] and, more importantly, with the publication of two major studies of the Upper House—Donald Shell, *The House of Lords*,[8] first published in 1988, followed by a second edition in 1992, and Donald Shell and David Beamish (editors), *The House of Lords at Work: A Study of the 1988–89 Session*[9] in 1993. The rest of this chapter inevitably and properly draws heavily on these two most recent studies with the intention of giving the House of Lords a more detailed and accurate treatment than is often the case in standard texts, leading to a discussion of the prospects for its reform, replacement or abolition.

---

[5] R. Stewart (ed.) *A Dictionary of Political Quotations* (London, Europa Publications, 1984).

[6] A. and V. Palmer (eds.), *A Dictionary of Historical Quotations* (London, Paladin, 1985).

[7] J. Morgan, *The House of Lords and the Labour Government, 1964–70* (Oxford, Clarendon Press, 1975).

[8] D. Shell, *The House of Lords* (Hemel Hampstead, Harvester-Wheatsheaf, 1992).

[9] D. Shell and D. Beamish (eds.), *The House of Lords at Work: A Study of the 1988–89 Session* (Oxford, Clarendon Press, 1993).

However applicable Gilbert's quip may have been to the House of Lords in the nineteenth century or, indeed, as recently as the 1950s, the first half is no longer true: the House of Lords does a great deal in particular and, in the judgement of many, does it well.

*Table 1.1: The growth of activity in the House of Lords, 1950–96*[10]

| Activity | 1950 | 1959–60 | 1995–96 | % increase 1950–59 | % increase 1959–96 |
|---|---|---|---|---|---|
| Average daily attendance | 86 | 136 | 372 | 58 | 173 |
| Sitting days | 100 | 113 | 136 | 13 | 20 |
| Sitting hours | 294 | 450 | 935 | 53 | 108 |
| Length of sitting (hrs/mins) | 2.57 | 4.00 | 6.53 | 36 | 72 |
| Sittings after 10 p.m. | 1 | 1 | 60 | – | 5,900 |

The data shown in Table 1.1 could not illustrate more vividly the massive increase that has occurred in the activity of the House of Lords since the 1950s. In fact, it would not be inappropriate to describe the Upper House in the earliest period as moribund to the point that some observers expected it to atrophy. That it did not was due partly to the impact of life peers, partly to the growth in government legislation in the 1960s and later, and partly to the initiative of the House of Lords in carving out new roles for itself.

THE FUNCTIONS OF THE HOUSE OF LORDS

Table 1.2 suggests that Parliament performs a variety of functions which, with the important exception of the judicial function, are performed by both Houses of Parliament. Because the judicial function is a quite separate role it is excluded from further discussion, except to say that were the House of Lords substantially reformed or abolished there would be no difficulty in setting up a separate "Supreme Court" to perform that role. All other functions are carried out collectively or individually in both Houses. More significantly, from a constitutional and political point of view, the table suggests that the House of Commons is more important than the House of Lords (and in most cases considerably more important) in carrying out these functions. The legitimising function, for example, is clearly a matter primarily for the Commons since it is elections which essentially give governments their legitimacy in the eyes of the public. However, unless the provisions of the Parliament Acts 1911 and 1949 are invoked, all laws are legitimised by being passed by both Houses of Parliament. Similarly, although MPs, by virtue of their election, can claim greater legitimacy

[10] M. Wheeler-Booth, "The House of Lords", in J. A. G. Griffith and M Ryle, *Parliament: Functions, Practice, and Procedure* (London, Sweet & Maxwell, 1989); Shell, n. 8 above, at Table 4.2; and House of Lords Annual Accounts.

than peers to represent public opinion, this does not prevent members of the Lords making representations on behalf of individuals or various interest or pressure groups.[11]

*Table 1.2: The functions of Parliament*[12]

| Function | Performed by | | | |
| | House of Commons | House of Lords | Collectively | Individually |
| --- | --- | --- | --- | --- |
| Legitimising | X[a] | x | x | |
| Representative | X | x | x | x |
| Financial | X | x | x | |
| Redressing of grievances | X | x | x | x |
| Legislative | X | x | x | x |
| Recruitment of ministers | X | x | x | |
| Scrutinising and informing | X | x | x | x |
| Judicial | | X | x[b] | |

Notes:

a—X indicates the more important of the two houses in performing a particular function, x the less important;

b—Performed exclusively by Law Lords (up to twelve Lords of Appeal, the Lord Chancellor and any former Lord Chancellors).

The financial supremacy of the Commons is clearly enshrined in the Parliament Act 1911 and the House of Lords devotes only a limited amount of time to financial business and, as noted earlier, members of the Cabinet are now drawn overwhelmingly from the House of Commons. Thus, given the constitutional convention that ministers must normally be in Parliament, the House of Commons is now the principal source of ministerial recruitment: in 1997 Tony Blair's government included twenty-two peers out of a total of one hundred and twelve, of whom two were members of the Cabinet. However, the House of Lords' most important functions are in the legislative process itself and the scrutinising and informing roles which go beyond legislation.

In order to examine these two functions it is necessary to break them down into more detail (see Table 1.3). The first four of these functions were those suggested by the Bryce Commission as appropriate to a second chamber; the remaining four are largely functions in which the role of the House of Lords has become increasingly important since the late 1950s. Of the eight functions listed in Table 1.3, the most controversial is inevitably the delaying power, but, as noted earlier, the formal delaying power has been used on only four bills since its introduction in 1911, including the Parliament Act 1949 itself. However, the

[11] N. Baldwin, "The House of Lords" in M. Rush (ed.), *Parliament and Pressure Politics* (Oxford, Clarendon Press, 1992).

[12] M. Rush, *Parliament and the Public* (Longman, London, 1986), at Table 3.1.

delaying power could be said to spill over into the second function—the examination and revision of legislation passed by the Commons, since any amendments made by the Lords delay the passage of the Bill concerned because the changes have to be considered by the Commons. The latter can, of course, accept or reject Lords' amendments and, where the Commons persists in its view, the House of Lords usually gives way. Nonetheless, governments of all complexions resent some of the amendments made in the Upper House, although Labour's objections tend, naturally, to be more fundamental.

*Table 1.3: The functions of the House of Lords*

| | Performed | |
|---|---|---|
| *Function* | *in Chamber* | *in Committees* |
| 1. Causing sufficient delay to enable the government or the public or both, to reconsider legislation passed by the House of Commons | X | |
| 2. Examining and revising bills passed by the House of Commons | X | x |
| 3. Initiating non-controversial legislation | X | x |
| 4. Holding debates on major issues and policies unconstrained by strict party discipline | X | |
| 5. The consolidation of existing legislation | x | X |
| 6. Dealing with private legislation | x | X |
| 7. Dealing with delegated legislation | x | X |
| 8. Scrutinising policy and administration | x | X |

Notes: X—major role; x—lesser role.

### THE LEGISLATIVE FUNCTIONS OF THE HOUSE OF LORDS

The rarity with which the formal delaying power of the House of Lords is used should not be taken to mean it is unimportant, since the threat is always there and becomes potentially more important when a minority government holds office, since the ability of such a government to claim an electoral mandate for its policies can be called into question. During the last lengthy period of minority government—February–October 1974 and 1976–9, the Lords did not use their formal delaying power, but did heavily amend much of the Labour government's legislation, although usually giving way when the Commons rejected Lords' amendments. Of much greater significance is that, in 1990, the House of Lords rejected the War Crimes Bill on second reading, thereby rejecting the Bill outright. The Bill sought to make individuals who had allegedly committed war crimes during the Second World War and were now resident in Britain liable to prosecution, even though at the time of the alleged crimes they were outside British jurisdiction. The strongly-felt objections in the House of Lords to the Bill were mainly on the ground that it was retrospective legislation. The government, however, decided to invoke the Parliament Acts and reintroduced the Bill in 1991. It was again rejected by the Lords, but received the Royal Assent under the terms of the Parliament Acts. The willingness of the government to override the Lords' veto and the fact that it was a Conservative government may be an indication that future governments might be more willing to use the Parliament Acts. Certainly, in the wider context of government legislation generally and specific disagreements with the House of Lords, there are signs that Conservative governments have become increasingly impatient with the Upper House, but not to the point of proposing any change.

Although the Lords' delaying power is constitutionally important and looms large in the textbooks, there is little doubt that in the routine work of Parliament the major legislative function of the House of Lords is in the examination and revision of government legislation passed by the Commons or introduced in the Upper House before being passed to the Commons for consideration. The scale of this work is shown in Table 1.4:

*Table 1.4: The House of Lords and government legislation*[13]

A. *Government bills*[a] *passed by first by the House of Commons*

| Period[b] | Total no. bills | No. of bills amend by Lords | % of bills amended | No. of amends. by Lords | Av. no of of amends per bill |
|---|---|---|---|---|---|
| 1970–3 | 79 | 31 | 39 | 2,366 | 76 |
| 1974–7 | 68 | 49 | 72 | 1,859 | 38 |
| 1979–82 | 82 | 39 | 48 | 2,231 | 57 |
| 1983–6 | 69 | 43 | 62 | 4,137 | 96 |
| 1987–90 | 61 | 38 | 62 | 5,181 | 136 (79)[c] |

B. *Government bills*[d] *introduced in the House of Lords*

| Period[b] | Total no. bills | No. of bills amend by Lords | % of bills amended | No. of amends. by Lords | Av. no of of amends per bill |
|---|---|---|---|---|---|
| 1970–3 | 39 | 29 | 74 | 488 | 17 |
| 1974–7 | 58 | 38 | 65 | 1,594 | 42 |
| 1979–82 | 33 | 20 | 61 | 1,604 | 80 |
| 1983–6 | 42 | 28 | 67 | 1,373 | 49 |
| 1987–90 | 29 | 18 | 62 | 2,687 | 149 (58)[c] |

Notes:
a—excluding financial Bills.
b—covering *full* parliamentary sessions, since figures for Bills and amendments for sessions in which general elections take place are distorted and unrepresentative.
c—mean figure for 1970–90.
d—excluding Consolidation Bills.

[13] N. 8 above, at Tables 5.1 a) and (b).

The figures shown in the table provide a far more complete picture of the role of the House of Lords in the examination and revision of government legislation than those simply for the exercise of the formal delaying power. The figures for the percentage of Bills amended illustrate part of the complexity of the picture. It is clear from Section A of the table that by no means all government Bills passed by the Commons are subsequently amended in the Lords, although it is noticeable that the figure for the only period of Labour government shown in the table—1974–7—is significantly higher than for the periods of Conservative rule. Even in the latter case the figure has risen markedly compared with the earliest period. Furthermore, the sheer volume of Lords' amendments has increased dramatically by no less than 119 per cent. Apart from those Bills which are not amended at all in the Upper House, those that are amended are often subject to substantial change—on average no fewer than seventy-nine amendments per Bill, ranging from thirty-eight per Bill in 1974–7 to 136 in 1987–90.

To complete the picture, account also needs to be taken of the nature and source of these amendments. Many are drafting amendments, clarifying the wording of a clause, but others make changes of substance, some involving significant change, some of a more detailed but still important nature. In practice, the majority of Lords' amendments are accepted by the Commons, but, inevitably, this figure is higher during periods of Conservative rather than Labour government. This is mainly because a majority of amendments agreed in the House of Lords are tabled by the government anyway. However, as many as a quarter of these are introduced by the government as a result of pressure on the government, either during the Bill's passage in the Commons or from clearly identified representations made by pressure groups. No research has been done to establish why the government moved other amendments, the source of which cannot be identified, but they clearly reflect further consideration by the government and an indeterminate number of cases will be the result of representations from outside interests.

Apart from using the Upper House to amend its own legislation, the government is, of course, sometimes defeated in the House of Lords, in that amendments are passed that it strongly opposes. Indeed, 148 of the 155 defeats it suffered between 1979 and 1990—95 per cent of the total—were on legislation.[14] Moreover, the number of defeats shows no sign of abating, averaging twelve per year between 1993 and 1996, but increasing since the election of the Labour government in 1997. Not all defeats are reversed in the Commons—some because, on reflection, the government decides to accept the amendment, others because the government is unwilling to find the time available in the Commons to reconsider. The latter is particularly likely when the end of the parliamentary session or year is close.

In examining and revising legislation already passed by the Commons the House of Lords is subjecting that legislation to additional scrutiny. Moreover,

[14] N. 8 above.

that scrutiny has recently been enhanced by the use of public bill committees, which can take oral and written evidence, for the committee stage of some Bills. That these changes are made is, in itself, important, but so is the fact that the House of Lords is the means of making them: if the Upper House were not used, the changes would either not be made or would, under existing arrangements, have to be made in the House of Commons, which is already short of time in which to consider legislation.

A similar point can be made in respect of Bills introduced first in the House of Lords, a high proportion of which are subject to amendment in the Upper House, but the average number of amendments per Bill is normally lower than for Bills from the Commons, as section B of Table 1.4 shows. Almost all these Bills are non-controversial or less controversial measures in which the House of Lords does the "donkey work", thereby saving the Commons valuable time. Here too the number of amendments made in the House of Lords has shown a dramatic increase, especially between 1970–3[15] and 1974–7.[16]

One type of Bill which is excluded from section B of the table is that known as a consolidation Bill. These are Bills which repeal redundant provisions of various statutes within a particular policy field and bring together the remaining extant provisions within a single statute. This work is shared with the House of Commons mainly through a joint select committee, but a significant part of the work on consolidation bills is undertaken by the Lords. In recent sessions between four and eight such Bills have been passed, though it must be said that they occupy only a very small amount of parliamentary time.

A more important category not covered in Table 1.4 is that of Private Members' Bills, that is Bills introduced by backbench Members of the House. Whereas the government normally secures the passage of ninety-four per cent or more of its legislation, sometimes even 100 per cent, the success rate of Private Members' bills is usually less than twenty per cent, sometimes less than ten per cent. The principal reason is time: the government loses one or sometimes two Bills because of the pressures of the parliamentary timetable, but the amount of time available for backbench Bills is very restricted. This has led to a reduction in the number of Private Members' Bills introduced by peers—in the early 1980s the number was more than twenty a year, but in recent sessions it has been less than half that number. Most successful Lords' Bills are on non-controversial, minor matters, which do not arouse partisan or governmental opposition. Although the success rate for Private Members' Bills introduced in the Lords is quite often higher than for those introduced in the Commons, the *number* passed is very small: in most sessions only two or three Lords' Bills receive the Royal Assent and the highest number in the period 1980–91 was five in 1980–1, with a mean of 2.5. Compared to this, the mean for Commons' Private Members' Bills was 11.8, ranging from nineteen in 1990–1 to eight in three other sessions. Moreover, very few Private Members' Bills passed by the Commons

---

[15]  N. 8 above.
[16]  D. Miers and J. Brock, "Government Legislation: Case Studies" in n. 9 above.

fail to pass the Lords—only six per cent between 1980 and 1991—and Commons' Bills are little amended by the Lords.

There are, however, in both Houses reasons for introducing Private Members' Bills other than the obvious one of directly seeking a change in the law. In general, tabling a Bill publicises the issue concerned and, if it is debated, provides an opportunity for airing views on the matter. In the House of Lords a number of Bills have been referred to select committees for consideration. The significance of this practice relates less to the consideration of the Bill itself and more to the impact the committee's report sometimes has on the subject-matter or policy concerned. For instance, the report on the Laboratory Animals Protection Bill 1979–80 led eventually to a government measure, the Animals (Scientific Procedures) Bill, being introduced in 1986. Similarly, the two Bills on charities in 1983–4 led directly to more satisfactory government legislation being passed in 1984–5, while the report on the Infant Life (Preservation) Bill 1987 contributed directly to debates on the Human Fertilisation and Embryology Bill 1990.[17]

However, second only to the role it plays in dealing with government legislation, which can take more than fifty per cent of its time, is the part the House of Lords plays in scrutinising delegated (or secondary) legislation, both domestic and that emanating from the EU Commission in Brussels. Most domestic delegated legislation is in the form of statutory instruments (SIs) and these are considered by a joint committee, drawing its membership equally from both Houses. The committee's task is to ensure that all SIs meet various technical requirements, such as whether an instrument is properly drafted, within the powers of the enabling statute, or whether it makes unusual use of the statutory powers concerned. Unlike most select committees, the Statutory Instruments Committee cannot call for witnesses and evidence, but it does have the power to demand written explanations on specific instruments from the government department concerned. It also has the legal advice and assistance of the Speaker's Counsel and the Counsel to the Chairman of Committees in the House of Lords. SIs are subject either to affirmative procedure, which means they will not come into effect unless specifically approved by Parliament, or to negative procedure, which means that they will come into effect unless specifically rejected by Parliament. However, only a minority of SIs are subject to affirmative resolution. Some affirmative instruments are adjudged to be hybrid instruments, that is affecting personal or local interests as well as the public interest. In the Lords these may be referred to the Hybrid Instruments Committee for further scrutiny, but there have been only three such referrals since 1973. There is no counterpart to this committee in the Commons.[18,19]

The most important work the House of Lords does on secondary legislation relates to that emanating from the European Commission in Brussels. Following

---

[17] D. Natzler and D. Millar, "Private Members' Bills" in n. 9 above.

[18] R. L. Borthwick, "Delegated Legislation" in n. 9 above.

[19] N. 8 above.

Britain's accession to the European Community in 1973, both Houses of Parliament set up select committees to deal with European secondary legislation. The House of Lords Select Committee on the European Communities operates through six sub-committees. Unlike the Joint Committee on Statutory Instruments, it ranges more widely than the technical merits of delegated legislation, often making substantive reports on policy matters, and takes a wide range of evidence in conducting its inquiries. The sub-committees are specialised, though the committee occasionally establishes an *ad hoc* sub-committee to deal with a matter not coming within the purview of the normal sub-committees. For example, in 1989–90 *ad hoc* sub-committees were set up to consider economic, monetary and political union in the EC and the European Company Statute. The committee also employs specialist advisers for most of its inquiries and in 1989–90 had the assistance of twenty advisers.

The European Communities Committee has built up a strong reputation as an effective instrument of parliamentary scrutiny. Although it is appointed to deal with secondary legislation, its terms of reference and the way in which it has developed mean that it operates very like an investigatory committee by ranging widely over EU policy and producing reports (at the rate twenty to thirty a year) which are both highly regarded and not infrequently influential in London[20] and Brussels.[21]

Membership of the EU has, of course, increased the volume of secondary legislation Parliament is expected to scrutinise, but there has long been a wider concern about the nature and use of such legislation. As a consequence, in 1991 the House of Lords appointed the Delegated Powers Scrutiny Committee to "give closer and more systematic scrutiny to the delegated powers sought in bills" (Select Committee on the Work of the House, 1991–2). This was an important development, extending significantly Parliament's scrutiny of secondary legislation. It is also a task to which the House of Lords, with its wide range of expertise and less partisan atmosphere, is particularly well-suited. In 1996, the committee's remit was extended to cover the government's deregulation programme, changing its name to the Select Committee on Delegated Powers and Deregulation.

There is one further type of legislation in the consideration of which the House of Lords plays an important part. This is in dealing with private legislation, that is Bills which apply only to named persons or a limited geographical area. In the former case, for instance, a private Bill may be necessary to authorise a marriage impermissible under existing law or to settle an estate which cannot be resolved through existing procedures, but most private Bills concern local developments, such as harbours and marinas, railways and other transit systems, or livestock markets. Occasionally, a so-called hybrid Bill is introduced, that is a Bill part of which is of general application, part specific. The relevant parts of such Bills are subject to separate public Bill and private Bill proceedings.

---

[20] N. 8 above.
[21] D. Shell, "The European Communities Committee" in n. 9 above.

A recent example of a hybrid Bill is the Channel Tunnel Rail Link Bill. Between twenty and thirty private Bills are passed each year and are dealt with by a separate quasi-judicial procedure, an important part of which involves the use of committees. The work on private legislation is divided, as far as possible, evenly between the two Houses and each uses separate committees to deal with opposed or unopposed Bills, but the Lords does the main work on personal Bills through a Personal Bills Committee.

In all these areas of legislation the House of Lords provides additional examination of primary or secondary legislation, whether government or Private Members' Bills, domestic or European delegated legislation, or private Bills. In a number of instances, it also saves the House of Commons time by examining legislation before it reaches the Lower House or facilitating the revision of Bills which have already passed the Commons.

### THE SCRUTINY AND INFORMATION FUNCTION

All debates and committee proceedings dealing specifically with legislation may be seen as part of the scrutiny and informing process, but that process extends to other matters through the debating of various issues, the debating of government policy and administration, the asking of Parliamentary Questions (which may lead to a short debate in the Lords), and through the use of select committees to conduct inquiries into particular issues or policies. Because debates, the asking of Questions, and select committee inquiries are conducted in public and their proceedings are published, the scrutiny thus exercised may also be said to perform an informing function, at least to the extent that those who wish to know more about these matters, whether members of the public at large or pressure groups, may inform themselves. No one should be under any illusion that the public pays a great deal of attention to parliamentary proceedings, although the televising of Parliament has probably produced a greater degree of awareness. However, the public record is there to be consulted and, certainly as far as many pressure groups are concerned, consulted it is.

The relative quality of debates in the Lords and Commons is ultimately a matter of opinion, although it is commonly suggested that the quality of debate in the Upper House is either generally or frequently superior. Be that as it may, there is a wide range of expertise in the House of Lords and its debates are undoubtedly less affected by partisan posturing. The same is even more true of Questions tabled for oral answer in the Lords. As with its role in dealing with legislation, the Lords provides an additional layer of scrutiny and publicity, more often than not adding to the contribution made by the Commons, since debates and Questions are not normally duplicated.

It is, however, through its use of investigatory select committees that the Upper House adds a more important, though limited, dimension to its contribution to the work of Parliament. Because the number of regular attenders in the

House of Lords is on average fewer than 200, the House cannot sustain the level of investigatory select committee activity found in the Commons, notably through the seventeen departmental select committees. Nevertheless, the Lords' contribution is widely regarded as significant in terms of quality.

The only permanent investigatory committee operated by the House of Lords is the Select Committee on Science and Technology. This was established in 1979, when the House of Commons abolished its then Science and Technology Committee with the creation of departmentally-related rather than subject investigatory committees. The Science and Technology Committee operates through three sub-committees, but these are not specialised and the 15 committee members are involved in inquiries according to their interests and expertise. The committee is widely regarded as successful and its reports are valued both inside and outside Parliament. It issues one or two major reports each year, ranging widely in topics, as the following examples illustrate: research and development in engineering (1982), remote sensing and digital mapping (1983), science and technology in local government (1985), UK space policy (1987), the "greenhouse" effect (1987), overseas aid (1990), innovation in manufacturing industries (1991), management of nuclear waste (1998) and resistance to anti-biotics (1998). In addition, the committee produces follow-up reports on earlier inquiries. To assist it in its work the committee may engage specialist advisers for particular inquiries, and in 1988–9, for instance,[22] employed seven such advisers.[23]

From time to time the House also appoints *ad hoc* select committees to consider particular policy matters, recent examples of which are the Select Committees on Murder and Life Imprisonment (1988–9), Sustainable Development (1994), Central–Local Government Relations (1995–6), the Public Service (1997–8). These too produce valued reports, drawing on both the expertise of members of the House of Lords and the oral and written evidence presented by specialists[24] in the fields concerned.[25]

## WHITHER THE HOUSE OF LORDS?

The cry at the beginning of the century was that the House of Lords should be ended or mended. No one would deny that its composition is anachronistic: heredity can no longer be justified as a basis for membership of the legislature in a modern society and, while the influx of life peers may have rejuvenated the House of Lords (though nor necessarily in terms of age), the case for phasing out the hereditary element[26] is very strong.[27]

[22] N. 8 above.
[23] C. Grantham, "Select Committees" in n. 9 above.
[24] N. 8 above.
[25] N. 23 above.
[26] N. 8 above.
[27] N. Baldwin, "The Membership of the House" in n. 9 above.

The general election of 1997 and its aftermath have done little to clarify Lords' reform. Labour's election manifesto contained four pledges on composition: first, the removal of the right of hereditary peers to sit and vote in the Lords; secondly, to make the House of Lords "more democratic and representative"; thirdly, to review the appointment of life peers to secure a balance which reflected the proportional division of votes between the parties at the previous general election; and fourthly, to maintain "an independent crossbench presence" through life peers. The legislative powers of the Lords would remain unchanged. It was envisaged that reform would be a two-stage process, first the swift removal of hereditary peers, followed by a period of consultation leading to more extensive reform. In the event, the disposal of the hereditary peers, originally intended to be achieved by a short Bill in Labour's first year, has been postponed until at least the second parliamentary session, although there have been discussions about further changes between the Labour and Conservative front benches in the House of Lords. This has produced a shift in attitude by the Conservative Party, which has now expressed a willingness to contemplate and support change, but beyond that there is no agreement between Labour and the Conservatives.

Before turning to what is likely to happen, two questions need to be addressed: does Britain need a second chamber and, if the answer is "yes", what form should it take?[28]

If the House of Lords were abolished Britain would not be alone in having a unicameral or single-chamber legislature, but almost all other cases are countries with fairly small populations, such as Denmark, Israel, New Zealand and Sweden. One of the commonest rationales for having a second chamber is in federal systems, in which the lower house is popularly elected in proportion to the distribution to the population and the upper house represents, usually, though not always, on an equal status the states or constituent parts of the federation. The most well-known case is the United States Senate, which consists of one hundred members, two from each state, regardless of population or geographical size. Whether the second chamber has any special powers is something that varies. Similarly, whether it is elected and, if so, whether it is at the same time and for the same length of time as the lower house also varies. If Britain were either to adopt a federal system or introduce comprehensive devolution, which can amount to *de facto* federalism, the case for a second chamber representing the various regions of the United Kingdom would be strong. Proposals for the setting up of a Scottish Parliament and a Welsh Assembly were approved by referendums in Scotland and Wales in September 1997 and, following legislation passed in 1998, elections will take place in 1999, with the devolved systems coming into operation in 2000. In addition, the Northern Ireland Settlement of April 1998 envisages a devolved legislature in Belfast, but proposals for English devo-

---

[28] The Constitution Unit, *Reform of the House of Lords* (London, University College London, Apr. 1996).

lution have been shelved. Nonetheless, the absence of English regional assemblies does not preclude a second chamber representing all the regions of the UK.

However, the case against the abolition of the House of Lords, leaving Britain with a unicameral Parliament, rests on two types of arguments: first, that the existing second chamber, whatever the anomalies of its composition, does necessary or sufficiently useful work to justify its retention; and secondly, that a single chamber dominated by party, as the House of Commons is, should not be allowed to exercise untrammelled power, limited only by periodic elections and the uncertain willingness of MPs to defy their parties.

The first argument is mundane but powerful: in the absence of the Upper House what the House of Lords currently does the House of Commons would have to do or leave undone. The additional scrutiny of primary and secondary legislation, of government policy and administration, and the airing of various issues would fall on the Commons or on no-one. In particular, the government would have to find ways of amending its own legislation through further or better scrutiny in the Commons, or subsequently amending Bills, or make even greater use of delegated legislation, or leave much legislation in an unamended and unsatisfactory state. The ability of the Commons to undertake this task must, however, be in doubt: already the House of Commons meets more often and for longer than any other legislature, and second place in that league table is held by the House of Lords. The alternative would be for the Commons to reform its procedures, particularly by using special standing committees, which can take evidence, but this would prolong the legislative process and governments show no sign of be willing to do so; political life is already too short. In any case, the Select Committee on the Modernisation of the House, set up after Labour's election victory, has yet to produce any proposals which would dramatically improve the efficiency of the Commons.

The second argument—curbing the power of a party-dominated House of Commons—should not be seen simply as arguing for a bulwark against dictatorship, a form of constitutional longstop. It is well established that governments of all complexions have used their majorities in the Commons to force through policies which were in serious conflict with public opinion. This raises questions relating to democracy and the nature of representation beyond the scope of this chapter, but the argument needs to be acknowledged. The Parliament Act 1911 contains a provision which allows the House of Lords to veto a proposal from the Commons to prolong the life of a Parliament (and, by inference, of a government) beyond five years, and such extensions occurred during both world wars. The Upper House did not demur in these two instances and has not otherwise been placed in a position of considering whether to frustrate a government seeking to prolong its life. Beyond that, although the House of Lords has from time to time modified unpopular policies, it cannot be said to have provided regular protection against a government determined to persist with demonstrably unpopular polices. Ironically, the very membership of the House of Lords, representing no-one as it does, hardly strengthens its case for standing in the way of the Commons; were there an elected second chamber that case would be immeasurably strengthened.

If Britain were to replace the House of Lords, it would almost certainly be with a fully- or partially-elected second chamber. The pressure for a fully-elected chamber is strong, but a case might be made for allotting membership to various individuals eminent in their field or using nominated members as a means of ensuring that the government party is adequately represented in the second chamber, rather on the lines of the 1968 proposal. However, it was, among other objections, the power of patronage that nomination gave the government and the political parties that led to the defeat of the 1968 reform. Yet it must be acknowledged that an elected second chamber would almost certainly place great patronage in the hands of the parties, if not governments, as MPs have almost without exception since the mid-nineteenth century been party rather than independent candidates. Who, then, would choose these candidates? By long tradition and practice candidate selection in Britain has been primarily a local[29] rather than a national matter[30] and one possibility is a second chamber consisting largely or entirely of regional representatives chosen mainly at regional level, as has been the case for selecting British candidates for elections to the European Parliament.[31] However, there are strong signs that the parties, particularly Labour, might take the opportunity to exert much greater central control over the selection of candidates and thus over who is elected to the second chamber, by adopting regional party lists, a system which will be used for the next elections to the European Parliament in 1999.

The implications of an elected second chamber and of regionally-based constituencies are of considerable importance. First, the House of Commons is acknowledged as the superior of the two Houses of Parliament precisely because it is the elected chamber; an elected second chamber would secure a significant degree of democratic legitimacy which the House of Lords at present inevitably lacks. Secondly, if elections for the second chamber were held at a different time, possibly on a staggered basis with a proportion of the membership retiring at regular intervals (as with the US Senate), then the more recently elected chamber might claim or be seen to have greater legitimacy because it reflected a more recent expression of public opinion. This expression of public opinion would be all the more powerful if, as has been proposed in a number of quarters, the second chamber were elected by a form of proportional representation rather than the first-past-the-post system used for the Commons. Consequently, more recently elected members of the second chamber might be less willing than peers currently are to defer to the will of the House of Commons. Thirdly, elections generally might encourage members of the second chamber to act even more independently than peers currently do. Conversely, as party nominees they

---

[29]   M. Rush, *The Selection of Parliamentary Candidates* (London, Nelson, 1969).

[30]   P. Norris and J. Lovenduski (forthcoming), *Political Recruitment: Gender, Race and Class in the British Parliament* (Cambridge University Press, 1995).

[31]   M. J. Holland, *Candidates for Europe* (Alton, Gower, 1986).

might feel a greater obligation to support their parties—partly moral, partly ideological, partly in fear of electoral defeat or deselection. Fourthly, unless a national party list system were used to choose candidates, elected members of the second chamber, unlike peers, would have constituencies and their constituents would presumably make demands upon them, much as they do with MPs. This might be no bad thing, but if constituencies were regionally-based then regional factors might play a significant part in the legislative behaviour of members of the second chamber. This too might not be a bad thing, but it might also produce forms of regional "NIMBY-ism" in the form of "not in my region", as well as a form of regional "pork barrel" politics in which regions with a clearer and stronger sense of identity would benefit at the expense of less clearly-defined regions.

These implications should not be seen as reasons for supporting the *status quo*. Indeed, they can be used powerfully in support of an elected second chamber. Their relevance to the future of the House of Lords is that they need to be considered in seeking answers to three fundamental questions. First, is what the House of Lords currently does important? Secondly, what purpose would a reformed second chamber have? And thirdly, if the answer to the first question is yes, is what the House of Lords does compatible with the purposes of a reformed second chamber? The answer to the third question is not necessarily no, but it would be unwise to ignore it.

What is likely to happen? The experience of the last century or more suggests not a great deal, but that experience also suggests that any change that takes place is likely to be at the instigation of one party rather than an all-party agreement: although there was much agreement between the parties in 1948 and 1968, the Parliament Acts of 1911 and 1949 and the Life Peerages Act of 1958 were the actions of the government of the day and not an inter-party settlement. Labour's commitment to reform is undoubtedly genuine and, to that extent, history is likely to repeat itself: reform will take place at the instigation of the party in power, even if it is, in this instance, with the reluctant support of the Conservatives. On the other hand, reform of the House of Lords is not especially high on the Labour government's agenda and the earlier linkage between devolution and a regional second chamber has all but disappeared, at least for the time being. Scottish and Welsh devolution are high on Labour's agenda, but English regional government is likely to be longer in coming, and in piecemeal form if and when it does. What has become much clearer since the 1997 election is that, other than getting rid of the hereditary element in the House of Lords, Labour has no detailed plans for a reformed second chamber. The election manifesto is clear to the extent that a mixture and an elected and nominated second chamber is envisaged, but in what proportion and, for the elected members, by what electoral system and for what term of office, remains unclear. Similarly, how a party balance reflecting the distribution of votes in the previous general election, combined with the continued presence of life peers and, at the same time, preventing any one party from having an absolute majority is to be achieved is also unclear. No doubt the Cabinet committee established to consider these matters is considering them. The shift from opposition to government is enormous and crucial: priorities have to be decided and external factors confronted; real decisions have to be made and the resulting policies are tested in practice rather than theory; and the cosy but frustrating world of opposition is replaced by the exhilarating but often equally frustrating world of government. The government is determined to replace the hereditary element and reduce one of those frustrations, but, if the House of Lords was Mr Balfour's poodle in 1911, it is no one's poodle today, and that may provide the spur for further change. Much, as Harold Macmillan once said, will depend on "events, events, dear boy" and a cynic could be forgiven for having a sense of *déjà-vu*.

FURTHER REFERENCES

The Constitution Unit, Checks and Balances in Single Chamber Parliaments: A Comparative Study (London, The Constitution Unit, University College London, 1998).

G. Drewry and J. Brock, "Government Legislation: An Overview" in n. 9 above.

*House of Lords Reform* (London, HMSO, Cmnd. 3799, 1968).

Select Committee on the Committee Work of the House, *Report*, HL 35–I, 1991–92.

M. A. J. Wheeler-Booth, "The House of Lords" in J. A. G. Griffith and M. T. Ryle, *Parliament: Functions, Practice and Procedures* (London, Sweet & Maxwell, 1989).

# 2

# The Membership and Work of the House of Lords

## NICHOLAS BALDWIN

"It is difficult to describe the . . . House of Lords. It is like trying to describe cricket to an Abyssinian through a Greek interpreter."[1]

### ORIGINS

Being the product of evolution rather than deliberate creation, it is not possible to stipulate exactly when the House of Lords originated, for Parliament itself had no sudden genesis. Rather, it came into being gradually "from the medieval court and council where Plantagenet kings consulted the great men of their realm to secure support and offered their people justice".[2] Nonetheless, the deepest parliamentary roots pre-date the Plantagenets, it being possible to trace them back to the consultative customs of the Anglo-Saxon people established from the time of Saxon settlement and dominion dating from the fifth-century incursions. The Saxon kings took council of the "Witan", or "Witenagemot", an assembly of the most important men—lay and ecclesiastical—of the kingdom, in total perhaps numbering up to as many as 100 individuals. The functions of the Witan were ill-defined, but included "discovering and declaring" the law—in short, it was a consultative, deliberative and law consenting assembly.

A new stage in the development of the nation's political institutions was ushered in when William, Duke of Normandy, defeated Harold, the Saxon claimant, at Hastings in 1066 and assumed the throne. It was William who introduced the feudal system, a system whereby the greater part of the country was granted to tenants-in-chief, or barons, who held their land directly from the king on condition that they held down the conquered territory. The barons assembled in the court of their sovereign to regulate the affairs of their tenancies, settle disputes between each other and organise the military subjection of the conquered lands. The tenants-in-chief thus assembled—lay and ecclesiastical—became the "*Magnum Concilium*" or Great Council. Summoned, presided

---

[1] Lord Willis, H.L. Deb., vol. 352, col. 1074 (20 June 1974).
[2] Ronald Butt, *A History of Parliament: The Middle Ages* (London, Constable, 1989), at 1.

over and guided by the king, the Council assisted in determining state policy, supervised the work of administration, acted as the highest court of justice and made or modified laws. (As with the Witan, the Council met only three or four times a year, and then only for a matter of days.) Eventually, political tensions were to emerge in the relationship between king and barons—brought to the surface through the misuse of autocratic power.

These tensions led in 1215 to "Magna Carta", an assertion of the limited nature of kingship. The fifty-six-year reign of Henry III (1216–72) was dominated by the struggle between the Crown and the barons. It was in the midst of this struggle that Parliament—including representatives of the counties and towns alongside the barons—emerged by name as an organ of government, acting as the highest court in the land and as a national forum deliberating on the great affairs of the realm. In it also, and with its assent, the king declared the law while it also emerged as the body with the right to approve—or not—any extraordinary taxation. At no time was "Parliament" definitively "established"; it merely evolved through a combination of the results of political conflict and the perceived usefulness of Parliament as a consultative forum between the king and the politically important sections of his realm.

Gradually, there took place a realignment of the membership—nobles, greater and lesser clergy and the knights of the shires and the burgesses—into two great groups, one of which became the House of Lords and the other the House of Commons—the one composed of men who attended in response to individual summons, and the other persons who, elected in counties and boroughs, attended in a representative capacity. This "bicameral" or two-house nature of the arrangement was to become firmly established.

Broadly speaking, one may say that by 1485, with the accession to the throne of Henry VII, the first of the Tudors, the great institutional foundations of the modern constitution had been laid. What came thereafter was in the nature of further growth and development within the existing framework, and, more particularly, the working out of new relationships between institutions, a process which led to altered balances of power and mechanisms of control.

## COMPOSITION

As previously stated, by the accession of the Tudor dynasty, Parliament was already clearly divided into two houses. In the House of Lords sat the king's officials, counsellors and judges, the magnates summoned to Parliament in their personal capacity as "peers of the realm", and the great ecclesiastics, archbishops, bishops and abbots. As far as numerical membership was concerned, there were two archbishops, nineteen bishops and up to thirty abbots, while the number of lay lords in attendance fluctuated owing to the number of minors at any particular time and the rates of both extinctions and new creations, but tended to range between forty and fifty; in total an approximate membership of one hundred.

During the reign of Henry VIII, as a result of the suppression of the monasteries, the House of Lords became, for the first time, a predominantly secular body.

Today, the membership of the House of Lords is still divided between ecclesiastical and lay members, between the two former categories of Lords Spiritual and Lords Temporal. The Lords Spiritual, or church peers, are the Archbishops of Canterbury and York, the Bishops of London, Durham and Winchester, and the twenty-one most senior among the other diocesan Bishops of The Church of England. The Lords Temporal are the Peers of England, Scotland, of Great Britain and of the United Kingdom. All peers of these types who are of full age (twenty-one), are not bankrupt, have not been convicted of a felony resulting in a term of imprisonment of twelve months or more (until pardoned or completion of sentence), and of British nationality are entitled to a seat in the House of Lords.

A further distinction can be made, namely between hereditary and non-hereditary peers. Hereditary peers are those whose title is held by virtue of inheritances (unless a hereditary peer of the first creation) where the title can be transmitted from one generation to another. The permanent or hereditary nature of the House of Lords was something which gradually became established, growing out of the right of individuals to receive personal writs of summons as great barons. Nowhere was it actually laid down that the King had to continue to summon an individual once summoned, or summon his heirs after him, and, indeed, omissions were not infrequent. Nevertheless, it duly became the usual practice to repeat the summons to an individual, and to issue a summons to his heir. In the natural course of events, that which had once been merely usual came to be expected, and as such it became rare for the King to withhold a summons from an individual once summoned or to not issue it to his heir. Finally, this became so rare that a denial of a writ appeared to be a denial of a basic right. Hence, the hereditary nature of the House grew out of the custom and little else.

Non-hereditary peers are those whose title ceases to exist upon the death of the title holder, regardless of there being an heir or not. Amongst the ranks of the Lords Temporal, there are two types of non-hereditary peers, or life peers, namely, those created under the Appellate Jurisdiction Act 1876 (as amended), and those created under the Life Peerages Act, 1958. The Appellate Jurisdiction Act of 1876 provided for the introduction of a limited number of Lords of Appeal in Ordinary, judges appointed by the Crown to assist the House of Lords in the hearing and determination of appeals. The individuals concerned are created peers for life, hold office during good behaviour, and can only be removed from office by an address of both Houses of Parliament. The Life Peerages Act 1958 enables individuals, men and women, to have peerages for life conferred upon them.

In the context of this chapter, those individuals created peers under the Appellate Jurisdiction Act 1876 will be termed "Law Lords" while those created peers under the Life Peerages Act 1958 will be termed "Life Peers". Similarly, those who have succeeded to their titles will be termed "Hereditary Peers" while those who have had a hereditary title bestowed upon them will be termed "Created Hereditary Peers".

Having made these formal distinctions, and following on from them, the total membership of the House can be presented (see Table 2.1). From this it is apparent that the membership of the House is predominantly male—females accounting for only 7.6 per cent (ninety-six) of the membership in April 1998. It is similarly apparent that the balance, both numerically and proportionally, is very much in favour of the hereditary as against the non-hereditary element—hereditary peers by succession accounting for fifty-nine per cent (750) of all members in April 1998.

THE POLITICAL BALANCE IN THE HOUSE OF LORDS:
PEERS AND THEIR POLITICAL AFFILIATION

Conservative dominance within the Lords was a product of history. At the beginning of the eighteenth century there had been a very small majority in the House for the Whigs. This had then been turned into an even smaller Tory majority by the creation of twelve peers for the specific purpose of securing a majority for the ratification of the Treaty of Utrecht in 1713. After a few years the Whigs were once again in a majority—a position they were able to maintain until Pitt the Younger became Prime Minister (1783), when creations took place on an unprecedented scale—during the seventeen years of his premiership 140 peerages were created, providing the Tories not merely with a majority, but placing them in a position of ascendancy in the House of Lords. The ascendancy was underlined by the natural conservative tendencies of a hereditary House and was increased by defections from amongst Liberal peers as a result of the infusion of radically minded individuals into the Liberal Party as a whole. In 1868, the House contained a majority opposed to the Liberal Government of between sixty and seventy, and although a number of Liberal creations took place, they in fact did little more than compensate for defections which occurred.

The events of 1886 and the issue of Irish Home Rule drove the great majority of Liberal peers to join the Conservatives, and the strength of the Liberal Government in the Lords was believed to be as little as thirty. The actual strength was put to the test in 1893 with a vote on Gladstone's second Home Rule Bill. It showed a majority of nearly 400—419 to 41—against the Government. By 1906, the membership of the House entitled to participate in proceedings stood at 602. Of these, only eighty-eight described themselves as Liberals, and in reality a number of these were extremely dubious supporters of the newly elected Liberal Government. There were 355 Conservatives and 124 Liberal Unionists, which left only thirty-five, including fourteen bishops and a number of Princes of the Blood Royal, who had no political label. Hence, there was at that time in the House of Lords a nominal Unionist majority of 391; Conservative dominance was a fact. Conservative dominance was complete following the

Table 2.1: Composition of the House of Lords
Peerage classification and numerical/proportional balance 1950—April 1998

| Peerage Category | 1950 N | % | 1960 N | % | 1970 N | % | 1980 N | % | 1990 N | % | 1998 N | % |
|---|---|---|---|---|---|---|---|---|---|---|---|---|
| Created Hereditary | 810 | 95.6 | 843 | 92.8 | 97 | 9.0 | 38 | 3.3 | 20 | 1.7 | 9 | 0.7 |
| Hereditary—Male | – | – | – | – | 741 | 68.7 | 751 | 64.2 | 743 | 62.7 | 734 | 57.7 |
| Hereditary—Female | – | – | – | – | 19 | 1.8 | 19 | 1.6 | 20 | 1.7 | 16 | 1.3 |
| Life Peer—Male | – | – | 25 | 2.7 | 155 | 14.4 | 277 | 23.7 | 304 | 25.7 | 382 | 30.0 |
| Life Peer—Female | – | – | 6 | 0.7 | 23 | 2.1 | 40 | 3.4 | 53 | 4.5 | 80 | 6.3 |
| Law Lord | 11 | 1.3 | 8 | 0.9 | 17 | 1.6 | 18 | 1.6 | 18 | 1.5 | 26 | 2.0 |
| Bishops | 26 | 3.1 | 26 | 2.9 | 26 | 2.4 | 26 | 2.2 | 26 | 2.2 | 26 | 2.0 |
| TOTAL | 847 | 100.0 | 908 | 100.0 | 1078 | 100.0 | 1169 | 100.0 | 1184 | 100.0 | 1273 | 100.0 |

Labour election victory in 1945, for the Government party was supported by as few as eighteen members within the House of Lords. The political affiliation of peers more recently is outlined in Table 2.2.

By far the largest political grouping in the contemporary House is the Conservative Party, accounting for 38.4 per cent (489) of members in April 1998. Today, the second largest party or grouping are the Crossbenchers. The term crossbencher is used to describe those members who are not formally aligned with any political party, but who belong to an unofficial group which meets each week, with a convenor—currently Lord Weatherill—in the chair, to discuss forthcoming business. These members receive written notice of future business, the difference between this notification and a party whip being that, in the case of the crossbenchers, the notification is issued without the additional matters on divisions and so on which are included in a party whip. Apart from membership of this group, no meaningful distinction can be made between those in receipt of the crossbench notice and other peers who describe themselves as independents—such as the Law Lords—who sit on the crossbenches, the Bishops, who have their own benches, and those from within the "no declared affiliation" category who are genuinely not aligned with any political party. Putting these two sets of figures together, a cross-tabulation of political affiliation by peerage category in the contemporary House of Lords can be obtained, as shown in Table 2.3.

From the information in Table 2.3, it is apparent that there is a marked contrast in the ratio of hereditary peers to life peers/created hereditary peers amongst the party membership, a ratio which stood at 1.78:1 in the Conservative Party, 1:8.8 amongst Labour Peers and 1:1.79 amongst Liberal Democrats. (Amongst Crossbench peers the ratio stood at 2.13:1.) Whereas 64.0 per cent (313) of Conservative peers had succeeded to an hereditary title, the equivalent figure amongst Labour peers was 10.1 per cent (16)—a stark contrast.

However, a substantial proportion of the possible membership of the House chooses, for various reasons, either not to attend sittings of the House or to attend only occasionally. This can be seen from an analysis of the attendance statistics during any individual session—here, by way of example, the analysis is for the 1994–5 Session shown in (Table 2.4).

The reasons for non-attendance are varied, including age or illness, lack of either time or interest, and distaste for the institution itself. The reasons for attending sittings of the House are similarly varied, peers attending because of a sense of duty or responsibility, out of interest and enjoyment, or even out of a sense of habit. Primarily the reasons some peers attend sittings of the House more frequently than others are the same as, or at least similar to, those reasons given by peers who do not attend at all, namely age, illness, lack of time, job not permitting political involvement and lack of interest.

There is an additional factor to be taken into account, namely the financial aspect of attendance at sittings. Members of the House are not paid a salary, nor

*Table 2.2: Composition of the House of Lords*
*Political affiliation numerical/proportional balance 1945—April 1998*

| Political Affiliation | 1945 N | % | 1955 N | % | 1970 N | % | 1980 N | % | 1990 N | % | 1998 N | % |
|---|---|---|---|---|---|---|---|---|---|---|---|---|
| Conservative[a] | 400 | 50.4 | 507 | 59.3 | 468 | 43.4 | 446 | 38.2 | 468 | 39.5 | 489 | 38.4 |
| Labour[b] | 18 | 2.3 | 55 | 6.4 | 120 | 11.1 | 156 | 13.3 | 115 | 9.7 | 157 | 12.3 |
| Liberal Democrat[c] | 63 | 8.0 | 42 | 4.9 | 38 | 3.5 | 41 | 3.5 | 55 | 4.7 | 67 | 5.3 |
| Others | – | – | – | – | 2 | 0.2 | 2 | 0.2 | 18 | 1.5 | – | – |
| Crossbench[d] | – | – | – | – | 110 | 10.2 | 211 | 18.0 | 240 | 20.3 | 294 | 23.1 |
| Non-Party[e] | 312 | 39.3 | 251 | 29.4 | 51 | 4.8 | 48 | 4.1 | 45 | 3.8 | 57 | 4.5 |
| No Declared Affiliation[f] | – | – | – | – | 289 | 26.8 | 265 | 22.7 | 243 | 20.5 | 209 | 16.4 |
| TOTAL | 793 | 100.0 | 855 | 100.0 | 1078 | 100.0 | 1169 | 100.0 | 1184 | 100.0 | 1273 | 100.0 |

a—Including Unionists, National Liberals, etc.
b—Including Labour and Co-operative, etc.
c—Formerly the Liberal Party.
d—Those in receipt of the Crossbench "notification of business" (excluding those in the non-party category).
e—Includes Archbishops, Bishops, Law Lords and Royal Dukes, all of whom are prevented by convention from declaring any political preference they may have.
f—The designation "no declared affiliation" should be applied to these peers with appropriate reservation. Strictly, it would be more accurate to describe them as "peers about whose party allegiance no information has been obtained from any of the Whips, where no information has been provided in reference books, and from whom no such information has been personally supplied".

Table 2.3: Composition and political affiliation—April 1998

| Peerage Category | | | | | | | | | |
|---|---|---|---|---|---|---|---|---|---|
| Political Affiliation | Created Hereditary | Hereditary by Succession | | Life Peer | | Law Lord | Bishop | Total | |
| | | Male | Female | Male | Female | | | Number | % |
| Conservative | 4 | 311 | 2 | 139 | 33 | – | 0 | 489 | 38.4 |
| Labour | 1 | 16 | – | 110 | 30 | – | – | 157 | 12.3 |
| Liberal Democrat | – | 24 | – | 35 | 8 | – | – | 67 | 5.3 |
| Crossbench | 2 | 191 | 9 | 84 | 8 | – | – | 294 | 23.1 |
| Non-Party | 2 | 3 | – | – | – | 26 | 26 | 57 | 4.5 |
| No-Declared Affiliation | – | 189 | 5 | 14 | 1 | – | – | 209 | 16.4 |
| TOTAL N | 9 | 734 | 16 | 382 | 80 | 26 | 26 | 1273 | |
| % | 0.7 | 57.7 | 1.3 | 30.0 | 6.3 | 2.0 | 2.0 | | 100.0 |

*Table 2.4: Levels of attendance—1994–5 Session*

| Days attended[a] | Number of Peers | % of Peers who attended (872) | % of total (1242) |
|---|---|---|---|
| None[b] | 370 | – | 29.8 |
| 1 only | 59 | 6.8 | 4.8 |
| 2–9 | 122 | 14.0 | 9.8 |
| 10–47   (7–33%) | 233 | 26.7 | 18.8 |
| 48–71   (34–50%) | 96 | 11.0 | 7.7 |
| 72–94   (51–66%) | 62 | 7.1 | 5.0 |
| 95–106  (678–74%) | 49 | 5.6 | 3.9 |
| 107–127 (75–89%) | 116 | 13.3 | 9.3 |
| 128–142 (90–100%) | 135 | 15.5 | 10.9 |
| Total who attended | 872 | 100.0 | 70.2 |
| TOTAL | 1242 | – | 100.0 |

a—The number of sitting days was 142.
b—Includes those Peers without Writs (including Minors), and Peers with leave of Absence.

do they receive a daily attendance fee. Rather, the position is that there is an expense allowance, the purpose of which is to enable lords to reclaim a reimbursement, within defined limits, of certain of the expenses they incur in attending sittings of the House, or of committees of the House. It is undoubtedly the case that the availability of the reimbursement of expenses has encouraged members to attend, and to do so more regularly than they would otherwise have been able to do.

Attendance statistics do not by any means give a complete picture of the participation of members in the work of the House. By no means all those who attend sittings of the House participate in debate; and, conversely, members who attend sittings less often may be active on select committees. Attendance at meetings of committees cannot be measured satisfactorily, as comprehensive statistics are not available, but it is clear from anecdotal evidence that a significant number of members play a full part in committee work and comparatively little part on the floor of the House. A major study into the 1988–9 session[3] showed that although the average attendance on each sitting day during the session was 316, this figure masked significant differences between days of the week: the average attendance on the nine Fridays when the house sat during the session was 177, while on the thirty-seven Tuesdays it was 354.

It is apparent, therefore, that there is a marked difference between the total possible membership and the actual achieved day-to-day membership. Because of this and because a significant number of members are not affiliated to any political party, considerable confusion exists over the question of the political complexion of the House of Lords. This is something to be returned to later, but

[3] See N. D. J. Baldwin, "The Membership of the House" in D. Shell and D. Beamish (eds.), *The House of Lords at Work* (Oxford, Clarendon Press, 1993), at 39–55.

before such further consideration, it is important to consider the functions of the House of Lords.

FUNCTIONS

The House of Lords has a number of functions which are relics of the past and which have now become largely obsolete, such as those of tendering advice to the monarch, acting as the court for the trial of persons impeached by the Commons for "high crimes and misdemeanours" and determining the validity of claims to the peerage. A further function which can be regarded as having its roots in the past, but in this case one which is still of immense significance, is that of final court of appeal. Technically, there is no distinction between the House of Lords in its judicial capacity and in its other activities, but in practice the judicial proceedings are quite separate from all other proceedings, as peers other than Law Lords do not participate in hearing appeals, legal sittings are separate from the sittings of the whole House, and the House of Lords may sit in its judicial capacity even after prorogation or dissolution.

The judicial function apart, the classic statement of the functions of a second chamber was given in the Bryce Conference Report of 1918, and the present activities of the House of Lords can be considered in the light of the four functions it found appropriate for a second chamber:

1. The examination and revision of bills brought from the House of Commons;
2. The initiation of bills dealing with subjects of a comparatively non-controversial character;
3. The interposition of so much delay—and no more—in the passing of a bill into law as may enable the opinion of the nation to be adequately expressed upon it;
4. To act as a forum for the full and free discussion of the large and important questions of policy at moments when the House of Commons may happen to be so much occupied that it cannot find sufficient time for them.[4]

About the second and fourth of these functions there is less controversy, less of a dispute over their existence and their use, than is the case, to a certain extent at least, with regard to the first function, and, as is certainly the case with regard to the third function. For this reason, the second and fourth functions are considered first.

The reason for allotting the second function—the initiation of bills dealing with subjects of a comparatively non-controversial character (and in this respect it means controversial on politically partisan lines)—to a second chamber was that such bills, having been fully discussed and put into a well considered shape prior to submission to the House of Commons, may have an easier passage

---

[4] Conference on the Reform of the Second Chamber, Report by Viscount Bryce (London, HMSO, Comd. 9038, 1918).

through the House of Commons than would otherwise be the case. The view often held is that because the work on such legislation is dull and not advantageous politically, members of the House of Lords are better suited to carry out the work than are members of the House of Commons. It is also pointed out that when such bills are examined first by the Lords, this saves the House of Commons a considerable amount of time.

The fourth function for a second chamber enunciated by Viscount Bryce was that of acting as a forum for debate. It has been said that such debates may be all the more useful if conducted in an assembly of experts—such as is, to a great extent, the House of Lords, certainly according to its apologists. Moreover, it has been pointed out that as there is little or no party discipline in the House of Lords and because peers have no electorate to consider, they can speak more freely than can members of the House of Commons.

The examination and revision of bills brought from the House of Commons was the first function named in the Bryce Report as an appropriate one for a Second Chamber to possess. It is this function which has often been regarded as the most important possessed by the House of Lords, particularly as the House of Commons usually operates under a fairly restrictive timetable and on occasions operates under rules which specifically limit the time available for discussion, with the result that some clauses in some bills receive either very little or in fact no examination in the Commons.

The close scrutiny of bills involves a great deal of work, often painstakingly dull, and it is said that the House of Lords performs an invaluable parliamentary function in this respect. In carrying out this function it deals with work which would otherwise either have to be done by the members of the House of Commons or which would simply be left undone, while, at the same time, in relieving the work-load of the members of the Commons, it enables them to concentrate on matters of a partisan nature.

However, a problem does exist with regard to this function because the question of how far the revision goes before it amounts to interference with the will of the Commons (interference by a predominantly hereditary Chamber in the activities of a popularly elected Chamber) is a perennial one. It is argued by some, for example, that when acting as a revising chamber the House of Lords has sometimes taken on the role of a wrecking chamber, for although it is recognised that some Lords' amendments are simply tidying-up amendments, some, the critics say, are very much more than this and can be very substantial indeed.

In addition, the belief has developed amongst some that the extent of the revising activities of the peers depends upon the political complexion of the government of the day. This belief dates back to constitutional wrangles of the late nineteenth and early twentieth centuries. Essentially, it is that the House of Lords is a partisan assembly, always ready to pass the Bills of one party—the Conservatives—and always ready to reject and maim the Bills of the other parties.

Similar controversy surrounds the third function mentioned, namely the power to delay legislation. Controversy exists because critics do not accept that a second chamber composed predominantly of hereditary peers should have the right to question the wisdom of elected representatives.

Clearly, therefore, the issue of the delaying power of the Lords, as well as, to a certain extent at least, their power to amend, is tied to the issue of the composition of their House—the fact that members are there by virtue of either patronage or the functioning of the hereditary principle and therefore have no "democratic" authority and there is an uneven party-political balance.

Determining the political balance is therefore of crucial significance if one is seeking to place the contemporary House of Lords in perspective. Before further consideration of this, however, in addition to the four functions listed in the Bryce Conference Report, the House of Lords is thought by some as having three other important functions, namely those of scrutinising the actions and activities of the Executive, scrutinising legislative proposals, directives and regulations emanating from the European Community and, finally, acting as a constitutional check. As such, it is important to look at these.

As far as scrutinising the activities of government is concerned, there are several ways in which members of the House of Lords engage in questioning ministers about government policy in addition to the opportunities provided by general debates. For example, up to four questions for oral answer may be asked each day, each of which can lead to supplementary questions. Unstarred questions, Private Notice Questions and questions for written answer are also utilised. In addition, the most important statements of government policy made in the House of Commons are usually repeated in the House of Lords, and on such occasions members have the opportunity to ask questions of the government for the purpose of clarification. All of these are ways in which members of the House of Lords can scrutinise the activities of the Executive, and all have been used by peers to keep issues to the forefront of government attention in order to press for some form of action.

In seeking to fulfil its scrutinising function the House of Lords has in recent years made use of a number of Select Committees, each with the task of undertaking scrutiny within a specific area of concern. The first such committee—and what many would regard as the most important—was the Select Committee on the European Communities which was established in April 1974 to scrutinise European Community secondary legislation. This Lords committee—with wider terms of reference than its Commons counterparts—has developed a sizeable network of sub-committees corresponding to the main areas of community activity, with a total membership of over 100 peers involved, each with considerable practical experience of the problems they examine. Supporters argue that the work of the Committee is of considerable value in ensuring that an in-depth monitoring of the Communities draft legislation takes place.

In respect of acting as a constitutional check, the House of Lords is viewed by some not only as a barrier against a possible elected dictatorship but also as a safeguard of the independence of the judiciary. These two propositions are derived from the facts that the House of Commons cannot extend the life of a Parliament beyond that of five years without the consent of the House of Lords (a factor which is not subject to the provisions of the Parliament Acts), and that senior judges can only be dismissed on an address to the Monarch from both Houses of Parliament.

EVOLUTIONARY ADAPTABILITY

An important—possibly the most important—feature of the British Constitution is the capacity for gradually adapting itself to meet changing conditions. Throughout history, the British Constitution has been adapting itself to its environment. Transitions have, as a rule, been gradual, deference to tradition habitual, and there has been a tendency to maintain throughout accustomed names and forms, to the extent that the constitutional history of Britain displays an unparalleled continuity.

In this respect, the House of Lords is but a microcosm of the British Constitution, for throughout it is apparent that it has been able to adapt to meet the changing conditions within which it has found itself functioning. This is so because, in contrast to other present-day second chambers which have been specially created institutions, with their powers and compositions clearly defined in constitutional documents and whose origins can be traced to some theoretical and practical purpose in the minds of those responsible for drawing up the constitution, the House of Lords was not established to meet the requirement of any particular theory of politics; it was not created by any national convention; it does not owe its existence to some paper scheme drawn up by politicians, academics or constitutional lawyers. Rather, it is a product of history. It has not been made; it has grown. Herein lies the key to why the House of Lords, this curious institution which has been the subject of a protracted, often ritual, campaign of abuse, is still in existence; the key to why it has not only remained, in essence, untouched by the hand of whole-scale reform, but also to why it has not fallen victim to inward decay; the key to why the House of Lords can correctly be depicted as the perennial survivor. It is because it has an inherent evolutionary adaptability. This is not to say that this evolution has been a neat continuous one; on the contrary, its development has been haphazard, spasmodic, irregular and uncertain. Nonetheless, from the beginning it has developed organically, gradually modifying, often indispensably, both the attitudes and behaviour of its participatory membership and its own procedures in response to the prevailing circumstances.

In recent years, this evolutionary adaptability has resulted in significant changes in both composition and behaviour. Today, although the House of Lords appears essentially unchanged from that which existed thirty, forty, even fifty years ago—indeed, some would say, much longer than that—in practice significant changes of both form and character have taken place, to the extent that many of the commonly held beliefs that have traditionally been applied to the House of Lords have in effect been rendered incorrect. The fact is, however, that because the House of Lords has throughout been able to retain its identity, the changes that have taken place have gone largely unrecognised, creating circumstances whereby perceptions of what the position is thought to be have not kept pace with what the position is in practice. The result of this is that contemporary arguments and observations on the subject of the House of Lords portray a tendency to ignore changes in both composition and behaviour that have taken place in recent years, and instead reiterate and re-emphasise the traditional received ideas. These changes, as highlighted by recent events during the 1980s and on into the 1990s, provide clear evidence not only of the development of what is a new professionalism and a new independence amongst the membership, but also, and as a result, the fallaciousness of much of the conventional wisdom associated with the subject.

THE HOUSE OF LORDS SINCE 1979

With the return of a Conservative government in 1979, backed by a solid Commons majority, it was assumed by many that the House of Lords would be little noticed. In fact, however, the reverse was the case, it being made abundantly clear during the 1979–97 period that the days when a Conservative government need have no fear of being defeated in the Lords had disappeared. Indeed, by the middle 1980s, some observers viewed the House of Lords as providing the most effective opposition to the government, the Lords being the focus of much of the opposition to the government's rate-capping scheme and its plans to abolish the Greater London Council and the six Metropolitan County Councils. In 1990, the peers rejected by 207 votes to 74 a government Bill—the War Crimes Bill—at Second Reading, the first occasion the peers had taken such a step—under any government—since the Parliament Act of 1949 imposed tighter curbs on the powers of the Lords.

During the first parliamentary session under the Conservative administration elected in 1979, the government was able to avoid being defeated on any significant legislative matter on the floor of the House of Commons. It was not able, however, to avoid such defeats in the House of Lords. The most notable of these occurred when the Lords objected to a clause in the Education (No. 2) Bill which would have enabled local authorities to impose charges for school transport, and voted by 216 votes to 112 to delete it. The division not merely saw two former Conservative Ministers of Education, Lords Butler and Boyle, vote against the government, but saw a total of 38 Conservative peers walk into the lobby in opposition to the government, a total of 28.7 per cent of all Conservatives voting. This division went a long way to emphasise the change in the political balance that has gradually evolved in the House in recent years. In a division which saw a high degree of activity by the government whips and which saw a high turn-out of members voting (itself a factor which conventional wisdom has as favouring the Conservatives), it is interesting to point out that even if all those Conservatives voting against the government had instead followed the party whip, the government would still have been defeated by twenty-two votes. In addition, even if all the Conservative peers, supported by all those peers with no declared party allegiance who voted in this division, had gone through the same division lobby, the government would still have been defeated by thirteen votes. The sheer scale of this defeat, with the prospect of having to face backbench dissent in the Commons and a second defeat if put before the Lords again, encouraged the government to climb down.

No further attempt was made to resurrect the clause and the Treasury was obliged to forgo an estimated public expenditure saving of up to thirty million pounds. In all, fifty defeats, ten of them significant, were inflicted upon the Conservative government by the Lords in the 1979–83 Parliament. Most were on specific points of particular concern to their Lordships—for example, the treatment of pensioners and the disabled, rural issues, respect for existing minority rights and matters of constitutional etiquette.

During the 1983–7 Parliament, further government defeats in the Lords ensued—a total of sixty-two. Perhaps the most significant was when the government's plan to cancel the May 1985 elections to the Greater London Council and six other Metropolitan County Councils was defeated by 191 votes to 143 on a Labour amendment which came before the House in its deliberations on the 1984 Local Government (Interim Provisions) Bill; a defeat made all the more striking by the fact that it occurred in the face of concerted government whipping. Indeed, as was observed at the time. "One of the principal consequences of [this] remarkable vote . . . has been to shatter the conventional wisdom on the House of Lords."[5]

The government then offered a compromise in the light of the defeat which allowed the existing Councils to continue for an extra year, but which still cancelled the election due in 1985. Such an example clearly indicated that the Lords have been both willing and able to administer salutary and timely rebuffs to Conservative and Labour governments alike.

During the 1987–92 Parliament, the Lords inflicted a further seventy-two defeats upon the government, including, for example, in April 1991 when, during consideration of The Criminal Justice Bill the peers defeated the government by passing an amendment to do away with the mandatory life sentence for murder, an amendment which the government later overturned in the Commons.

During the 1992–7 Parliament, the Lords again defeated the government on a number of occasions: nineteen times during the 1992–3 Session, sixteen times during the 1993–4 Session, seven times during the 1994–5 Session, ten times during the 1995–6 session and ten times during the short 1996–7 session. For example, in

---

[5]  Geoffrey Smith, *The Times*, 2 July 1984.

1993, during passage of the Railways Bill, the peers voted to give British Rail an equal chance to bid for rail franchises alongside the private sector, twice defeating the government on the issue and thus ensuring that the government came forward with a compromise solution. During the 1993–4 Session the Police and Magistrates' Courts Bill and the Criminal Justice and Public Order Bill both suffered defeats or forced concessions at the hands of their Lordships—for example, on the proposed power for the Home Secretary to appoint Police Authority chairmen; to end local government majorities on Police Authorities; to introduce a new offence of male rape; to challenge in the courts the film censor's criteria on video violence and to allow judges to draw the attention of juries to a defendant's exercise of the traditional right to silence when charged with a criminal offence.

During the 1995–6 Session and consideration of the Family Law Bill, the principle of dividing pension entitlement at the time of divorce was approved by the peers by 178 votes to 150, a majority of twenty-eight against the government in a division which saw twenty-one Conservative peers defy their party whip. Originally scorning the Lords action, it became apparent to the government that the amendment had a lot of support in the House of Commons and that reversal of the defeat could not be guaranteed. It was an assessment that led to a decision not to attempt to try to overturn the Lords amendment. Finally, again during the 1995–6 Session, during the passage of the Asylum and Immigration Bill peers voted by 158 votes to 155 to give people arriving in the United Kingdom three days—instead of a single day—to claim refugee status before losing any entitlement to claim welfare benefits; it was a government defeat by three votes. The amendment was however overturned in the Commons, a move with which the peers then complied.

In all these cases the House demonstrated considerable self-confidence in playing one of its legitimate roles as constitutional critic and check upon the power of the government of the day. Indeed, the modern House of Lords has been prepared to create difficulties for Conservative governments—a fact in clear contravention of the tenets of conventional wisdom. Why is this so? What brought about such a change?

ANALYSIS

During the years immediately after the passage of the Reform Act of 1832, the House of Lords acted in a way which gave rise to little conflict between the two Houses. However, towards the latter half of the nineteenth century until 1914, it is difficult to describe its activities other than in terms of conflict between the Unionist opinions and landed interest which were prevalent among peers at the time and the Liberal majorities in the House of Commons. Indeed, as the policies advocated by the Liberal government became increasingly objectionable to the established interests represented by Conservatives in the Lords, the conflict became sharper, precipitating the constitutional crisis of 1909–11. The settlement of that crisis came with the passage of the Parliament Act of 1911. The significance of this Act was two-fold. First, it created procedures whereby obstruction by the Lords could be overcome, and, secondly and more importantly, it served to act as a deterrent to obstruction by the Lords. It is upon these twin pillars that the activities of the Lords have evolved and developed since 1911, to the extent that today, the reform, challenged at its inception as undermining the entire constitutional edifice of the nation, can be regarded as one of the very cornerstones of that constitutional edifice. It can be seen as such because, more through gradual evolution than by design, it led to the development of a chamber which is neither too dependent nor too independent, which has influence but not authority. This was not, however, self-evident at the time.

Although assertive during the period 1911–14, the onset of the War followed by a long period in which the Conservative Party, save for two brief intervals, was the dominant element in government, precipitated a state of quiescence on the part of the Lords. The election of a Labour government in 1945 did not shake the peers from this state, a state which owed much to the fact that the peers were waiting for their House to be reformed—the preamble to the Parliament Act of 1911 having stated that it was intended only as a temporary measure, a stop-gap, before a thorough-going reform to substitute for the House of Lords a second chamber constituted on a popular, instead of hereditary, basis could be carried out. Although a number expected the 1945 Labour government to initiate such a scheme, it was not until after the return of a Labour government following the General Election of 1966 that a serious attempt at reform was instigated, firm proposals based upon inter-party talks being brought forward as the Parliament (No. 2) Bill during the 1968–9 Session. The proposals involved, however, received a critical and, in some respects, hostile reception in the House of Commons, in large part because they were perceived as a means of making the Lords more effective (and thereby likely to have more authority and ability to use their powers), and the legislation was ultimately dropped. Because of the circumstances surrounding the collapse of this attempt at wholesale reform, the perception being that the government had had its fingers burned, the subject of reform came to be regarded as an issue governments would be hesitant to get involved with again, and as such was seen as having been placed on the "back burner".

The episode had a profound effect on many of the peers. The position, as they saw it, was that they remained unreformed through no fault of their own (to a very great extent they had favoured the reforms proposed), while the circumstances of the collapse made it apparent that they were likely to remain unreformed for the foreseeable future. As one member explained:

> "The failure of the [reform] proposals had the effect of freeing us from the lethargy that had encumbered and inhibited us for so long. From this point we were determined not to pussy-foot about any longer but instead to get on with the job in hand."[6]

[6] Labour life peer to author.

This attitude was not purely and simply a reaction to events; rather, it was the result of a number of changes that had taken place during the intervening years. The most important of these changes was the addition of life peers to the membership following the passage of the Life Peerages Act in 1958. The effect upon the composition of the House was marked (see Table 1). Lloyd George had described hereditary peers as "[d]ug out of the cellars of the House of Lords . . . stuff bottled in the Dark Ages . . . not fit to drink . . . cobwebby, dusty, muddy, sour".[7] The innovation of peerages for life proved to be an ingenious method whereby, continuing the analogy, old bottles were filled with new wine, and as such had a significant effect on the House. As one hereditary peer explained, "there was a tremendous revival . . . looking back [it can be said that] the Life Peerages Act really saved [the] House as an entity, and for its future . . . [because] it injected considerable new life into the work of the House".[8]

Although today the "popular" view of the House of Lords is of a place full of landed aristocrats up from their country estates, mainstream politicians of a bygone age, wealthy patrons of party funds, friends of former Prime Ministers and titled fugitives from the pages of P. G. Wodehouse, to portray the membership in such terms would be inaccurate. The addition of a large number of life peers, although not fundamentally altering the nature of the composition of the House (as, for example, direct elections would have done), has undoubtedly enriched it by bringing in members of more varied background and experiences.

Since the passage of the Life Peerages Act the House of Lords has acquired newly ennobled bankers, engineers, diplomats, lawyers, businessmen, economists, trade unionists, military commanders, politicians, academics, educationalists, scientists, administrators and senior civil servants on a scale unprecedented before the passage of the Act. As a result of this blend of hereditary and life peers, the House has members with very considerable knowledge of almost every aspect of life. Because of this it has become the custom for these experts—or at any rate these people with considerable knowledge—to attend and speak on their specialised subjects, often leading to a very high level of debate. It is difficult—although certainly not impossible—to find a topic for debate on which there is at least one peer, and more often than not several peers, who is either a recognised authority or at least has considerable practical knowledge, and today any major debate in the House is likely to include speeches from experts.

The introduction of life peers has also gradually caused the style of the House to alter, particularly because a number—a growing number—of the new creations have been "working peers", individuals created peers with the specific task of being working legislators, distinguishing them from those names which appear in the Honours List at the New Year and on the Queen's Birthday. Many of the life peers have formerly been MPs or have been active in local government or party politics, and as such have tended to approach their role as members of

---

[7] Lloyd George, quoted in I. Gilmour, *The Body Politic* (London, Hutchinson, 1969), at 297.
[8] Lord De Clifford, H.L. Deb., vol. 352, col. 1104 (20 June 1974).

the Lords with a degree of professionalism previously unfamiliar to the House, and this in turn has had something of a knock-on effect among the hereditary element. This "new professionalism" remained largely unrecognised, however, until the beginning of the 1970s, first because it could not materialise with any effect until a significant number of life peers had been created and, secondly, the threat/promise of reform had until then been present. Since 1970, the members have approached their work in a manner and with a determination previously unknown: see Tables 2.5 and 2.6.

*Table 2.5: Sessional statistics 1950/1–1995/6*

| Statistical item | 1950–1 | 1960–1 | 1970–1[a] | 1980–1 | 1990–1 | 1995–6 |
|---|---|---|---|---|---|---|
| Average Daily Attendance | 86 | 142 | 265 | 296 | 324 | 372 |
| Number of Sitting Days | 100 | 125 | 153 | 143 | 137 | 136 |
| Number of Sitting Hours | 294:45 | 599:00 | 966:02 | 919:53 | 885:52 | 935:27 |
| Average Length of Sitting | 2:57 | 4:47 | 6:18 | 6:25 | 6:28 | 6:53 |
| Sitting after 10pm | 1 | 5 | 38 | 53 | 42 | 60 |
| Monday Sittings | – | 21 | 22 | 28 | 29 | 30 |
| Friday Sittings | – | – | – | 11 | 9 | 7 |

a—The 1970–1 Session was longer than usual because it began after a June General Election.

From Table 2.5, it can be seen that the number of peers attending sittings has greatly increased; indeed, between 1950–1 and 1995–6 there was an increase of some 332 per cent in average daily attendance, itself both a sign and a cause of the "new professionalism". In addition, members are spending more and more time at the Lords and are involved in an increasing amount of business when there. Whereas peers could at one time count on a working week of Tuesday to Thursday and a working day often not beginning until 4.00 pm and possibly ending before 7.00 pm, now the House sits more often, the working week has expanded, the sittings begin earlier and go on much longer in order to accommodate the new professionalism of the membership: between 1950–1 and 1995–6 there was a 217 per cent increase in the number of hours the House sits and a 113 per cent increase in the average length of sittings.

In addition, the business arrangements of the House have, little by little, been adapted to meet these changes, the membership being anxious not only to improve its own procedures but to evolve existing functions and to develop new ones. The fact that the House is a self-regulating body with few standing orders (for example, it has no Speaker, no guillotine, no closure) has enabled the membership to do just this.

Changes have also taken place with regard to the political balance found amongst the membership: see Table 2.2 above. By far the strongest political grouping in terms of numbers is indeed the Conservative Party, although the growth in the number of peers sitting on the crossbenches—an increase by the beginning of 1998 of more than 167% over the 1970 level—is important to note.

*Table 2.6: The work of the House of Lords 1950/1–1995/6*

| Type of work | 1950–1 | 1960–1 | 1970–1[a] | 1980–1 | 1990–1 | 1995–6 |
|---|---|---|---|---|---|---|
| Starred Questions[b] | 119 | 290 | 511 | 537 | 531 | 498 |
| Questions for Written Answer | 38 | 73 | 283 | 857 | 1304 | 2471 |
| Unstarred Questions | 12 | 12 | 39 | 31 | 42 | 26 |
| Motions leading to Debate | n/a | n/a | 46 | 47 | 71 | 77 |
| Government Bills Introduced[c] | 6 | 7 | 11 | 12 | 10 | 13 |
| Private Member Bills Introduced | 2 | 2 | 14 | 23 | 8 | 19 |
| *Amendments made* | *1951–2* | *1962–3* | *1970–1* | *1980–1* | *1990–1* | *1995–6* |
| Government Bills Commons | 30 | 456 | 558 | 418 | 544 | 422 |
| Private Members' Bills Commons | 27 | 29 | 15 | 49 | 24 | 4 |
| Government Bills Lords | 75 | 283 | 207 | 940 | 1012 | 1133 |
| Private Members' Bills Lords | 0 | 8 | 75 | 53 | 5 | 108 |
| TOTAL | 132 | 776 | 855 | 1460 | 1585 | 1667 |

a—The 1970–1 Session was longer than usual because it began after a June General Election.
b—In 1954, the limit was put up to three per day on any Sitting Day; previously it had been three only on Tuesdays and Wednesdays. In 1959, the limit was raised to four per day on any Sitting Day.
c—Excluding Consolidation Bills.

However, because there is a marked difference between the total possible membership—1,273 in April 1998—and the actual achieved day-to-day membership—in the region of 380 in 1998—and because a significant number of members are not affiliated to any political party, as pointed out previously, considerable confusion exists over the political complexion of today's House of Lords.

The outcome of any division depends upon two basic factors, namely the number of members voting and the way in which they cast their votes. These basic factors in turn depend upon a number of variables, such as the subject under discussion, the advocacy of certain individuals, the day of the week and the hour of the day. Any exposition of the political complexion of the House of Lords is invalidated unless it takes into account these factors. When they are taken into account, it becomes apparent that the complete Conservative control evident in 1945, indeed evident into the 1960s, has disappeared; gone are the days when a Conservative government need have no fear of defeat in the Lords. Indeed, as we have seen, in the period between 1979 and 1997 the Lords were often an embarrassment, irritant and obstruction to the Conservative government.

Although in the past there was a built-in Conservative majority, at present, and at best, because of the developments highlighted, there is only ever a potential Conservative majority in the House. Certainly, it is easier for the Conservatives to win a division than it is for any other party—indeed, in this regard, the position of the Conservative Party in fact improved (strengthened) between the latter part of the 1980s and the return to power of a Labour government in 1997—but it is not inevitable. The days have long since passed when either a Conservative government or a Conservative opposition can count on having an automatic majority in the House of Lords. In short, one of the unsung secrets of the contemporary House of Lords is that the Conservatives no longer have an automatic majority; indeed, no single party can rely unreservedly on its support.

The new professionalism, linked with the altered political balance, has meant that peers have not only recognised but have responded to political developments. In short, the House of Lords has adapted its behaviour, chameleon-like, to its changing political environment, taking into account not only the political complexion of the government with which it is faced, but also such factors as whether or not the government at a particular time or on a particular issue has a secure majority in the House of Commons, and the way in which the government of the day organises the business timetable in both the Lords and the Commons. The House of Lords—the peers—weighs up such factors, judging how best to act and react to them. A change in one of the factors leads to corresponding changes, though often imperceptible, in its own mode of procedure.

During the 1970s, for example, the Lords were faced with three specific, though inter-related, developments in the Commons, namely, minority government, a significant increase in the levels of intra-party dissent in the division lobbies and the fact that, as a result of these two factors, government defeats were no longer infrequent occurrences. The Lords responded accordingly using these factors to their advantage, amending legislation against the government's wishes in the hope that the amendments would receive support in the House of Commons; support which was, on a number of significant occasions, forthcoming. Because this was the case, the Lords were also unable to secure compromises from the government merely by threatening to return items to the Commons, thereby placing the government in danger of being defeated—the perception being that the government would be more open to making concessions in order to avoid the risk of returning legislation to the Commons, particularly on matters where it had had considerable difficulty securing a Commons majority the first time.

During the 1980s, circumstances within the House of Commons altered, in that there were large majorities for the government. The peers responded to this change, adapting their behaviour accordingly with a view to providing effective opposition—certainly effective scrutiny—which they felt the House of Commons, given the political balance, was unable to provide. As one observer noted:

"The heart of democracy [the House of Commons], pumping the blood stream round the system, has [because of the high Government majority] ceased to function properly . . . the Lords see themselves as the by-pass valve, restoring health to the organism."[9]

Through these changes, through its evolutionary adaptability, the House of Lords developed a new strength and vigour, and an inner confidence in itself as an institution and in what it was doing. The constitutional confrontation between the two Houses of Parliament in the late nineteenth and early twentieth centuries was not, in essence, the result of differences between two partisan political philosophies, but rather was the result of a failure on the part of the Lords to recognise and accept the implications of the political trends of the time, namely the inevitability of the transference of political power to the elected House of Commons.

It is during the past thirty years, as a direct result of the external reforms that have taken place and of the internal changes brought about by them, that the peers have fully accepted and adapted to the limitations inherent within their position; indeed the House of Lords is able to function today largely because its members recognise and accept the constraints within which it works.

In the process of adaptation, the House of Lords has itself changed, evolving into what legislative "revolution" has always failed to bring about, namely a more balanced second chamber. As the professionalism and independence of its members grew, so the House of Lords developed an effective capacity for influencing—though not determining—the course of events.

CONCLUSION

In 1867, Walter Bagehot wrote that:

"the danger of the House of Lords is that . . . it is not safe against inward decay. . . . If most of its members neglect their duties, if all of its members continue to be of one class . . . if its doors are shut against genius that cannot found a family, and ability which has not [wealth] . . . Its danger is not in assassination, but atrophy; not abolition, but decline."[10]

A study of the House of Lords in recent years provides clear evidence that it is in danger neither of atrophy nor decline; indeed, quite the reverse becomes apparent. The House of Lords has portrayed throughout a remarkable ability to evolve and adapt to changing circumstances. What also becomes evident is its quite extraordinary character, a character derived from the fact that it is not the brainchild of any constitutional draughtsman but is instead a strange amalgam

---

[9] Hugo Young, "Praise The Rebel Lords But Pass The Electoral Ammunition" *The Guardian*, 9 July 1984.

[10] Walter Bagehot, *The English Constitution*, first published 1867 (London, Fontana/Collins, 1975), 149.

of the provisions of a small number of *ad hoc* statutes, together with precedents, habits, conventions, customs, traditions, usages, understandings and beliefs. Although the House of Lords has been altered by what can be termed external measures—such as the Reform Act of 1832, the Parliament Acts of 1911 and 1949, and the Life Peerages Act of 1958—it has been the internal reactions to them, the capacity to adapt to the changes they heralded, that have formed and continue to shape the character of the House.

The House of Lords as it exists today is the result of this evolutionary process. Certainly it is an illogical institution, to the extent that no-one would set out to devise a second chamber like it, but it is its very irrationality that in a strange, even perverse, way is its strength. It encompasses a delicately balanced combination of limited effectiveness with ultimate impotence through which it is, in a rather haphazard and improbable way, able to make a significant contribution to the process of British government. Whether one judges this contribution as a benign or malignant aspect of the body politic, few doubt that if it did not exist, it would almost certainly need to be replaced with a new parliamentary institution of comparable purpose and utility.

# 3

# The Second Chamber:
# Paradoxes and Plans

RODNEY BRAZIER*

SETTING THE SCENE

There has been no shortage of official analyses of the strengths and shortcomings of the Upper House, or of attempts to improve it. The preamble to the Parliament Act 1911 set the scene for the replacement of the House by an elected chamber, "but", as the preamble lamented, "such substitution cannot be immediately brought into operation". That bare statement of intent was clothed with a detailed plan by the Bryce Committee after the First World War.[1] After the Second World War, a number of reform matters were settled in principle between the leaders of the political parties.[2] Twenty years later still, the comprehensive reform plan which had been agreed by the front benches[3] was placed before the House of Commons in the Parliament (No. 2) Bill, only to have backbench MPs from both sides ensure its ignominious withdrawal.[4] Subsequently the political parties went their separate ways. The Conservatives decided that doing nothing was the best policy, the party leadership declining to adopt the scheme put forward by Lord Home and a Conservative Party committee in 1978 for a partly-nominated and partly-elected second chamber.[5] By the late 1970s, the Labour Party had plumped for abolition, a policy reversed a decade later in favour of an elected second chamber with limited legislative authority; then, new Labour decided to remove hereditaries as the first stage towards creating an elected chamber with as yet unspecified powers. The Liberal Democrats, true to

* This chap. is adapted from chap. 5 of my *Constitutional Reform* (2nd edn., Oxford, Oxford University Press, 1998).

[1] *Report of the Conference on the Reform of the Second Chamber* (London, HMSO, Cd. 9038, 1918).

[2] *Agreed Statement on the Conclusion of the Conference on the Parliament Bill 1947* (London, HMSO, Cmd. 7380, 1948).

[3] *House of Lords Reform* (London, HMSO, Cmnd. 3799, 1968).

[4] The text of the Bill is given in Rodney Brazier, *Constitutional Texts* (Oxford, Clarendon Press, 1990), at 529–40.

[5] *The House of Lords: Report of the Review Committee* (London, Conservative Political Centre, 1978). Doing nothing (or at any rate nothing very much) has been advocated also by a number of crossbench peers, chaired by the Earl of Carnarvon: see their report *Second Chamber* (1995).

their radical traditions—exemplified in the preamble to Asquith's Parliament Act—wish to see a second chamber elected by proportional representation and possessing major legislative powers. Schemes have also been proposed by those outside government.[6]

Over the years, paper plans have been supplemented by legislative action over the composition and powers of the House of Lords—not, indeed, of a comprehensive or radical kind, but piecemeal and useful none the less. So, the House of Commons was made pre-eminent in legislation, and omnipotent over money,[7] by the Parliament Act 1911. Since the invention of life peerages in 1958, the House of Lords has gradually changed from being a thinly-attended[8] and rather sleepy place into a chamber with an average daily attendance of some 300 members which gets through a substantial amount of work. That transformation was enhanced by the introduction of attendance, travel and office allowances and expenses. Peeresses in their own right and Scottish peers have been full members since 1963, in the same year in which it became possible for hereditary peers to disclaim their peerages for life.[9] None of that has, however, touched the central anachronism that one House of Parliament has a large majority of members who are there only because they are the children of their parents, or who can claim some other line of descent in the hereditary peerage. The House is unelected, unrepresentative and unaccountable. Why, in a century in which democracy has burgeoned and flourished around the world, has the seemingly indefensible survived?

Those who have grappled with the problem of Lords reform might sympathise with Trollope's Plantagenet Palliser. He brought to politics, as seen through the Palliser novels, a burning passion to decimalise the Victorian currency. He failed. As Trollope put it, "When in power, he had not succeeded in carrying his measure, awed, and at last beaten, by the infinite difficulty in arranging its details".[10] Lords reform has beaten both Liberal and Labour ministers so far, partly because of the complexities of arranging its details, but perhaps mainly because of a number of peculiarities and paradoxes which beset the upper House. Thus, the hereditary composition of the House of Lords was stated to be temporary in the Parliament Act 1911; but the hereditaries are there still. The United Kingdom has exported to the nations of the Commonwealth large numbers of second chambers based on election; but she has been unable to create one for herself. Everyone (apart from unicameralists) believes that the

---

[6] See, e.g., Institute for Public Policy Research, *A Written Constitution for the United Kingdom* (London, IPPR, 1991), at chap. 6; Brigid Hadfield, "Whether or Whither the House of Lords?", 35 *Northern Ireland Legal Quarterly* 313; Dawn Oliver, *Government in the United Kingdom* (Buckingham, Open University Press, 1991), at 54–6. The fullest and most recent independent analysis is the Constitution Unit's *Reform of the House of Lords* (London, Constitution Unit, 1996), which must be read by everyone with an interest in the subject.

[7] See Rodney Brazier, "The Financial Powers of the House of Lords" (1988) 17 *Anglo-American Law Review* 17.

[8] E.g., the average daily attendance of peers in the 1950–1 Session was a mere 86.

[9] Peerage Act 1963.

[10] Anthony Trollope, *Phineas Redux* (1874), at chap. 1.

House of Lords rightly has the power to delay Commons Bills in appropriate circumstances so that (for example) public opinion may be sounded on them; in doing so, reliance is placed on an unelected and unrepresentative House to frustrate the wishes of the very chamber which is elected in order to represent public opinion. The government majority in the House of Commons damns hereditary and nominated peers when they do delay Commons Bills, but no House of Commons has been able to agree on how to replace such peers with elected representatives. Oppositions want the House of Lords to act against legislation passed at the request of an elective dictatorship, but do not want peers to interfere with *their* legislation when *they* are in office. Many Members of Parliament would like to see a reformed second chamber, provided that it did not exercise its new powers as a rival to the House of Commons; but a newly-created second chamber would fairly assume that it had been given powers in order to use them from time to time. A reconstituted second chamber could not be elected by the same method and at the same time as the House of Commons, because it would then be a pointless duplicate of that House; but if it were elected by a different method and at different times that could result in a chamber with a political make-up different from that of the Commons, thus making conflict between the two Houses inevitable. If the second chamber were to be elected by proportional representation, the objection that is currently made that the House of Lords has no political legitimacy would disappear; but if it *were* so elected the new House would have *greater* political authority and be more representative than a House of Commons which remained elected by the first-past-the-post method. In view of all that, if Plantagenet Palliser had been given the option by his creator of either grappling with such peculiar traits and paradoxes or of trying to decimalise the currency, might he not still have elected to pit his wits against pounds, shillings, and pence?

Most liberal democracies have legislatures consisting of two chambers.[11] Those that do not usually have small populations, such as Denmark, Sweden and New Zealand. Even states which have been forced to embark on radical constitutional reconstructions, like Germany after the Second World War (and, indeed, in 1990), or France in 1958, have generally retained a second chamber. Perhaps that trend is explained as much by the forces of tradition as by any need to provide a legislative check on the lower chamber. Again, most second chambers are elected in one way or another, but in a minority of states some members are appointed by the government and a few are entirely composed in that manner. The United Kingdom goes with the trend in being a bicameralist state; and the House of Lords on an average day, made up of a majority of peers who have been nominated to be there, is not in that regard a unique place in the parliaments of the world. What, of course, does make it unique is its potential majority of hereditary members who could turn up to alter the course of proceedings.

---

[11] For the historical reasons, see Donald Shell, *The House of Lords* (Hemel Hempstead, Harvester Wheatsheaf, 1992), at 1–9; and, for comparative information see n. 6 above, the Constitution Unit, at chap. 3.

The question which should be addressed is not whether the House of Lords is unusual among the world's legislatures, but whether it is an effective and appropriate part of the parliament of a democratic country approaching the year 2000.

It is possible to state the functions of the House of Lords with some precision. The 1968 White Paper, for example, listed seven functions.[12] Undoubtedly, the most important work of the Lords today is its consideration and revision of public Bills sent up from the Commons. That work accounts for at least half of peers' time each session, and on average about 1,500 amendments are made every year by them. This is work well done, in that the vast majority of Lords amendments are accepted by the government and the House of Commons—unsurprisingly, as most of them are proposed by Ministers in the Lords.[13] The legislative work of the House is complemented by the introduction there each session of about a dozen, usually uncontroversial, government Bills. This reduces the pressure on the Commons, and gives peers work to do while they wait for the first Commons Bills of the session to be sent up. The government faces scrutiny through questions from peers, and through Lords select committees, of which those on the European Community and on science and technology are generally acknowledged to be outstanding successes. It is often claimed that the quality of debate in the House of Lords is higher than that in the other place, a claim which in its nature cannot be proved. Debates are certainly of a different quality—much less party-political, joined by experts from many walks of life, not in general constrained by worries about whether a particular speech or point might upset the Whips, or might help or hinder the speaker's hopes for ministerial office. All this scarcely represents a picture of an otiose second chamber, but rather describes one which contributes usefully to the shape of legislation and to discussions of the issues of the day.

THE LORDS ATTACKED AND DEFENDED

Critics of the House of Lords always ask the central question of how appropriate it is in a democracy to have a chamber which is dominated by hereditary and mainly Conservative peers. In that form, that is a loaded question which like many loaded questions asserts rather more than is compatible with the facts. Fifty years ago, the party composition of the House of Lords gave the Conservatives some 400 adherents, the Liberals 80, and Labour a mere 15.[14]

---

[12] They were (1) to be the supreme court of appeal; (2) to provide a forum for debate; (3) to revise public Bills passed by the Commons; (4) to initiate less controversial legislation; (5) to consider subordinate legislation; (6) to scrutinise the activities of the executive; and (7) to consider private legislation.

[13] E.g., in the 1988–9 Session the Lords made 2,401 amendments to Bills, most of which were acceptable to the Commons: see Lord Belstead, Leader of the House of Lords, at H.L. Deb., vol. 518, col. 634 (25 Apr. 1990).

[14] N. 11 above, Shell, at 13.

Today, that party mix is very different. Leaving out of account those peers with leave of absence[15] and those who have no writ of summons,[16] the Conservatives can claim almost 500 supporters, while Labour has about 110, and the Liberal Democrats 55. But another crucial difference from half a century ago is that there are currently about 300 crossbenchers and a further 80 or so peers with no affiliations. Of course, nothing like the maximum possible complement of some 1,100 peers, or anything like the maximum total of 775 hereditary peers, ever present themselves. The average daily attendance is about 300, in which life peers and hereditary peers of first creation usually have a small majority over hereditary peers. In that working House, the Conservatives will be able to count on a small majority.[17] This transformation from a House overwhelmed by hereditary Conservatives has been achieved by the invention of life peerages.

Thus, the House of Lords is not daily dominated by hereditary and, in the main, Conservative peers. But what of the backwoodsmen, caricatured as living deep in the shires, Conservative to a man (occasionally to a woman), and ever ready to answer the summons from the Conservative Chief Whip to sweep to Westminster to save the nation—or at least to save the Conservative Party? The old, and largely accurate, jibe was that the House of Lords snoozed while a Conservative was in Downing Street, but sprang to life to thwart policies of Liberal, and later of Labour, Prime Ministers. Certainly, some policies of Labour governments have been delayed (or worse) by the Lords in fairly recent memory: the fates of measures such as the House of Commons (Redistribution of Seats) Bill in 1969 or the Aircraft and Shipbuilding Industries Bill in the 1975–7 sessions, or the Trade Union and Labour Relations (Amendment) Bill in 1975–6, all testify to that. But, since the advent of Mr Edward Heath's government, the House of Lords has interfered with Conservative measures, too. It did so most spectacularly over the Bill to cancel Greater London Council elections in 1984 (the unelected House thwarting the elected chamber for acting undemocratically—another paradox[18]), and over the War Crimes Bill in 1990–1.[19] Although bare statistics about legislative defeats show nothing of their nature or importance,[20] who would have even dreamt in 1979 that, by 1989, Mrs Margaret Thatcher's Bills would have been amended against her wishes in the House of Lords on 125 occasions?[21] Labour governments have endured numerically more setbacks, it is true, but at least a degree of greater evenhandedness with respect to both parties seems to have come about. In doing so, the House

[15] Usually some 80 to 100 peers have leave of absence in any given session.

[16] In 1995 85 peers lacked such a writ.

[17] Within the ranks of life peers, the Conservatives can claim some 140 adherents, Labour some 100, the Liberal Democrats about 30, with over 100 crossbenchers.

[18] For the defeat see H.L. Deb., vol. 453, cols. 1033–70 (28 June 1984).

[19] See H.L. Deb., vol. 519, cols. 1080–1208 (4 June 1990); H.L. Deb., vol. 528, cols. 619–742 (30 Apr. 1991).

[20] For information about legislative defeats of the government in the House of Lords from 1974 to 1991, see H.L. Deb., vol.512, cols. 534–6 (written answers, 6 Nov. 1989) and H.L. Deb., vol. 532, cols. 62–4 (written answers, 19 Nov. 1991).

[21] See Lord Belstead, Leader of the House of Lords, at H.L. Deb., vol. 146, col. 534 (6 Nov. 1989).

of Lords can claim with some justice that it has forced governments of both colours to think again over some of their legislation, in a proper exercise of the powers enshrined in the Parliament Acts. Moreover, it is also important to keep the exercise of the Lords' revising function in proportion. In an average session, almost regardless of which party is in government, anything from half to two-thirds of public Bills brought from the Commons are passed by the House of Lords with no amendments of any kind.

That Conservative as well as Labour governments are vulnerable to checks in the House of Lords from time to time may be explained by several factors. The number of crossbenchers has increased, and crossbench peers can act truly independently. The power of party in the second chamber is much weaker than in the Commons, partly because peers cannot be cajoled or disciplined in the same way as their Commons counterparts. In recent years peers have been lobbied more intensely than ever before, because lobbyists believe that amendments are more likely to be carried in the Lords than in the heavily-whipped Commons. As a consequence of all this, rhetoric about the uniquely anti-left nature of the modern House of Lords has a slightly old-fashioned ring about it. Certainly, the Chief Whip in the Lords in a Conservative government can mobilize battalions of peers rarely seen at Westminster to vote the government line. He did so notoriously in 1988 to defeat a vital amendment (moved by a Conservative backbench peer) which would have related the planned poll tax to a person's ability to pay: the second-highest turn out of peers this century ensured a government victory by 317 votes to 183. Thirty-one peers who voted in the division had not made their maiden speeches, and all but three of them voted with the government. The government Chief Whip claimed in the aftermath of that vote that, because attendance at the House of Lords is voluntary, he could rely on a three-line whip being answered adequately only if he were to send it out no more than twice a year. An ability to do even that, so as to bring in so many relative strangers to the House to do the Conservative Party's bidding, is twice more than is justifiable.

The authority of the House of Lords is weakened in three major respects. It is anomalous, unrepresentative, and Conservative led. No modern state seeking to create a new legislature would devise anything as odd as a House most of whose members existed on the basis of heredity, while the rest existed on the unrestricted patronage of the head of government. True, the accidents of heredity can produce some young peers: in a survey some years ago, seventy hereditary peers were listed as being under forty (and over half the hereditary peers were under sixty), whereas no life peer was under forty, and only thirty-nine were under sixty: indeed, the average age of life peers was seventy.[22] But it is not convincing to assert that, because they do not owe their place in Parliament to prime ministerial patronage, hereditary peers must be independent, for although some are, others are as slavishly devoted to their parties as any recipient of a Prime

---

[22] N. 11 above, Shell, at 40. The average age of all peers in that year was 63.

Minister's favour. The fact that heredity has thrown up a Communist baron[23] needs to be set against the more important facts that the majority of hereditary peers would usually support the Conservative Party, and that only about a dozen of them take the Labour whip. Being an unelected House, it is not designed to be representative; but it is not even loosely representative of society. The House of Lords is dominated by well-off, well-educated men: it is not a cross-section of society, in the sort of way that we like to think that juries are. The greatest source of new personnel is the House of Commons, former Members (and especially ex-ministers) being translated there as life peers for a kind of semi-retirement. The principle of having life peers is defensible: the way in which they are chosen is not. The repeated requests to Mrs Thatcher and Mr John Major from Labour Leaders of the Opposition for the creation of more life peers to reinforce Labour's thin ranks either were refused, or were agreed to but each time in a list containing more Conservative creations than Labour ones. That was absurd, and Mr Tony Blair has understandably recommended the creation of significant numbers of Labour life peers since May 1997. It cannot be right that one party is permanently in a stronger position in the House of Lords than any other, even if that does not guarantee the sacrosanctity of all Conservative legislation in that House.

What, though, are the main benefits which are conferred on the constitution by the House of Lords? I will pick out two. One is the presence of life peers. People outside the practice of politics, especially men and women rising in their careers, can be inducted into Parliament without having to become professional politicians or having to embrace the burdens of elections and constituents. People earning their living, or living and working away from London, are not going to be attracted to Parliament if they have to commit themselves to being there regularly, and the paraphernalia of elections and the demands of constituents would scarcely be an added incentive. The expertise which they possess would not, by and large, be available in Parliament if the second chamber were based on any elective principle. (Whether the mechanism of life peerages is adequately used to bring in sufficient numbers of younger people, women, members of minority groups and representatives of all the regions of the United Kingdom is another question which will be addressed later.) The other benefit is the unpredictability of the House of Lords in the matter of legislation. In its tendency to treat the legislation of both parties with something approaching an impartial rigour, the House of Lords has become the only counterweight in the British constitution to elective dictatorship. While the government can, in general, rely on the Commons to do as they are told, Ministers have no such felicity in relation to the Lords (although it is right that the elected House should normally get its way in the end). It would be very different if the second chamber were elected. Presumably, if one party held sway in both Houses, ministers could sleep soundly at night in the knowledge that their Bills were sure of safe

---

[23] The second Lord Milford.

passages through Parliament; but when different parties dominated each House, turmoil—or at least delay—would be caused to the government's legislative programme.

## WHAT CAN BE DONE?

So what is to be done about the House of Lords? Since the acceptance by the Labour Party at its annual conference in 1989 of the need for an elected second chamber, we are all bicameralists. Abolition of the second chamber would not be a sensible way forward. Without a second chamber, elective dictatorship would be utterly unfettered. Legislation, moreover, would become even worse than it is now: even at its present rate of overworking, the House of Commons manages to pass badly-written legislation, tracts of which are cut off by the guillotine from debate and amendment. When he was Leader of the House of Commons, Mr Richard Crossman estimated that if the House of Lords were to be abolished at least two additional stages would be needed in the Commons to deal adequately with legislation. Meshing in such stages scarcely seems feasible: a second, revising chamber of some sort is, as most other states believe, essential.

At the other extreme from the option of abolition was the late Conservative government's policy of doing absolutely nothing about the Lords. Mrs Thatcher ignored the 1978 Home Committee proposals. Even the mauling by the Lords of the Bill to cancel Greater London Council elections, and the rejection of the War Crimes Bill, did not goad her into action. Doing nothing is obviously an option. Adherents to that approach must rely on a generalised statement that the House of Lords "works", and must reject as unconvincing the criticisms which have been made of that House.

Two of the political parties do have plans to reform the second chamber. Without doubt the more radical scheme emanates from the Liberal Democrats. Their constitutional reform document[24] proposes a new Senate, which would consist of about 225 members, directly elected (naturally enough) by proportional representation. Scotland, Wales, Northern Ireland and each of the English regions would return specified numbers of Senators, each of whom would serve for six years and with one third retiring every two years. There might also be a number of co-opted Senators. Commons ministers would attend and participate as appropriate but without votes in Senate proceedings. As would befit such an illustrious body, substantial powers would be vested in it: indeed, the present suspensory veto of about a year possessed by the Lords would, in this Senate, be *doubled*, although its powers over financial legislation would be the same as those of the House of Lords. By contrast, the replacement chamber envisaged in the Labour Party's last full (and subsequently abandoned) policy document on the subject

---

[24] *Here We Stand: Proposals for Modernising Britain's Democracy* (London, Liberal Democrat Federal White Paper No. 6, 1993), at 23–4.

would have been very different.[25] The Lords would have been abolished, and a new second chamber would have been elected, almost certainly not by the first-past-the-post method, but by some system of proportional representation. The Plant Report of 1993 suggested the use of the regional list system, which might have resulted in a chamber of 320 members. That chamber's powers over most Commons legislation would have been limited to referring Bills back to the lower House for one reconsideration,[26] after which such Bills would have passed into law in the form desired by the Commons: thus the present Lords suspensory veto would have been cut substantially. But new Labour abandoned that detailed plan in opposition, and it came to power in 1997 committed to a two-stage reform programme. In the first stage, the hereditaries would be removed from membership of the House of Lords and, in the second, there would be consultation on the shape of a replacement and elected chamber.[27]

An elected second chamber would constitute a House of Parliament with the political legitimacy which popular election brings. It would be representative of the electorate—indeed, if it were elected by proportional representation it would be more representative than the House of Commons itself. The political advantage enjoyed over the centuries by one party in the second chamber would be ended. Those would all be notable gains. But such schemes would share certain disadvantages. First, the pool of talent which is prepared to make part-time contributions to Parliament as nominated peers would, without doubt, be largely lost because most such amateurs would have no inclination to turn professional. Secondly, conflict between the House of Commons and an elected second chamber would be unavoidable; even a second chamber with weaker powers than the House of Lords would have to irritate the Commons on occasion if it were to have a reason for being at all. And a new second chamber would be overwhelmingly party-political, for how many crossbench, or independent, members would be elected—especially under a regional list system? By analogy with the House of Commons, hardly any.

The Labour government may introduce a Bill in the 1998–9 session to remove hereditary peers from the House of Lords.[28] Such a Bill was promised in the Party's 1997 general election manifesto, and its passage would be procured, if necessary, under the Parliament Acts.[29] If such a Bill were to be passed, it could prove to be as temporary as the Parliament Act 1911 (which, it will be recalled, was to hold the

---

[25] See *Meet the Challenge: Make the Change* (London, The Labour Party, 1989), at 55–6. The 1989 paper was supplemented by the *Plant Report: Report of the Working Party on Electoral Systems* (London, The Labour Party, 1993), at chap. 4. The 1989 document was to be abandoned by new Labour in the early 1990s.

[26] The exception would have been Bills to amend specified civil rights laws, which the second chamber could have delayed until after a general election.

[27] The merits and demerits of all feasible methods of consultation are considered in detail in n. 6 above, the Constitution Unit, at chap. 7.

[28] A draft short, five-clause, Bill to do just that is ready: n. 6 above, the Constitution Unit, at Appendix A.

[29] Indeed, under the Salisbury convention the House of Lords should not seek to defeat any Bill for which a government has manifesto authority.

ring until an elected chamber was created). It would be much more difficult for a government to move to that next stage: the time might never prove ripe: we might end up with a House whose membership was based entirely on prime-ministerial nomination, but without any of the counterbalances to that power which were envisaged in the 1968 scheme. Would the government of the day expect to nominate any additional peers necessary to give it a majority in the House, or (as in the 1968 proposals) would the government just have a majority over the main opposition party, but not over the Opposition plus the crossbenchers? Moreover, no doubt life peerages would be offered to a number of existing hereditary peers after the Act excluding hereditary peers had been passed, so that their expertise could be retained in the new House: but who would choose the reprieved ones? Ministers are apparently considering setting up an independent commission to advise the Prime Minister on the creation of new life peers, a welcome departure (if it comes to fruition) from unrestrained prime-ministerial patronage.[30]

### GRADUAL CHANGE: A NOTION OF REDUCTION

The importance of the second chamber must not be exaggerated. It is much the less powerful and the less significant House. The House of Commons is rightly pre-eminent and is the (admittedly somewhat worn) cradle of British democracy, which needs and deserves all the urgent reformist energy that can be mustered. The fair complaint that the House of Lords caused trouble only for non-Conservative governments has been rectified to an extent. (That complaint might, of course, revive: indeed, the previous Leader of the House of Lords, Lord Richard, criticised hereditary peers for some legislative amendments that have been carried against the government's wishes.) Several of the unacceptable incidents of the unreformed House have gradually been removed. Attempting to bring about radical change to the House of Lords may just not be worth a government's parliamentary time and the trouble involved in securing it against the objections of the Opposition; moreover, even if cross-party front bench agreement were to be achieved, the events of 1968–9 show that such agreement may promise everything yet still deliver nothing. The fundamental obstacle in the way of comprehensive Lords reform is still that there is no consensus among the parties or in the country about what a second chamber is for. Without such common ground there can be no general agreement about any final replacement.[31] Accordingly, what I believe should be done is to continue in the gradualist tradition of limited and pragmatic reforms, wherever possible pursued through agreement between the parties.[32]

---

[30] Since 1964 Prime Ministers have been responsible for the creation of over 700 new peers.

[31] N. 6 above, the Constitution Unit, at chap. 4.

[32] The Labour government is committed by its 1997 manifesto to consultation through a joint select committee of both Houses, although that government's first Leader of the House of Lords, Lord Richard, personally favours the use of a Royal Commission.

Assuming that elections do not reach the House of Lords (as I suspect they may not), the ways in which people are nominated for life peerages will remain of central importance. The procedures leading up to the publication of lists of working peers hold the key and, typically of so much of the British constitution, would not require legislation to change them. At present, these procedures are informal and based on barter between the parties, the leaders of the opposition parties trying to get as many of their supporters as possible accepted for nomination as life peers, while Prime Ministers have ensured usually that people who will take the government whip are in the majority in each list. It would be desirable if these discreet procedures could be made rather more formal, and if they could be based on a number of precepts. Thus, the party leaders should acknowledge that all the parties represented in the Commons have a legitimate expectation of representation in the House of Lords (subject to some minimum number of Members of Parliament and votes obtained at the previous general election to qualify). They should accept that the active party strengths in the House of Lords, together with votes and seats won at the previous general election, should be taken into account in drawing up lists of working peers. In doing that, the party leaders should try to increase the numbers of non-Conservative peers so as to correct to some degree the historical party imbalance in the Lords. A rough and ready formula for replenishing the Lords, with those aims in mind, would be preferable to any tit-for-tat exercises of patronage. Part of a new compact between the party leaders ought to be a concerted attempt to find more women, younger people and members of ethnic minorities, for nomination as life peers, together with a strategy to ensure that all the nations and regions of the United Kingdom had active representation in the second chamber. There could be a part here for the Public Appointments Unit of the Cabinet Office. The political parties can be relied on to look after their own, but that Unit, if given the Prime Minister's authority, might seek out non-party people, using advertising for the purpose. Voluntary groups and others could put in suggestions, and of course individuals could nominate themselves. Perhaps the party leaders might also agree that certain people should go to the House of Lords by virtue of their offices, such as the Governor of the Bank of England, the General Secretary of the Trades Union Congress, and so on. It should not prove controversial to reduce the number of Bishops in the House—for it was agreed in 1968 to cut their presence from twenty-six to sixteen (still a remarkably generous number)—or to try to get leaders of other faiths into the Lords, again perhaps *ex officio*.

What these more formalised procedures should aim at, in a word, is reductions—reductions in the party imbalance in the second chamber, reductions in the average age of life peers, reductions in the imbalance between the sexes, and reductions in the over-representation of the Church of England. This notion of reduction might usefully be carried further. Thus the Lords of Appeal in Ordinary, other peers who may sit judicially, and serving judges ought to be excluded from membership. It is wrong in principle that judges are able to intervene in the process of legislation, especially given the growing tendency for some of them to participate in debates on even politically controversial topics. Some legal expertise, which is of particular relevance to the form of legislation, would be lost by their going, but then, as it has been estimated that 10 per cent of the House of Lords are qualified lawyers,[33] the loss of even a couple of dozen judicial peers would be of rather less significance than some might suppose.

A notion of reduction as a principle to guide changes in the House of Lords ought to apply so as to cut the number of peers entitled to attend its proceedings. Measures must be taken against backwoodsmen, in order to end the disgrace of the attendance of those who are not seen at Westminster for months or even years on end suddenly being called up by the Conservative Chief Whip to outvote those who attend regularly. It is indefensible that a peer who is not able or prepared to present himself or herself for a certain number of parliamentary days retains full voting rights. The 1968 White Paper envisaged a minimum attendance requirement of one-third of all sittings each session for voting peers.[34] No one could object to reluctant peers keeping their right to speak (but not to vote) on their rare appearances (although it would be an interesting exercise to see just how many of the worst offenders actually have been moved to add their voices to their votes on such occasions). The Report by the Group on the Working of the House[35] recorded that, counting only those peers who attended at least one-third of the sittings, the party composition of the working House in the 1985–6 session would have been Conservatives 168, Labour 88, and Liberal/SDP Alliance (as they then were) 51, with 73 crossbenchers. On the same basis, there would have been 217 life peers and 163 hereditary peers entitled to vote. The crossbenchers would have held a balance of power between left and right. Now perhaps a one-third requirement would be too onerous, and a lower proportion might be agreed on. It would also be for consideration whether life peers should be subject to the same attendance requirement as hereditary peers, or to a lower one. Younger or middle-aged life peers (and potential life peers) earning their living nowhere near London are to be encouraged to attend (and to become members). A careful balance would need to be struck. An additional advantage of a scheme based on an attendance requirement (or requirements) would be that the leave of absence procedure, invented over 30 years ago to solve the backwoodsmen problem and having conspicuously failed to do so, could be scrapped.

These ideas will be criticised as being too timid. Certainly, when set against the bold nostrums put up by the Liberal Democrats and by the Labour Party, that is a fair adjective to use. Dreaming up schemes is a simple and agreeable pastime. But reform plans ought to be formulated with the realities of the polit-

---

[33] N. 11 above, Shell, at 48.

[34] As a recompense, voting peers would have been paid a salary of £2,000 a year. Peers remain unpaid; it should be considered whether life peers who meet minimum attendance requirements ought to receive a parliamentary salary.

[35] H.L. 9 (1987–8), Table II.

ical situation clearly in mind if they are ever to stand a reasonable chance of being implemented and of lasting. If the political parties could be persuaded to ponder Lords reform together and calmly, rather than separately and only in the light of their own final solutions, ways around several noble paradoxes might actually be found.

# 4

# *Second Chambers—A Comparative Perspective*

PAUL CARMICHAEL and ANDREW BAKER

## INTRODUCTION

The debate about the legislative role of the British House of Lords has focused on abolition or varying degrees of reform. There is no consensus over what form reform should take. In part, the disagreement stems from uncertainty and misinformation about what precisely is the function of a second chamber, as well as on questions of composition, role, powers and relationships with the first chamber, the executive and the judiciary. To further the debate, questions asking why second chambers exist, what is their use and what role they perform need to be answered. In order to gain a richer perspective, comparisons from abroad are essential. This, in turn, raises questions over the extent of, and reasons for, the significant variation between different systems. Above all, it begs the question of ideal types—is there an archetypal form of second chamber which satisfies academic commentators and policy practitioners? The comparative study of parliamentary structures and legislatures has produced a well established and voluminous literature. For example, Blondel, Lowenburg and Patterson, and Mezey all developed thematic comparative analytical frameworks for researching parliamentary processes.[1] This chapter is concerned specifically with second chambers. With adaptation and synthesis, we aim to construct a framework that will provide the basis for analysing and distinguishing between various forms of second chamber. Space constraints prevent a comprehensive treatment. However, it has been possible to focus primarily on a select group of states, namely, the Republic of Ireland, France, Germany, Italy and the United States of America, with some reference to countries with unicameral and other systems. First, however, the debate over bicameralism must be set within the wider contextual framework of the role of parliaments and of representative government. Hence, we begin by reviewing the *raison d'être* of bicameralism, tracing its historical and theoretical roots.

[1] J. Blondel, *Comparative Legislatures* (New Jersey, Prentice Hall, 1973); P. Laundy, *Parliaments in the Modern World* (Aldershot, Dartmouth, 1989); G. Loewenberg and S. C. Patterson, *Comparative Legislatures* (Boston, Mass., Little, Brown, 1979); M. L. Mezey, *Comparative Legislatures* (Durham, N.C., Duke University Press, 1979).

UNICAMERALISM AND BICAMERALISM

The concept of representation marked a fundamental break in the state form. For Bobbio, it was a "genuine Copernican revolution in the evolution of the relationship between rulers and ruled" because it postulated a new principle of legitimacy, namely, that of popular consent.[2] Progressively, elected representative assemblies have become the cornerstone of modern liberal democracies. The authoritative process of government and of the wider state is seen, at least theoretically, to derive its legitimacy from the fact that those in government owe their position to the elected will of the people, as reflected in the composition of the legislature. For Norton, legislatures are viewed as "constitutionally designated institutions for giving assent to binding measures of public policy" whilst elections are a usual but not a "defining characteristic".[3] Blondel argued that in the "overwhelming majority of countries, constitutions state that the "legislature", "parliament" or the "congress" is the expression of popular sovereignty, and either that it is the top decision-making body or, at least, that its status is on a par with that of the executive".[4] In reality, some legislatures have been abolished; in many cases, they are wholly manipulated; in the majority, they are controlled, and only in a small number of polities are they "an essential element in the national decision making process".[5] The symbolism evoked by the idea of a national representative forum explains the enduring appeal of legislatures in all types of constitutional regime.

Bryce's first truly empirical study of western governments suggested strongly that legislatures were weak, decadent and in decline, giving a *prima facie* case for resurrecting some golden age of parliaments.[6] Blondel asserted that this breakdown is a direct product of the age of big government and large-scale intervention in both society and economy. He added that: "[i]t is simply impossible for assemblies to be sovereign with respect to modern social and economic legislation: they can only participate in a general process of decision making".[7] In the main, legislatures are confined to exercising influence via scrutiny of the administration. Nevertheless, despite the reality of often docile legislatures in the face of executive dominance, especially in those polities where the legislature and executive are intertwined (as distinct from presidential systems), some attempt at reinvigorating the elected element of the polity appears overdue.

Ostensibly, determining the structure of a legislature ought to be straightforward enough. In a system of democracy predicated upon the representative

---

[2] N. Bobbio, *Democracy and Dictatorship* (Cambridge, Polity Press, 1985), at 115.

[3] P. Norton (ed.), *Parliaments in Western Europe* (London, Cass, 1990), at 1.

[4] J. Blondel, *Comparative Government* (London, Prentice Hall/Harvester Wheatsheaf, 1995), at 249.

[5] *Ibid.*

[6] Lord Bryce, "The Decline of Legislatures" in P. Norton (ed.), *Legislatures* (Oxford, Oxford University Press, 1990).

[7] N. 4 above, at 252.

principle, "one people" ought to imply "one legislature". Indeed, for Meny, "the theory of representation seems incompatible with the idea of more than one chamber of representatives".[8] Certainly, to create more than that would appear to invite conflict. Critics of bicameralism assert that it fosters unnecessary "complications, delays and expense without any compensating advantage for the regime".[9] The dilemmas associated with having two chambers of a parliament prompted the French prelate and revolutionary Emmanuel Sieyès (the Abbé Sieyès) to remark that "if a second chamber dissents from the first it is mischievous; it if agrees with it, it is superfluous".[10] More recently, a meeting of the Commonwealth Parliamentary Association in 1991 supported a unicameral system for smaller countries "dismissing upper chambers variously as a waste of money and manpower, ineffective, undemocratic and a needless duplication of effort".[11] Blondel's rather casual treatment of the topic is puzzling and does little to sustain his contention that "it is questionable as to whether there is any longer a real case for a second chamber, except in countries where there are sharp geographical cleavages (hence their value in a federal context)".[12] Despite the predicament over number of chambers, the formation of legislatures (or, more accurately, "representative fora") has been marked by the emergence of both unicameral and bicameral structures.

The question of structure is not simply a matter of exercising preference within a vacuum. Miller and Hammond contended that the impact of the configuration of governmental institutions on the stability of legislative policies can be discerned from analysing unicameral and bicameral systems.[13] Using simple mathematical logic, they demonstrate how there is "no equilibrium policy" in a unicameral system. Hence, "because some policies which are unstable in unicameral institutions are stable in bicameral institutions, we may conclude that the choice of institution can matter".[14]

Most countries of the world are unitary systems, whilst some 20 are federations.[15] Of 178 unitary states, some 51 are bicameral.[16] Bicameralism is strongest in South America, the Caribbean (but not central America) and the "Atlantic" countries (North America and Europe). Where they exist, second

---

[8] Y. Meny, *Government and Politics in Western Europe* (Oxford, Oxford University Press, 1993), at 188.

[9] M. Ameller, *Parliaments* (London, Cassell/Inter-Parliamentary Union, 1966), at 13.

[10] G. FitzGerald, "When the Tame Pussy-Cat Seanad Grew Some Claws" in the *Irish Times* (20 May 1995).

[11] Commonwealth Parliamentary Conference of Members from Small Countries Summary Report, *The Parliamentarian* (January 1992), cited in Constitution Unit, *Reform of the House of Lords* (London, The Constitution Unit, 1996), at 22.

[12] N. 4 above, at 254.

[13] G. Miller and T. Hammond, "Stability and Efficiency in a Separation of Powers Constitutional System" in B. Grofman and D. Wittman (eds.), *The Federalist Papers and the New Institutionalism* (New York, Agathon Press, 1989).

[14] T. Hammond, "Formal Theory and the Institutions of Governance", *Governance* 9(2) 107–85 at 125–6.

[15] J. Derbyshire and I. Derbyshire, *Political Systems of the World* (Edinburgh, Chambers, 1989).

[16] The Constitution Unit, n. 11 above.

chambers tend to be much less powerful than the main chamber because of the representative nature of the lower house. That said, the quality of the representativeness of the first chamber varies enormously between states. At best, "we are bound to recognise that the lower chambers approximate no more than imperfectly to the ideals of liberal philosophy".[17] Essentially, the origins of second chambers differ from, on the one hand, the recognition of the federal or regionalist nature of the state in question (as in the USA, Germany, Spain) and, on the other, on the historical legacy of constitutional development (UK and France). Some second chambers exist almost as co-equals, for example, Italy. Some are clearly the poor relation—in France and Britain, "the official two-chamber system marks what in effect virtually amounts to a one chamber system".[18] Uniquely, the US Senate possesses greater powers in certain respects than the House of Representatives, whilst the German Bundesrat occupies the mid-range position—no right of legislative initiative but with major and inviolate veto powers.

Since the first and, in many respects, most fundamental distinction between types of second chamber is whether they exist in unitary or federal states, the justification for the presence, and the historical roots of the respective types, of bicameralism vary considerably. We focus first on unitary states.

BICAMERALISM IN UNITARY STATES

Notwithstanding the obvious case of federations (considered below), there is a correlation between size of population and the existence of bicameral systems and, indeed, the "size of population appears to be a significant factor in considering the need for a second chamber at all".[19]

Increasing the size of a lower house is often not a viable proposition, especially in populous states where there is a risk of it becoming unwieldy. On this basis second chambers can have a number of advantages. Their existence can facilitate greater citizen involvement, if only through an increase in the number of contact persons. They also allow additional scope for representatives (of either house) to become involved in the activities of the chambers and in the wider legislative process. The creative tension which can exist between two chambers has the potential for both positive and negative outcomes. There is no *a priori* rule to ensure that the tenor of these relationships is harmonious.

Historically, bicameralism developed in England in the thirteenth century with the establishment of a chamber for the high aristocracy—the early medieval King's Council of feudal magnates—the Lords Spiritual and Lords Temporal. Even today, the British House of Lords retains a large number of hereditary peers "making it a unique phenomenon in contemporary constitu-

---

[17] N. 8 above, at 192.
[18] *Ibid.*
[19] N. 16 above, at 22.

tional law"[20] although its aristocratic character has been diluted by the introduction of Life Peers. The advent of the House of Lords could be seen as the first step in a process of democratisation with England being a model that was eventually replicated across Europe. For Finer *et al.*, "it is arguable that the widespread adoption of an upper house throughout most of Europe and, then, through the wider world springs from the historical accident that Britain had a bicameral legislature in 1815, when her institutions were regarded as a model for western Europe".[21] However, a historical overview of the development of second chambers reveals a more complex picture. Rather than contributing to the democratic process, second chambers all too often restricted it, and deliberately so. State formation in western democracies was accompanied by a process of widening the franchise in response to popular pressures in that direction. Despite this, the process of constitution-building invariably remained the preserve of a small landed élite. In each case, bicameralism could be attributed to the sense of preserving a class advantage, hence the terminology of "upper" and "lower" houses. Frequently, the introduction of a second chamber was the product of a pragmatic class compromise, from an aloof and unrepresentative dominant élite seeking to counter the increasing assertiveness of a first chamber buoyed by universal suffrage. The introduction and maintenance of a second chamber made the process of democratisation more palatable to the aristocracy, given the partial preservation of the exclusive nature of political office and that group's continuing privileged access to it.

Accordingly, Ameller contended that bicameral systems are "essentially designed to restrain and moderate the ebullience of popular sovereignty which would operate in too ruthless a manner if there were only a single chamber".[22] To that extent, monarchical and presidential appointments reinforce the innate conservatism of second chambers (as in the UK and Canada). Similarly, narrowed electoral bases do likewise. For example, some second chambers are chosen by members of the first chamber acting as the electorate. In others, such as France, an electoral college of local/sub-national councillors elects the second chamber. Or, in the case of mass suffrage, the franchise might be limited (in whole or in part) to university graduates (for example, Republic of Ireland), to those citizens who own a given amount of property or to those citizens aged over a threshold (for example, Italy). All share an implicit wish for conservatism in constitutional and legislative affairs.

The most fundamental and simple justification for the existence of a second chamber is that "it acts to prevent the excessive concentration of power in the hands of a single institutional actor and compensates for the apparent deficiencies elsewhere in the system".[23] In theory, second chambers do this by checking

[20] N. 9 above, at 8.
[21] S. E. Finer, V. Bogdanor and B. Rudden, *Comparing Constitutions* (Oxford, Oxford University Press, 1995), 59.
[22] N. 9 above, at 12.
[23] N. 16 above, at 22.

the power of an ascendant chamber whilst providing the legislature as a whole with an additional tier or extra dimension to offset the power of the executive. Such claims are based on the belief that the more branches government has, the more difficult it becomes for any one group entirely to monopolise its operation. Bicameralism thus augments polyarchy by contributing to a diverse and pluralistic institutional structure.

In cases where the composition is chosen along similar lines to the first chamber, the powers of second chambers tend to equal or surpass those of the lower house. For example, in Italy, this has translated into an ability to bring down a government. Some states, such as Iceland and Norway, have what might be termed a "unicameral bicameral" system in which the second chamber is composed exclusively from a limited number of members elected to the lower house. The rationale is that the process of having to subject legislative proposals to two rounds of scrutiny and consideration makes for a more thorough and effective process.[24] There are a number of other justifications and advantages of second chambers. Given the risk of overloading the legislature, a second chamber can relieve the pressure. It can review and put a brake on hasty or ill-considered legislation. This might be particularly so if other constituencies of interest which are not, or for constitutional reasons cannot be, provided for in the lower house can be represented in the upper house. On this basis it can be argued that second chambers serve as a "repository of wisdom", allowing accomplished meritocrats, otherwise not given to party politics, to cast an authoritative eye over legislative proposals.

The disadvantages of second chambers can be summarised equally concisely. One perspective is that their conservative disposition can impede or obstruct otherwise progressive measures. This is particularly problematic where the composition of the upper house differs from that of the lower house because any subsequent thwarting of the popular will, as represented by the first, would be undemocratic. Delays in decision-making resulting from a bicameral structure can exacerbate the scale of a problem of national importance, especially when the problem requires immediate action; "double consideration may result in an unacceptable degree of redundancy and delay".[25] Financially, two chambers involve extra cost to the public revenue. Furthermore, in certain instances it can be claimed second chambers serve no constructive purpose, often operating as nothing more than a convenient mechanism for distributing consolation prizes for political failure, appeasing politicians ejected from more active public office.

Many of the considerations outlined above would be of equal relevance in federal states. However, such forms of government have their own distinct justification for the presence of two chambers. It is to the position within federal systems which we now turn.

---

[24] N. 9 above, at 13.
[25] N. 1 above, Lowenberg and Patterson, at 125.

The role of bicameralism in federations is vital. Save for anomalous cases such as the former Yugoslavia, bicameralism is a virtual prerequisite for the success of a federal arrangement. The historical roots and theoretical justifications of bicameralism in federations are distinct from those of unitary states, although many of the advantages and justifications for bicameralism in unitary states apply with equal force. The crucial additional factor is that the inherent duality of the constitutional structure is reflected in a ubiquitous bicameralism. The two-tier essence of the federal principle is inevitably translated into two parliamentary chambers. Bicameralism allows the representation of the nation in a different form. That is, "the obvious rationale is that the component units of the federation shall be represented as such, in contradistinction to the population at large".[26] Generally, this involves having a chamber directly elected by the people as a whole, and another regionally-based chamber composed of representatives from each of the constituent elements of the federation. Such a parliamentary structure reflects the power relationship between centre and periphery that is integral to any notion of federalism, namely a division of powers between the central and local governance structures. To that extent:

> "because this representative responsibility of a federal second chamber is so important, it is perhaps more accurate to describe the role of such chambers in relation to first chambers as complementary rather than compensatory. Indeed, 'complementation' is regarded by most commentators as the key feature of an effective bicameral system whether federal or not".[27]

Historically, federal parliamentary structures have their roots in the formation of the constitution of the United States. The Philadelphia Convention (in 1786) was a response to disagreements (between the founding large and small states) over the number of representatives each state should have in a single chamber. The eventual solution, the "Great Compromise", involved the creation of two chambers, a national one and a separate entity to represent the various states.

Latterly, the endurance of bicameral arrangements in federations attests to the "tenacity of organisational forms well after their original purpose had disappeared" as well as new justifications, such as a belief in the merits of "checks and balances, distrust of majority rule, belief in the virtue of multiple points of access to government, and a preference for slowing the output of legislation".[28] Beyond the existence of two parliaments—the variations between different federal states with regard to parliamentary structure and organisation are immense. An absolute embodiment of federal principles in an existing parliamentary structure in any state would require the fulfilment of a number of

---

[26] N. 21 above, at 58.
[27] N. 16 above, at 22.
[28] N. 21 above, at 121.

desirable criteria. First, the chamber representing the regional units of the federation should have an equal number of representatives from each state, irrespective of size or population; secondly this chamber's powers should be equal to those of the assembly representing the people as a whole. In reality, few federations meet such criteria in very much the same way as few democracies completely embody democratic principles. In fact, it is possible to hypothesise that in most federal states there has been a general centralisation of power which has reduced the extent to which federal principles are embodied. Translated into parliamentary structure this equates with only a partial application of the principle of equal representation of the various territorial units and the development of a situation that closely resembles an upper/lower house relationship between the two chambers, with the national chamber in the ascendancy. In some cases, this has been accompanied by the partial replacement of universal suffrage as a method of appointment with a less transparent method often based on personal or oligarchic judgement.

FOCUS ON NATIONAL EXAMPLES

Table 4.1 outlines the arrangements obtaining within western liberal democratic states with respect to the composition of their national legislatures. A comprehensive treatment cannot be afforded here but, it has been possible to look in a little more detail at five individual cases. In making our selection, we have endeavoured to reflect the variety across the western world: small, medium and large polities; unitary and federal systems; "Anglo-Saxon" and continental systems; bicameral and unicameral legislatures; and, amongst the systems which are bicameral, ones which differ according to the power, role, functions and timing of appointment of the second chamber. Necessarily, any choice is selective and in no way exhaustive or fully representative. However, the choice is informed also by a wish to make for effective comparison with the British position. Hence, our first choice, the Republic of Ireland, rests on the fact that the governmental institutions of this country remain heavily informed by the British influence prior to the state's inception (1922). France is a unitary and centralised state of comparable population and economic strength to the UK but with a unique hybrid constitution based on presidentialism and rationalised parliamentarianism. Also, UK–France comparative analyses are commonplace. As Europe's largest, richest and most powerful state, Germany possesses a federal system imposed under Anglo-American ægis. Also, it offers parallels with the embryonic governmental structure of the European Union. For all its political travails, Italy offers a useful comparison. Its population and economic performance are similar to the UK, whilst both states have experienced fissiparous regional tendencies of late. Also, Italy's second chamber enjoys equal status with the first. Being the world's classic federation and its strongest democracy, the United States of America is an obvious candidate for comparison.

Table 4.1: A comparison of selected national parliaments

| Country | Lower House Composition determined by | Size | Upper House Composition determined by | Size | Comments |
|---|---|---|---|---|---|
| United Kingdom Parliament House of Commons House of Lords | Direct Election Simple Plurality | 659 | Hereditary and appointed | c.1273* | *Includes 759 hereditary peers, 26 bishops, 462 life peers |
| Austria Parliament Nationalrat (National Council) Bundesrat (Federal Council) | Direct Election PR List | 183 | PR (List) by provincial legislatures | 64 | |
| Belgium Chambres Legislatives House of Representatives Senate | Direct Election PR List (d'Hondt) | 150 | PR List (d'Hondt) 40 directly*; 21 community senators*; 10 co-opted. | 71 | *25 Dutch-speakers, 15 French-speakers. *10 Flemish, 10 French, 1 German. |
| Denmark Folketing | Direct Election PR (List) | 179 | – | – | |
| Finland Eduskunta | Direct Election PR (List) (d'Hondt) | 200 | – | – | |
| France Parlement Assemblée Nationale Sénat | Direct Election Double Ballot | 577 | Electoral College (National Assembly Deputies; General Councillors; and, delegates of Municipal Councils). Double Ballot: absolute Majority on 1st ballot, simple majority in 2nd; PR List in departments with 5+ seats. | 321 | |
| Germany Parliament Bundestag Bundesrat | Direct Election PR (Additional Member) 330 single member seats + 330* by PR (List) at Land level (Niemeyer method) | 672* | State Government Nomination | 68 | *Currently 672— varies due to rounding effect in ensuring proportionality |

*Table 4.1: cont.*

| Country | Lower House | | Upper House | | |
|---|---|---|---|---|---|
| | Composition determined by | Size | Composition determined by | Size | Comments |
| Greece Vouli Chamber of Deputies | Direct Election PR (local, regional and national quota allocations) | 300 (min.200)* | | | *288 elected and 12 appointed |
| Ireland Oireachtas Dail Seanad | Direct Election PR (Single Transferable Vote) | 166 | Limited franchise: 43 from 5 panels of candidates representing vocational interests (STV); 6 by University constituencies (STV); 11 by prime minister's nomination. | 60 | |
| Italy Camera dei Deputati Senato della Repubblica | Direct Election | 630 | Direct Elections Majoritarian + 1/4 by PR | 315 (326)* | *Includes 9 appointed by the President plus 2 *ex officio* (ex-Presidents) |
| The Netherlands States General Eerste Kamer (First Chamber) Tweede Kamer (Second Chamber) | Direct Election PR (List—national) | 150 | Provincial Councils PR (List) | 75 | |
| Norway Storting* | Direct Election PR (List) | 155 (116 Lagting, 39 Odelsting) | | 39 | Storting forms 2 divisions after an election—Lagting (39 seats); Odelsting (116 seats) |
| Spain Cortes Generales Congress of Deputies Senate | Direct Election PR (List) (d'Hondt) | 350 (300–400) | 208 Direct Election Simple Plurality 48 by Regional Assemblies | 256 | |

| | Lower House Method | No. | Upper House Method | No. | Notes |
|---|---|---|---|---|---|
| Sweden<br>Rigsdag | Direct Election<br>PR (List) | 349 | — | — | |
| Switzerland Federal Assembly<br>National Council<br>Standerat—Council of States | Direct Election<br>195 by PR (List)<br>(Hagenbach-Bischoff)<br>5 by Simple Plurality in 5<br>single member<br>constituencies | 200 | Direct Election within cantons<br>2 by PR<br>41 by various majority systems<br>3 by assemblies of canton citizens | 46 | |
| Australia Parliament<br>House of Representatives<br>Senate | Direct Election<br>Alternative Vote—single<br>member constituencies | 149 | Direct Election<br>PR (STV) | 76 | |
| New Zealand Parliament<br>House of Representatives | Direct Election<br>PR (Mixed Member<br>Proportional)<br>(From Oct.1996) | 120* | — | — | *Old system of 99<br>seats elected by<br>simple plurality. |
| Japan Diet<br>House of Representatives<br>House of Councillors (Senate) | Direct Election<br>Simple Plurality | 511 | 152 by Direct Election<br>Simple Plurality<br>100 by PR (List) | 252 | |
| United States of America Congress<br>House of Representatives<br>Senate | Direct Election<br>Simple Plurality | 435<br>(440*) | Direct Election<br>Simple Majority (2 per state) | 100 | *4 elected district<br>delegates and 1<br>elected Puerto Rico<br>Commissioner |
| Canada Parliament<br>House of Commons<br>Senate | Direct Election<br>Simple Plurality | 282<br>(295) | "Summoned" by Governor-<br>General on advice of PM and<br>Cabinet based on "approved"<br>lists from provinces | 104<br>(max.<br>112) | |

Source: Gering and Canivan; Inter-Parliamentary Union
References:
V. Gering and L. Canivan, *Methods of Election to Upper Chambers (A Brief Guide)* (London, Electoral Reform Society, 1996); Inter-Parliamentary Union, *Parliaments of the World* (Geneva, Inter-Parliamentary Union, 1986); Inter-Parliamentary Union, *World Directory of Parliaments* (Geneva, Inter-Parliamentary Union, 1995).

Additionally, the USA provides an example of a second chamber which is the more powerful of the two houses of its legislature. Finally, evidence is considered from unicameral states.

### The Republic of Ireland

Under the Irish constitution of 1937, *Bunreacht na hEireann*, provision is made for two chambers within the national legislature, the *Oireachtas*, namely the *Dáil* (the lower house) and *Seanad* (the upper house). The *Seanad* is sixty strong, comprising forty-nine elected and eleven appointed senators. Six of the sixty are elected by graduates of higher educational institutes. Eleven are nominated by the *Taoiseac* (the Prime Minister), as a way of co-opting MPs into government (such as James Dooge in 1982). The remaining forty-three senators are elected from a system of panels (the composition of which is not stipulated in the constitution). The five panels are: (a) cultural and educational; (b) agricultural; (c) labour; (d) industrial and commercial; and (e) administrative. The electorate for these panels consists of members of the new *Dáil*, outgoing senators and county councillors. The parallels of this aspect of the Irish system with the situation in other states having a British influence are interesting. As the Constitution Unit noted, "provision is made in several Commonwealth countries for the nomination of professional groups or sections of society" such as from the worlds of literature, science, the arts and social services.[29] Elections are held ninety days after the *Dáil* is dissolved, using Single Transferable Vote in a secret postal ballot. Senators must be at least twenty-one years old. For Chubb, "[b]y and large, it is merely another selection of party politicians chosen in an unnecessarily complicated and not particularly democratic manner".[30]

The powers of the *Seanad* are minimal, its chief ability being to delay legislation, and then only for a short period. This power is itself much reduced in financial matters. Crucially, however, where the *Seanad* regards a bill as being of national importance, it can, with the support of one third of the members of the *Dáil*, petition the President to refer the measure to the people instead of signing it. On consultation with the Council of State, such a Bill would go to a national referendum or must be enacted within eighteen months and after fresh elections to the *Dáil*. This has never occurred. Also, the *Seanad* has powers to make "recommendations" but these can be ignored by the *Dáil*. Impact is more in terms of affecting government thinking, and hence willingness to consider amendments. Other than money and constitutional Bills, any Bill can be initiated in the *Seanad*. Frequently, the government does this to relieve pressure on the congested *Dáil* and to ensure a more thoroughgoing treatment. Provision exists for simple and non-controversial Bills to become law on the basis of having passed through only one house. The *Dáil* has refrained from exercising its

---

[29] N. 16 above, at 23.
[30] B. Chubb, *Government and Politics of Ireland* (Harlow, Longman, 1992), at 212.

formal prerogatives and a joint conference is regularly convened on occasions of disagreement.

One former *Taoiseach* spoke of a "tame pussy-cat role" for the *Seanad* in the Irish legislative process.[31] As a result, the *Seanad* is held in low esteem as people think it is a home for defeated TDs (MPs). FitzGerald makes the point that, in fact, fewer than twenty-five per cent of its members have been such. Provision for up to two senators to serve in the cabinet (though not as *Taoiseach*, *Tanaiste* (Foreign Minister) or Minister of Finance) gives the *Taoiseach* considerable room for manœuvre even though only three such appointments have occurred since the formation of the State. For FitzGerald, "the Independent element in the *Seanad* has always been an important factor . . . [having] provided a refreshing element of non-partisanship".[32]

## Germany

The Basic Law, Germany's Constitution, was set down in 1949 under Anglo-American occupation government. Central to the Constitution was the determination to diffuse power within the polity, both vertically, through the formation of a strongly federal state, and horizontally, through powerful independent national institutions. As part of this process, provision was made for a democratically elected legislature based upon federal bicameralism. Hence, the German Parliament consists of two houses, the *Bundestag* and the *Bundesrat*. As befits this federation, the Bundestag fulfils the functions of a diet, being democratically elected by universal suffrage in quadrennial polls, and providing a parliamentary government. The Bundesrat upholds the federal principle by representing the interests of the sixteen *Länder* (states) of which the German federation is composed. In fact, the *Bundesrat* (or federal council) is a comparatively small intergovernmental committee of sixty-eight members (comprising three to six members per state) which acts as a second chamber of parliament. Members must be at least eighteen years old. Article 50 of the constitution states that: "[t]he *Länder* shall participate through the *Bundesrat* in the legislation and administration of the Federation and in the affairs of the European Union". *Bundesrat* delegates, as they are known, are not, in fact, directly elected. Instead, they are appointed by their respective state governments in the *Ländtag* (the state parliaments in the *Länder*) and are mandated to serve the interests of their respective *Länder* (Article 51). Indeed, *Bundesrat* delegates must vote according to how they are instructed by their nominating *Land*. The individuals within any delegation are not necessarily fixed for a set period. Hence, it is permissible for officials from the state governments to serve as delegates in lieu of the formally appointed members, the state level cabinet members. The parallel with the operation of the European Union's Council of Ministers is striking.

[31] N. 10 above.
[32] *Ibid.*

Moreover, rather than having a set nationwide electoral cycle, the composition of the *Bundesrat* changes regularly when that of any *Land* government changes.

The powers of the *Bundesrat* are considerable and inviolate. Much of this flows from the need for a two-thirds majority to be secured for constitutional change and a veto over much legislation, including the federal budget.

More than any other institution, the *Bundesrat* exemplifies the "co-operative" character of the German constitutional system. The checks and balances, the mixture of federal and *Land* competences, and the blurring of administrative and legislative spheres—these all show the complex relationships involved in fashioning a consensus. Constitutional reform requires a two thirds majority in both houses of the Federal parliament.[33]

Government-sponsored parliamentary Bills go to the *Bundesrat* first, so that the various *Land* governments can scrutinise them before the *Bundestag* itself. Similarly, after approval by the lower house, the upper house must give its endorsement. A *Bundesrat* veto exists on constitutional bills, those involving *Länder* finance (that is, spending and taxes), and those where the *Länder* would be expected to administer legislation. On other bills, whilst a two-thirds *Bundesrat* majority can veto a proposal, a two-thirds *Bundestag* majority can overrule the veto. In practice, a Mediation Committee comprising equal numbers from both houses sits to secure a compromise. The whole process is suffused with consensus and compromise. A Constitutional Court is appointed by the two houses (half from each) to ensure that the spirit, if not the letter, of the constitution is observed.

## France

The powerful constitutional position of the French president, together with the impact of the *cumuls des mandates*, contributes to the relative weakness of the French parliamentary system, particularly its Senate. Indeed, Bornstein remarked that the "French legislature is one of the weakest in the Western world as a result not only of the changes in its role introduced by the 1958 constitution but also of three decades of majority control by parties subservient to various presidents".[34]

France possesses a bicameral legislature comprising the 577-seat National Assembly (lower house) and the 321-seat Senate (upper house). Provision for a Senate is made in Article 24 of the 1958 Constitution of the Fifth Republic. It states that the Senate shall be elected by indirect suffrage and ensure representation of the territorial units of the Republic. French people living outside France shall be represented in the Senate. Senators must be at least thirty-five

[33] G. Smith, W. Paterson, P. Merkl and S. Padgett, *Developments in German Politics* (Basingstoke, Macmillan, 1992), at 45.
[34] S. Bornstein, "The Politics of Scandal" in P. Hall, J. Hayward, and H. Machin (eds.), *Developments in French Politics* (Basingstoke, Macmillan, 1990), at 274.

years old. In practice, the election of the Senate is operationalised through the indirect election of senators for a period of nine years apiece, with elections occurring every three years for one third (107) of the Senate. Senators are chosen from the *grands électeurs*. This is an electoral college of local and other subnational government politicians, including Deputies in the National Assembly, *département* councillors, and city council delegates. The composition of the electoral college is disproportionately weighted towards the numerous small rural communes which are inherently conservative and which ensure an in-built anti-socialist majority. Under the principle of *cumuls des mandats*, ninety-three per cent of senators in 1982 were municipal councillors. Party discipline is much looser than in the rather rigid National Assembly. The Senate Speaker presides for a period of three years (the period of office being concurrent with the triennial election cycle), with four vice-presidents or deputies to assist. This group is important in that it forms the conference of presidents which formally determines the allocation of committee seats and the organisation of parliamentary debates.[35] That said, the number of permanent committees is limited to six in the Senate (as in the National Assembly), with each member sitting in only one committee so as to "avoid specialised committees shadowing departments or falling into the hands of interest groups as happened in the Fourth Republic".[36]

Theoretically, both chambers are equal. Superficially, for example, this is reflected in the appointment of the French Constitutional Council, where the Senate determines the same proportion of membership (one-third) as the National Assembly and President. Equally, in the event that the French President dies, resigns or becomes incapacitated, the President of the Senate assumes the role of State President, albeit temporarily. However, apart from those formal indications of strength, in practice, as Wright remarked, the "framers of the Fifth Republic clearly assigned a subordinate role within parliament to the upper house. . . . The Senate is a closed, autonomous, elitist body, jealous of its prerogatives and suspicious of any outside interference".[37] This is particularly true of the legislative process in which only the National Assembly can deal with money Bills first and only it can censure the government. In effect, the French Senate is "largely confined to amending and delaying legislation".[38] Formally, legislation must be approved in both houses. And, in cases of disagreement, the Bill might be shuttled between the two chambers until a text is agreed. A special conference committee might even be convened by the government (the sponsor of most Bills) and a second reading might be sought. However, in the final analysis, the National Assembly can, *in extremis*, proceed by simple majority and has the final say, save for constitutional measures and those affecting the powers of the Senate itself. Meny contended that this amounted to an "ingenious mechanism" whereby the government can "block or

---

[35] M. D. Hancock (ed.), *Politics in Western Europe* (Basingstoke, Macmillan, 1993), at 116.
[36] M. Keating, *The Politics of Modern Europe* (Aldershot, Edward Elgar, 1993), at 137.
[37] V. Wright, *The Government and Politics of France* (London, Unwin Hyman, 1989), at 149–50.
[38] N. 36 above, at 136.

unblock the [legislative] process at will, according to the prevailing political circumstances".[39] In effect, the mechanism is more elaborate than those within other states but, in reality, does little to confer genuine delaying power on the Senate since, ultimately, the Senate is reduced to being a pawn of the government's politicking. As Meny observed "the two-chamber system provides the executive with an extra means of implementing its own decisions".[40]

The one major obstacle to unfettered governmental power comes in the case of constitutional amendments where both houses must be in agreement, with a national referendum being held unless both houses can agree, in joint session, by a three-fifths majority. Nor has the Senate been averse to flexing its constitutional muscle in this respect as de Gaulle found to his cost in 1969, for example. Certainly, the Senate has offered a trenchant defence of local government in France, being a vigilant defender of the rights of local authorities. Equally, during the early Mitterrand era, the Senate became "the citadel of the opposition", according to Jean-Louis Quermonne.[41]

### Italy

Although the Executive does not dominate the legislature in the same way as occurs in the UK or France, for example, the effect of dithering and indecision "causes it to be dispossessed of its powers. Its theoretical rule . . . is replaced by an admission of impotence".[42] A weakness in the executive *vis-à-vis* the legislature has led to government by decree.

*Table 4.2: April 1996 Italian General Election results*[43]

| Party or Coalition Grouping | Chamber of Deputies | Senate |
| --- | --- | --- |
| Olive Tree (Centre Left) | 284 (45.1%) | 157 (49.8%) |
| Freedom Alliance (Centre Right) | 246 (39.0%) | 116 (36.8%) |
| Northern League | 59  ( 9.4%) | 27  ( 8.6%) |
| Communist | 35  ( 5.6%) | 10  ( 3.2%) |
| Others | 6  ( 1.0%) | 5  ( 1.6%) |

Under the post-war constitution, the Italian legislature is bicameral, comprising a Chamber of Deputies (lower house) of 630 members and a Senate (upper house) of 326 members (including nine appointed by the President and two *ex officio*, ex-presidents). Both houses are directly elected for five years in synchronous polls. Formally, both houses are equal in status. In 1993, in a bid

---

[39] N. 8 above, at 213.
[40] *Ibid.*, at 214.
[41] N. 37 above, at 151.
[42] N. 8 above, at 195.
[43] Reuters, cited in the *Irish Times*, 23 Apr. 1996.

to overcome the chronic instability which has paralysed effective and stable government in Italy since the war, the old system of proportional representation was replaced by an essentially plurality based voting system. Thus, seventy-five per cent of the seats in the Senate (like the Chamber of Deputies) have been determined by a plurality system using single-member constituencies, with a variant of the old regional-based PR system used to fill the remaining twenty-five per cent of seats. Essentially, Senate elections use the twenty-two regions as constituencies—each region is entitled to one senator per 200,000 population and all but three regions having fewer than six senators, leading to slight over representation of smaller regions. A candidate receiving sixty-five per cent of the votes in his/her district is declared elected. If no one attains this, the vote shares are sent to the regional capital to be pooled with all the other votes for that party within the districts where the district polls were inconclusive. Seats are then allocated proportionally. If a party is entitled to, say, four seats, then the four candidates of that party who polled the highest share of the vote in each of their respective districts will be elected. This favours the proliferation of smaller parties. There is no threshold minimum and no overall majority. It also encourages intra-party factionalism. Party strength is roughly similar in each house (see Table 4.2) reflecting the broadly similar electoral base. Unlike the stress on protecting the territorial dimension and/or special interests in France or Germany, for example, in Italy, the Senate exists as little more than a delaying chamber. Originally elected for a six-year term, the Senate now sits for five years maximum, and elections coincide with the those for the Chamber of Deputies. Elections for the Senate are confined to citizens aged over twenty-five years old (senatorial candidates themselves must be forty plus years old).

The Senate enjoys the same powers as the Chamber of Deputies although, arguably, the lower house is the most important in so far as it makes and breaks governments. That said, the parliament is truly bicameral, since the cabinet is equally responsible to both houses. There are some joint committees between the two chambers. Most legislative work is done in committees. Indeed, the committees act as miniature legislatures, virtually having the ability to decide the fate of a bill. The committees are important in setting the parliamentary timetable. The presidents of each chamber liaise with the Conference of Presidents (that is, the chairs of the various parliamentary committees) to agree the parliamentary timetable. Chamber presidents are invariably partisan figures which, again, can make securing agreement difficult. Italy has no formal mechanism for securing compromise or conciliation between the chambers. Hence, despite frequent disputes between them, there is no intermediary conference to reconcile them, unlike France and Germany. Consequently, Bills can pass round the system indefinitely, compounding the instability. Only other constitutionally established fora which can be adapted for the purpose (such as the Commission for regional questions) can unblock the impasse.

## The United States of America

The USA is the archetypal federation. Formally, the USA possesses a congressional system of government, first and foremost, reflecting that, in a system of government predicated on the separation of powers, the Founding Fathers regarded the legislature as the most important branch of government. Indeed, Andrew Hamilton once remarked of the US legislature that "[h]ere, sir, the people govern". Hence, in Article 1, Section 1, of the Constitution, all legislative powers are vested in Congress which consists of the Senate (upper house) and the House of Representatives (lower house).

While the 435-strong House of Representatives is composed on a national basis of population, the Senate is 100 strong, composed of two senators per state, irrespective of the size, population or economic (or, formerly, military) might of each state. Each senator serves a six-year term with one third facing elections occurring every second year (the lower house is re-elected every two years). Vacancies are filled by appointees from the state legislature of the state where the senatorial vacancy arises. Residency and age restrictions mean that candidates for Senate must be at least thirty years old, with nine years of US citizenship. The US Vice-President presides over the Senate. Analysing the composition of the Senate reveals that it remains like a white men's club with few black members and virtually no women.

Although the Senate was designed as a check on the popularly-elected assembly, initially it was in the shadow of the lower house. Progressively, however, its powers developed and its prestige grew accordingly. Today, the power and general importance of the US Senate cannot be overestimated. Indeed, unlike the national examples considered hitherto, the USA is distinct inasmuch as the Senate is in the ascendent. That is, of the two houses of Congress, the Senate remains the more powerful. Simply, the Senate must concur if legislation is to proceed. All Bills except revenue Bills can be initiated within either house. In cases of intra-Congressional dispute, a conference committee of House Representatives and Senators from their respective standing committees convenes to propose a compromise bill which both houses can approve. The Senate can amend, or ultimately reject, any bill. Whilst the President can veto Congress, a two thirds vote in both houses can overrule a presidential veto. The formal separation of powers between the executive and legislature is important in other ways. First, it imbues the constituent houses of Congress with considerable autonomy as to how they organise and operate their own internal affairs. Secondly, it creates a legislature which, almost uniquely, "strives to write its own legislation and monitor the vast governmental apparatus".[44] America's congressional government is, in fact, committee government, so powerful and expansive are congressional committees. The committees, established during

---

[44] H. Davidson, "Congress in Crisis . . . Once Again" in G. Peele *et al.* (eds.), *Developments in American Politics 2* (Basingstoke, Macmillan, 1994), at 141.

the nineteenth century, have come to wield enormous influence over the American system of government to the extent that they are instrumental in exacerbating (even creating) the "gridlock" from which the whole system is said to suffer.

Senators enjoy remarkable support services, all of which assist in the twin tasks of individual self-promotion and the collective power of the legislature versus the executive. A senator can expect to have around thirty-six staff (range thirteen to seventy-one), up to one third of whom work in the home state. Senatorial incumbents are a formidable force, able to ensure their re-election through diligent application of an enormous arsenal of resources at their disposal. The operation of Congress, as distinct from other legislatures, is differentiated by the pervasiveness of parochialism. Davidson quoted the former House Speaker, Tip O'Neill, who remarked that, in the USA, "[a]ll politics is local"[45] since, notwithstanding national influences, most congressional elections are fought on essentially local issues. Even in the selection of candidates for both houses of Congress, national parties have long since relinquished control to their local organisations. Because members of the House of Representatives face re-election every two years, it reinforces their exceptional sensitivity to local issues and interests and raises the prospects of pork-barrelling. Even in the Senate, whilst the constituency is the much larger state, the "two congresses problem" is clear. This problem stems from the fact that citizens see their own legislators as agents of personal or localised interests whilst congress as a whole is regarded as a law-making instrument and judged primarily on the basis of citizens' overall attitudes about politics and the state of the nation. Hence, the distinctions and differences, if not the rivalries, between the two houses have abated somewhat of late. For its part, the Senate has become less leisurely and more tightly organised. Senators have a greater concern with cultivating a "home style", spending more time in their states and concerning themselves with matters directly relating to their states in order to ensure that they are not defeated at election time.[46]

### A Brief Note on Unicameral Systems

Amongst western democratic states, Denmark, Finland, Greece, Iceland, Malta, New Zealand, Norway, Portugal and Sweden possess unicameral legislatures. That said, elements of bicameralism operate within some of these countries. For example, on convening after an election, Norway's parliament divides into two chambers although eighty per cent of work is done in plenary session. Much the same principle operates in Portugal and Finland, where each have internal large committees which serve like an internal second chamber in a nesting effect. Unicameralism is now established throughout Scandinavia where a "deliberate

---

[45] *Ibid.*

[46] J. D. Lees, *The Political System of the United States* (London, Faber and Faber, 1983), at 207; R. F. Fenno, *Home Style* (Boston, Mass., Little, Brown, 1978).

movement . . . towards the institution of a single chamber within the framework of the parliamentary system" has been under way since 1906.[47] Sweden completed the process in 1970 when the Riksdag became unicameral. Previously, the first chamber was indirectly elected by the assemblies of the country's twenty-four provinces. Today, any constitutional amendments to the Instrument of Government and Act of Parliament require that there is a majority vote in the Riksdag on two successive occasions, punctuated by an intervening election.

Of "Anglo-Saxon" nations, New Zealand is unique in having a unicameral system. Frequently, New Zealand is presented as an antipodean equivalent of the UK, not least in constitutional terms given its uncodified constitution and retention of the British Royal Family as its source of monarchical chief executives. However, just as unicameralism detracts from this image, so the more recent constitutional changes to the electoral system (namely, from plurality to proportionality) mark a further departure from the traditional Westminster model. Given that the justifications for bicameralism include promoting moderation in highly populous states, New Zealand's small population, at barely three million, makes a direct application of its experiences to the UK less appropriate.

SECOND CHAMBERS—DEMOCRACY AND EFFICIENCY:
TOWARDS A RESEARCH AGENDA

Currently, despite the extensive literature on legislatures, that which is devoted to second chambers in particular is limited, save for some notable exceptions. Frequently, second chambers go unreported or merit only a casual treatment, not least because there is a belief that they are superfluous, and hence relatively unimportant. This is remarkably shortsighted. This short chapter has revealed wide divergences in national practice in just a handful of cases. Simply, if second chambers were of such little consequence, one might have expected to see their demise. To some extent, outside federations, this process has begun, witness events in Scandinavia. However, in many states, they remain and, in some, they continue to enjoy substantial powers. Hence, there is a strong case for undertaking a wider and more meaningful examination of this important topic. To that end, we would propose the following research agenda.

Methods of appointment and powers of a chamber are the two single most important criteria when assessing how democratic are particular second chambers. Both of these criteria need to be systematically divided into a series of subcategories if they are to be usefully applied in comparative assessment of second chambers. We will attempt to move in this direction by constructing a comparative analytical framework to be used for further research. Assessments of the contribution of second chambers to the democratic process can be further assisted if we construct the conceptual tool of a bicameral continuum, along

---

[47] N. 9 above, at 13.

which various second chambers can be located in accordance with the extent to which they embody core democratic principles and values, such as political equality, representativeness and control by the populace.

Two extreme scenarios could be described which would constitute the respective limits of this bicameral continuum. At one end would be a second chamber recruited by non-democratic means, either by an oligarchic/personal judgement or by hereditary principle, wherein the unelected chamber would have powers greater than those of a first chamber that was selected by democratic means (fair, honest, direct, periodic election), which was subject to a degree of accountability and which had a legitimate claim to represent the nation. In effect, the unelected, unrepresentative chamber would have ascendancy over the directly elected, representative one and this legislative structure would have negative implications for the democratic nature of the entire polity.

At the other end of this continuum, the scenario would consist of a formal bicameralism which closely resembled a unicameral system. That is, every member of parliament would be directly elected simultaneously, with the separation into two houses occurring thereafter by newly elected members of parliament appointing a proportion of their number to sit in another chamber. To all intents and purposes, the political complexion of the two houses would be identical, as would be their powers. Theoretically, then, such a form of bicameralism would nest within a unicameral arrangement. The justification for this is that the work of legislation is done more thoroughly if it is done twice in two separate houses, albeit simultaneously, whilst, in principle, it reflects the notion that power should be diffused, making less likely the rise to prominence of authoritarian elements. The democratic representativeness of the second chamber is at least equal to that of the first chamber.

In practice, virtually all countries possessing a second chamber can be located at some point along this continuum, between these two extreme types. However, thus far, we have undertaken what might be termed a macro-level analysis, that is, assessing second chambers in broad terms. From this macro perspective, we have distinguished between unitary and federal bicameralism, whilst establishing the relevance and significance of the concepts of representative democracy and legislative efficiency in any assessment of second chambers. We have identified the importance of analysing the historical process of state formation, including the need to assess the motivations and strategies of those directly responsible for shaping constitutional arrangements, and the extent to which they were a response to the particular social, economic and geographical factors obtaining within each country. However, as an additional dimension to the research, it would be fruitful to undertake micro-level analysis, that is, a closer and more detailed scrutiny which analyses the diurnal procedural operations of particular second chambers. A number of criteria can be identified which offer us assistance in the completion of this comparative task.

By definition, analysis of second chambers cannot proceed in isolation. Rather, the venture requires comparison with first chambers. Such analysis is predominantly macro level and consists of two fundamental components: a comparison of the powers of the two chambers and a comparison of the composition of the two chambers. Micro-level analysis involves examining the structure, organisation and operation of the second chamber. Within each of these categories a number of sub-headings provide a useful comparative analytical framework. Future more detailed research could make use of this.

Under the composition of the chamber, we can assess the following: size of chamber; length of office; method of appointment; criteria of eligibility for candidature (including the objectives of any eligibility rules); the method for nomination of candidates; organisation of territorial representation; electoral system (if elected); occupational incompatibility regulations; expulsion/resignation procedures; extent of remuneration; seating arrangements and the shape of the chamber including specially allocated seats in the chamber. Comparative analysis of the respective division of powers in two chamber systems can be facilitated by the use of the following sub-categories: level of procedural independence, that is, the level of autonomy that the chamber has with regard to the formation and application of its rules of procedure; a chamber's level of financial independence including its control over, and its ability to audit, its own expenditure; the collective control it has over the length of its sittings and sessions; available administrative resources including secretarial support, research staff, information and library resources; the level of transparency including the publication of debates and media access; legislative function, initiating bills, law-making, delaying, approval function, amending and delegating legislation; extra-parliamentary consultation; status on emergency matters; veto powers; constitutional, judicial and legal role; role in the budget; relationship with the head of state; relationship with the executive/government; the dissolution of the chamber; the chamber's role in foreign affairs; powers to nominate government officials and judges. Obviously, there is some overlap with the previous two factors in terms of structure, organisation and operation of the chamber, but additional considerations include: the convening of joint sittings of the two chambers; number of readings; procedures for committees meeting outside the chamber (chamber's committee structure); procedures for conducting debate; restrictions on speeches; methods of voting; quorum and voting majority.

CONCLUSIONS

This short comparative study of second chambers has illustrated the difficulties and complexities in attempting to construct bicameral models to act as standard types of second chamber. Most bicameral arrangements are the product of a uniquely national process of state formation and constitution building, making it difficult to fit them into conceptually neat categories. However, almost all can be placed at a point on a bicameral continuum between two extreme types in accordance with the degree to which they satisfy democratic principles.

More fundamentally, this chapter has shown that second chambers cannot be dismissed as being irrelevant to comparative constitutional politics. Their existence makes a contribution to the unique nature of national institutional configurations, and it would be wrong to ignore them in the study of the structure and exercise of power in political systems across the world. This is despite the fact that the debate on the representative qualities of second chambers and their contribution to the democratic process has been partially overtaken by the relative ease with which executives can dominate their legislatures (be they unicameral or bicameral) and that second chambers, almost without exception (save for some federations), have seen their powers attenuated. Even in federations, second chambers seldom enjoy equivalent power to their lower counterparts (the USA, Germany and Switzerland being the obvious exceptions).

During the implementation stage of policy formulation, the executive still has to negotiate the legislative process. The existence of second chambers complicates that process and will almost certainly be included in the calculations of the executive. However, save for the vital need for public comprehension, one might expect the vital business of law-making to be complex if it is to be effective. The presence of a second chamber ensures that the whole process has to be repeated, either in whole or part. Some bills may require the agreement (expressly, by act of commission, or tacitly, by act of omission) of the second chamber to become effective. The complexity of the process is compounded by the fact that the composition of the two chambers may be different, as may be their modes of recruitment, social composition, ideological affiliation etc. Above all, the ease with which legislation can proceed will be heavily conditioned by the relative importance of the two chambers. That is, is one superior to the other, or are they co-equal, is there supremacy for one house (such as the Commons in the UK) or a committee of mediation of both (*Navette* in France, *Vermittlungsausschuß* in Germany)? Such considerations continue to exert an influence on the strategies and objectives of policy-makers, and second chambers should not be confined to the status of an inconsequential constitutional relic in the study of comparative public policy. Hence, the case for further research is indisputable.

For both proponents and opponents of change, the venerable antiquity of the British constitution is central to their respective cases. As the second oldest of our national institutions, the House of Lords figures prominently in the debate. As in all arguments, the burden of proof rests with those advocating change. If debate is not to sink into a mire of polemical argument, then a proper appreciation of the issues is required. In its contribution to the debate over the future of the British Upper House, the Constitution Unit confidently asserted that the "argument for bicameralism has been won in the UK" but added the important caveat that "there is little obvious consensus about the roles the UK's second chamber should fulfil or about the principles that should inform any attempt at the reform of the House of Lords".[48] We would agree. Equally, we agree also

---

[48] N. 16 above, at 32.

that the determination of the future role of the upper house would benefit immeasurably from a rational appraisal of the evidence from overseas. Indeed, both sides of the argument make frequent reference to practice abroad although this is invariably a selective and tendentious process on their part. As comparative public policy analysts, it is incumbent upon us to present a more rigorous framework for objectively analysing the wealth of evidence from overseas. This chapter represents a small contribution to developing the research agenda on the unfolding debate. Again, however, to quote the Constitution Unit, we would stress that "no exercise in comparative politics can hope to find an "off the shelf" answer to the question of how best to reform the House of Lords".[49] Any particular national system owes much to the peculiar combination of history and culture of the state concerned and to propose the transfer of features of a particular foreign system or, indeed, an eclectic sample from abroad to the UK, would be both crass and naïve without considering the full import of the consequences.

[49] N. 16 above, at 27.

# 5

# The Sub Judice Rule in the House of Lords

PATRICIA M. LEOPOLD*

## INTRODUCTION

The House of Lords, unlike the House of Commons, has by and large retained its old procedures. It has not followed the Commons down the path of constant procedural change. In consequence, peers "still remain as free as MPs were in the mid nineteenth century".[1] As Michael Wheeler-Booth states: "[u]nlike most other legislative Chambers, the House of Lords has not codified all its practice and procedure in the written word; many practices continue to be governed by custom and common sense rather than the rule book".[2] It is for this reason that it is interesting to consider how the *sub judice* rule, a restriction on the freedom of speech in the Lords, came to exist, how it developed and how and why it was changed in 1995. In its own small way, this illustrates how the Lords has changed in the last thirty years; it also raises questions as to the future development of reform of procedure in the House of Lords.

The *sub judice* rule has to be considered in the context of Article 9 of the Bill of Rights 1689, which applies to both Houses of Parliament. This provides that "freedom of speech, and debates or proceedings in Parliament ought not to be impeached or questioned in any court or place out of Parliament". As Sir Elwyn Jones, later Lord Elwyn Jones, told a House of Commons Select Committee in 1971: "[i]t is the fundamental responsibility of Parliament to be the supreme inquest of the nation with the overall responsibility to discuss anything it likes".[3] There are, however, limitations on freedom of speech which have been accepted by Parliament itself, and one of these is the *sub judice* rule or, more accurately, convention which broadly prevents members from discussing matters awaiting adjudication in the courts.

* The author would like to thank Donald Shell, Department of Politics, University of Bristol, for reading and commenting on an earlier draft of this chapter.

[1] D. Shell, *The House of Lords* (Hemel Hempstead, Harvester Wheatsheaf, 1992), at 99.

[2] Then Clerk of the Parliaments, In the Preface to the *Companion to the Standing Orders*, 17th edn., 1994).

[3] Evidence from Sir Elwyn Jones to the Select Committee on Procedure, Fourth Report "Matters *Sub Judice*" (H.C. 298 1971–2 Q.153), and cited with approval by the Committee in its report, para. 25, p. xii.

THE DEVELOPMENT OF THE *SUB JUDICE* RULE 1844–1963

The origins of the *sub judice* rule lie in the House of Commons. Between 1844 and 1963, it would appear that a convention, or self-denying ordinance, had developed in the House of Commons whereby matters that were awaiting or under adjudication in a court of law would not be referred to in the Commons.[4] Like many aspects of Commons procedure that developed in the late nineteenth century, the development of this convention was in response, at least in part, to the Irish situation and the activities of Irish Nationalist MPs.[5] The House of Lords in contrast did not have a substantial minority of its members unwilling to abide by the spirit of the old procedures, and in consequence it was able to avoid the path, then followed by the Commons, of increasing regulation. During this period, the scope and application of the *sub judice* rule was determined by the Speaker of the Commons by reference to the precedents and the likely prejudicial effect of the comments in Parliament on the court proceedings. The purpose of the rule appears to have been the desire of Parliament to prevent comment and debate from exerting an influence on juries and from prejudicing the position of parties and witnesses.[6]

Until December 1961, there had been no instance of the Speaker applying the *sub judice* rule to prevent comments on a civil case which was before the courts. The decision of the Speaker in 1961 to apply the *sub judice* rule to a parliamentary question which referred to aspects of a case where a writ for libel had been issued, caused disquiet in the Commons.[7] However it was the opinion of the Speaker that only the House of Commons could alter the application of the *sub judice* rule, and the House agreed to refer the rule to its Select Committee on Procedure. In its subsequent report, the Procedure Committee accepted that there was a need for a *sub judice* rule of some sort to provide guidance for the Chair, but it did not consider that it could be left to the good sense and feeling of the House.[8] The Committee was unhappy with respect to the application of the *sub judice* rule to civil cases, since it meant that motions, questions etc. were out of order from the time that a writ was issued, which in effect limited members, possibly for a considerable period of time, in what they could say in connection with a civil action. Also, it left the way open for an individual who wished to prevent members from, for example, pressing in Parliament for an investigation into his questionable activities to do so by issuing a writ, thereby activating the *sub judice* rule. The Committee therefore recommended that the *sub judice* rule should apply only once a case had been set down for trial, or

---

[4] For further details see the memorandum from the Clerk of the House to the Select Committee on Procedure, "The Rule Relating to Reference in the House of Commons to Matters Considered as *Sub Judice*", H.C. 156 (1962–3), Appendix I.

[5] See Redlich, *The Procedure of the House of Commons* (1903), i, pt. II.

[6] N. 2 above, at para. 9.

[7] H.C. Deb., vol. 650, cols. 912–15, (4 Dec. 1961); vol. 651, cols. 46–7 (11 Dec. 1961).

[8] N. 3 above, para. 6.

otherwise brought before the court, for example by notice of motion for an injunction. The proposal was that until a civil case had reached that stage it could be referred to, unless it appeared to the Chair that there was "a real and substantial danger of prejudice to the trial of the case". These, and other more minor recommendations, were embodied in a resolution of the House of Commons in 1963.[9]

In 1963, the House of Lords agreed, without debate, with a recommendation from its Select Committee on Procedure that the practice on the *sub judice* rule should be similar to that in the Commons.[10] In consequence, an entry was made in the House of Lords *Companion to the Standing Orders*[11] setting out the new restrictions on matters that were *sub judice*. There is no record of any particular deliberation by the committee on the need for, or the content of, the new *sub judice* rule in the Lords. Although there is no evidence that there had been any problems in the Lords in respect of cases before the courts, this is probably more a reflection of the state of decline in the power and influence of the Lords in the period from 1911 to 1963 than an indication of the success of the Lords in self-regulation. In 1963, the Lords was only beginning to reassert itself after the atrophy of the 1950s.[12]

### THE DEVELOPMENT OF THE *SUB JUDICE* RULE 1963–94

From 1963 until 1972, it seems that the newly formulated *sub judice* rule gave rise to few problems. However there were judicial and legislative developments in this period that eventually persuaded the House of Commons, but not the House of Lords, to look again at the *sub judice* rule. The main development was:

> "an increasing tendency for Ministerial action to find expression in measures, whether in the financial, economic or planning fields, which can ultimately lead to a Minister becoming a party to court proceedings in which . . . questions of Ministerial policy are involved".[13]

However, the convention of ministerial responsibility initially helped to reduce the likelihood of ministers having to account to the courts for decisions taken by them or in their name. It has been suggested that in the post-war period when judges were asked to pass judgment on issues of policy then:

---

[9] 297 H.C.J. (1962–3); see the Appendix to this chap.

[10] First Report from the House of Lords Procedure Committee (1963–4); H.L. Deb., vol. 755, col. 1109 (10 Dec. 1963).

[11] See the Appendix to this chap.

[12] For an account of how the House of Lords has changed since the 1960s see N. Baldwin, chap. 5 in P. Norton (ed.), *Parliament in the 1980s* (Oxford, Blackwell, 1985); Shell, n. 1 above, at 20; and J Vincent, "The House of Lords", XIX *Parliamentary Affairs* (1966), at 475.

[13] Fourth Report from the Select Committee on Procedure, n. 3 above, at 17 (Evidence).

"the simplest way was . . . to defer to the opinion being advanced by the Executive, and when the opinion was that of a Minister responsible to Parliament the judges found reassurance in the awareness of potential, if often inefficacious, political checks".[14]

This began to change. The 1973 edition of de Smith noted that:

"over the past ten years, and especially since 1967, there has been a striking increase both in the frequency with which judicial review has been invoked and in the readiness of the courts to intervene".[15]

It also observed that:

"The courts are increasingly disinclined to interpret statutes as giving Ministers conclusive power to determine the limits of their own powers, especially where the issue lends itself to objective judicial ascertainment."[16]

The 1963 *sub judice* rule, in that it did not make any particular reference to or exception for civil cases which involved the review of a ministerial decision, reflected the situation as it was in 1963. Prior to 1972, there had been no evidence that the Speaker had applied the *sub judice* rule in such a way as to restrict comment in the House where a minister had been involved in court proceedings.[17] However, it was clear that this was dependent on the Speaker being willing to exercise his discretion in favour of free speech, and the 1963 resolution did not provide guidance for him from the House on the exercise of his discretion in this type of case. It was, in part, the realisation that the 1963 *sub judice* rule could, and in 1972 did, prevent Parliament from discussing cases before the courts involving ministerial action taken under statutory powers, that led the House of Commons to ask the Select Committee on Procedure again to review the *sub judice* rule,[18] in particular in respect of its application to cases where a minister

---

[14] S. A. de Smith, *Judicial Review of Administrative Action* (London, Stevens, 1973), at 29.

[15] *Ibid.*, at 27.

[16] *Ibid.*, at 39.

[17] The only case where there had been a potential problem was the *Mersey Docks and Harbour Board* case (1970) where the minister announced to the House that the government intended to apply to the courts for the appointment of a receiver. The Speaker had exercised his discretion to allow a debate which covered the policy of the Minister; see the report from the Select Committee on Procedure, n. 3 above, at p. xi.

[18] The case which brought the matter to a head was *Secretary of State for Employment* v. *A.S.L.E.F.*, an appeal from a decision of the National Industrial Relations Court (N.I.R.C.). The Secretary of State had made an application to the N.I.R.C. claiming to be acting under powers given to him by the Industrial Relations Act 1971. The decision of the N.I.R.C. was appealed and the Court of Appeal had to decide if the minister complied with the conditions laid down by the statute. The Secretary of State had applied very quickly to the N.I.R.C. under the emergency provisions, and both it and the Court of Appeal had dealt with the case at short notice. Lord Denning M.R. in the Court of Appeal suggested that in cases like this, where a Minister applied quickly to a court without first telling Parliament of his intention, the case would become *sub judice* and Parliament would be unable to discuss his actions; consequently it was important for the courts to inquire closely whether the minister was within his lawful authority. Although this was probably a too restrictive interpretation of the *sub judice* rule, it drew the attention of the House of Commons to the problems inherent in the strict wording of the 1963 resolution.

had made an application to the National Industrial Relations Court under his statutory power.

The committee in its report accepted that:

"One of the principal functions of the House of Commons is to debate matters of national policy. Insofar therefore as the existing sub judice convention inhibits the House from exercising this function in matters of national importance, an argument exists for modifying it to remove this inhibition as far as possible".[19]

Although the committee was primarily concerned with the *sub judice* convention and the N.I.R.C., its recommendation went beyond the particular case of the Industrial Relations Act 1971 and the N.I.R.C. In particular, it stated that:

"In view of the increase in Ministerial involvement in court proceedings and other changes and developments in the last ten years . . . some relaxation in the provisions of the [*sub judice* resolution] is now called for".[20]

Consequently, it suggested that there should be a further relaxation of the *sub judice* convention in respect of civil cases, including those before the N.I.R.C.[21] This was accepted by the House and the resolution of 28 June 1972 provided that reference could be made to a matter awaiting or under adjudication in a civil court, in so far as it related to a:

"Ministerial decision which cannot be challenged except on grounds of misdirection or bad faith, or concerns issues of national importance such as the national economy, public order or the essentials of life".[22]

The Commons also accepted the committee's suggested guidelines for the Speaker to apply when exercising his discretion. The second paragraph of the 1972 resolution provides that the

"Chair should not allow reference to such matters if it appears that there is a real and substantial danger of prejudice to the proceedings and should have regard to the considerations set out in paragraph 25 of [the Select Committee Report]".

Paragraph 25 states:

"In any case in which a Minister has made an application to a court or has initiated proceedings on a matter of national importance . . . certain considerations should influence Mr. Speaker in the exercise of his discretion as to whether to restrict comment in the House".

These considerations are first that it is the "fundamental responsibility of parliament to be the supreme inquest of the nation with the overall responsibility to discuss anything it likes". This is, in effect, a reassertion of the privilege given by Article 9 of the Bill of Rights. Secondly, the Speaker should consider whether

[19] N. 3 above, at para. 20.
[20] *Ibid.*, at para. 22.
[21] But excluding defamation cases which were to be treated in the same way as criminal cases, n. 2 above, at para. 23.
[22] See Appendix to this chap.

there was a danger that the argument that a minister would present to court would be prejudiced by discussion in parliament.[23]

The 1972 resolution, like that of 1963, needs to be seen in the context in which it was passed. By its reference to ministerial decisions which could not be challenged in court "except on grounds of misdirection or bad faith", it reflected the law on judicial review as it then existed in respect of the way in which ministers were accountable to the courts. Also, it reflected the wording of the Industrial Relations Act 1971, which provided specific powers to the minister when industrial action would be likely to be injurious to the national economy, imperil national security or create a risk of public disorder.

In its 1963 *sub judice* rule, the House of Lords stated that:

> "The House has agreed that the practice governing Motions and Questions relating to matters sub judice should be similar in both houses of Parliament".

However, despite this it did not review its *sub judice* rule in the light of the 1972 Commons' amendment. Consequently, it did not contain the relaxation of the rule with respect to civil cases and, in particular, it contained no reference to the position when a minister's decision was being challenged in the courts. In a way, this is rather surprising since, unlike the situation in 1963, the Lords in 1972 was an active chamber, and the Industrial Relations Bill was subject to more protracted debate than any other Bill before the House.[24] The explanation probably lies in the way in which the 1972 resolution sought to give to the Speaker in the Commons a particular discretion to determine when the *sub judice* rule should be relaxed. The absence in the Lords of a Speaker, or any other official with effective powers, would have made it difficult to adapt the 1972 resolution to suit House of Lords procedures.

A minor amendment to the *sub judice* rule in the Lords was accepted in 1990. This followed a recommendation from its Select Committee on Procedure.[25] As the rule then stood in the Lords, a petition for leave to appeal to the Judicial Committee of the Lords was only *sub judice* from the moment leave to appeal was given, whereas in the Commons the *sub judice* rule applied from the time a petition for leave to appeal to the Lords was presented. In the light of the unanimous advice of the Law Lords, the Committee recommended, and the House accepted, that this discrepancy should be rectified.[26]

---

[23] The Committee also made specific recommendations on the application of the *sub judice* rule to applications under Part VIII of the Industrial Relations Act. 1971, which are no longer relevant, see paras. 26–8.

[24] See Shell, n. 1 above, at 24; M. Moran, *Politics of Industrial Relations* (Basingstoke, Macmillan, 1977); and J. Morgan, *The House of Lords and the Labour Government 1964–1970* (Oxford, Oxford University Press, 1975).

[25] First Report from the Select Committee of the House of Lords on Procedure of the House, H.L. Paper 24 (1989–90) paras. 10, 11.

[26] See *ibid.* and the Appendix to this chap.

Although there have been many examples of the application of the *sub judice* rule in the House of Commons, and some complaints about its application, the Commons has not looked seriously at its *sub judice* rule since 1972.[27] The rule in the Commons therefore is out of touch with a variety of legal and parliamentary developments that have occurred since then.[28] However, the flexibility given to the Speaker in the 1972 reform has probably prevented the type of outcry that occurred in the Lords in 1994.

It would appear that the 1963 *sub judice* rule gave little trouble in the Lords until 1994, when it was discovered that it appeared to restrict discussion in the Lords of the decision of the Home Secretary to extradite two British women, the Misses Hagan and Croft, to the United States. Their case was first raised by Lord Dean in the course of a parliamentary question to the Minister of State, Home Office. Lord Dean asked the Minister whether the government would reconsider the decision of the Home Secretary to extradite the women to the United States.[29] The case was not *sub judice* at this stage,[30] and in the course of a brief discussion several peers stated their views on how the Home Secretary should exercise his discretion. Lord Dean specifically requested that, if the women were to be extradited, the extradition should be delayed until the House had a chance to debate the substance of the matter; no such assurance was given. The matter was raised again two weeks later, after the Easter recess, when Lord Dean instituted a short debate on the criteria applied by the Home Secretary when exercising his discretion over extradition cases. The case was by this time subject to judicial review proceedings and *sub judice* within the terms of the House of Lords 1963 sub judice rule.[31] The problem identified in the House of Lords in the debate was that by the time the judicial review proceedings were complete and the case was no longer *sub judice*, if the decision went against the women, they would be extradited without the House ever having had the opportunity to discuss the matter.

In the course of this debate, several peers had to be warned that by referring to the case of Hagan and Croft they were in danger of breaching the *sub judice* rule. Indeed, feelings got sufficiently heated with respect to comments by the Earl of Longford, that Lord Skermersdale moved the motion: "[t]hat the noble

---

[27] In 1996 the House of Commons Select Committee on Procedure considered whether there should be a new rule, amounting to an extension of the *sub judice* rule which would apply where a court order such as an injunction prohibiting a child being named, had been made. H.C. 252 (1995–6).

[28] For an account of some of the developments in the House of Commons see my essay "The Changing Boundary Between the Courts and Parliament" in R. Buckley (ed.), *Legal Structures: Boundary Issues Between Legal Categories* (Chichester, Wiley 1996).

[29] H.L. Deb., vol. 553, cols. 1204–7 (31 Mar. 1994).

[30] It had been *sub judice* for some time before this date while the women had pursued a claim for habeas corpus.

[31] H.L. Deb., vol. 553, col. 1596 (13 Apr. 1994).

Earl be no longer heard".[32] This motion is described in Erskine May as rare and one only moved in exceptional circumstances.[33] The motion is only used where a Lord is thought to be seriously transgressing the accepted practice of the House.[34] The motion once moved is debatable and, if it is agreed to, the Lord in question is prevented from speaking further on the substantive motion. The motion in respect of the Earl of Longford was only the eleventh occasion that such a motion had been moved this century. Also, it was the first example of it being used to prevent a peer transgressing the *sub judice* rule. The more usual use of the motion is where a peer, contrary to the views of his fellow peers, will not give way to another peer, or the content of a speech is not relevant to the question before the House. The fact that this type of motion is so unusual in itself illustrates both how tolerant peers are, collectively, of irrelevant speeches and how successful the Lords has been at self regulation. In the absence of a presiding officer, peers are expected to comply, and on the whole do comply, with the few rules that regulate debate. In the event, the motion with respect to the Earl of Longford was withdrawn, and an alternative motion, for the House briefly to adjourn, so that representations could be made to "those who are more intimately concerned with this matter", was agreed.[35]

Before the motion was withdrawn, several peers had intervened to criticise both the use of the motion and the substance of the *sub judice* rule. The Leader of the House, Lord Wakeham, had intervened to explain that: "[t]he rules are quite clear . . . a matter is before the court and as such there is a real and substantial danger of prejudice to the trial of the case".[36] He went on later to say: "[t]here is no flexibility given to me and the rules are quite clear".[37] This did not appease matters, and on the resumption of the debate, criticism of both the content of the *sub judice* rule and the lack of flexibility in its application continued. The matter came before the Lords again some weeks later on 6 June, the day before the High Court decision was announced.[38] On this occasion, the House was given a more extensive opportunity to debate the matter of the proposed extraditions. Lord Wakeham told the House that reference could be made to the case of Hagan and Croft as an example of the way in which the Home Secretary exercised his discretion in extradition cases, provided no reference was made to the merits of the applications for judicial review.

This change of heart can be explained by events surrounding the particular case. By the time of this debate, the case had been heard by the High Court and there had been:

---

[32] H.L. Deb., vol. 553, at col. 1601.
[33] *Parliamentary Practice* (22nd edn., London, Butterworths, 1997), at 454.
[34] See the 17th edn. of the *Companion*, n. 2 above, at 77.
[35] H.L. Deb., n. 31 above, at cols. 1605–6.
[36] N. 30 above, at col. 1602.
[37] N. 31 above, at col. 1604.
[38] H.L. Deb., vol. 555, cols. 1052–74 (6 June 1994).

"wide publicity relating to the matters which led to the Home Secretary's decision and there has been no suggestion that publicity has posed any danger of prejudice to the various proceedings in English courts".[39]

Consequently, Lord Wakeham suggested that it would be possible:

"to discuss the case of Miss Hagan and Miss Croft as an example of [the exercise of the Home Secretary's discretion in extradition cases] without offending against our sub judice rules by discussing the matters under adjudication by the High Court in their application for judicial review".[40]

This explanation of the change of heart by the Leader of the House is very like an application of the criteria laid down by the Commons in 1972 for the guidance of the Speaker in respect of the application of the *sub judice* rule to civil cases. The House was therefore able to discuss the earlier court proceedings in the case, but not the current proceedings. In this debate, it was clear that peers were not trying to influence the High Court, but were trying to influence the Home Secretary in the exercise of his discretion in the case.

The difficulties encountered by the Lords in debating the exercise of the Home Secretary's discretion had demonstrated to peers that there were clear defects in the application of the *sub judice* rule. The greatest defect was that the *sub judice* rule did not allow for any discretion in its application where a matter was technically *sub judice*, but, since it concerned a ministerial decision, raised something which was the legitimate concern of Parliament. This was the very point appreciated by the Commons some twenty-two years earlier. The Lords Select Committee on Procedure was therefore invited to review the *sub judice* rule.

As is more common in the Lords than the Commons, the subsequent report from the Select Committee on Procedure[41] contains nothing in the way of background information or discussion on the *sub judice* rule in the Lords. The committee recommended that the *sub judice* rule in the Lords should be relaxed, not just to bring it into line with the 1972 amendment in the Commons, but in such a way that it would go beyond that amendment and more accurately reflect developments in judicial review that had occurred since 1972. The Procedure Committee's recommendation was that the paragraph in the *Companion* dealing with *sub judice* in civil cases should have the following addition:

"This is subject to the proviso that where a ministerial decision is in question, or a case concerns issues of national importance such as the national economy, public order or the essentials of life, reference may be made at the discretion of the Leader of the House, who must be satisfied that there is no real and substantial danger of prejudice to the proceedings. The Leader of the House should be given at least twenty-four hours' notice of any proposal to refer to a matter which is sub judice. It is undesirable that the exercise of his discretion should be challenged in the House."[42]

[39] *Ibid.*, at col. 1052.
[40] *Ibid.*
[41] Select Committee on Procedure of the House, First Report, H.L. Paper 9 (1994–5).
[42] *Ibid.*, para. 2, and see Appendix to this chap. The latest edition of the *Companion* (1994) was published before the Lords accepted the Committee's proposal.

This proposal differed from the 1972 Commons amendment to the *sub judice* rule, since it left out the words "which cannot be challenged in Court except on grounds of misdirection or bad faith" found in the 1972 resolution. The proposal from the Lords' Procedure Committee was designed therefore to give the Lords greater opportunities to debate cases of judicial review of ministerial action than the 1972 resolution allows in the Commons.

When the recommendation from the Procedure Committee came before the Lords,[43] there was broad agreement that there should be this relaxation of the *sub judice* rule. The interest and concern in the Lords in 1995, that one of its own practices had the effect of limiting it in its ability to hold ministers to account, is in marked contrast to the lack of interest in reforming the *sub judice* rule in 1972. In its own way the whole incident illustrates how the Lords has become a more significant chamber in the course of the last 25 years. Interestingly, the House of Commons, despite its "relaxed" *sub judice* rule, never managed to discuss the case of Hagan and Croft. So far as this case was concerned, the publicity both within and outside Parliament came from the Lords.

However, one aspect of the Procedure Committee's proposal caused controversy. This was the proposal to give to the Leader of the House an unchallengeable discretion to decide whether or not a proposed reference to a case would endanger or prejudice court proceedings. This proposal was contrary to the position whereby the House of Lords is self-regulating; it does not have a Speaker with powers of order, instead it relies on each individual member to act in accordance with the rules and conventions of the House. As the former Clerk of the Parliaments puts it:

> "The House is self-governing: all its Members are equal and procedural questions relating to the conduct of business are decided by the 'sense of the House' in accordance with the Standing Orders".[44]

Virtually all those who took part in the debate were concerned that the Lords should remain a self-regulatory body which collectively agreed upon its day-to-day procedures. To give the Leader of the House this power was seen as giving him a role comparable to that of the Speaker in the Commons, which it was suggested could have repercussions in the future.[45] A further concern was that the Leader of the Lords is also a cabinet minister and a member of the governing party, and in consequence his role is a delicate one, especially when matters of party political controversy are under discussion.[46] However, it became clear in the course of the debate that if a Peer wished to raise a matter that was *sub judice*, there had to be some mechanism for deciding whether this would, or would not, prejudice a case before the courts, and the proposal from the

---

[43] H.L. Deb., vol. 560, col. 108 (10 Jan. 1995).

[44] N. 2 above.

[45] Significantly twice in the last 25 years the Lords has rejected the need for a Speaker with powers of control: H.L. Paper 227 (1970–1); H.L. Paper 9 (1987–8).

[46] N. 45 above (1970–1), para. 4.

Committee was accepted as the most practical. A compromise was agreed whereby the Lords would relax the *sub judice* rule as suggested by the committee, but would ask the Procedure Committee to review its operation after "a reasonable period of experience".[47]

A connected matter raised was what was meant by the suggestion in the committee's report that the Leader of the House would exercise his discretion after "advice and consultation". In the debate. this was elaborated on by Viscount Cranbourne, then the new Leader of the House, who suggested that the Leader would not pronounce in his personal capacity. He suggested that it would be inappropriate to take advice from the Opposition leaders or the Convenor of the Cross-Bench Peers, since they were political figures; rather the appropriate source of advice would be the Clerk of the Parliaments and the counsel to the Chairman of Committees. Consequently, the advice would "bolster the Leader's position as an independent figure representing your Lordships as a whole rather than representing the party of the government of the day".[48]

Lord Simon drew attention to the position whereby a decision from the Court of Appeal could be appealed to the House of Lords. Legally, the judicial decision of the Judicial Committee of the House of Lords is a decision of the whole House, although by convention it operates like a court of law, and it is 150 years since the lay Lords have attempted to influence a decision of the Appellate Committee. Lord Simon suggested that it would be inappropriate for any Lord of Appeal, whether or not a Lord of Appeal in Ordinary, to express any view on the merits of a case pending before the House of Lords. He went on the suggest that it would be still more improper for a lay member of the Lords to do so. Consequently, it was his opinion that it would be extremely improbable that the Leader of the House would ever advise the waiver of the rule in any case which was pending before the Judicial Committee of the Lords. There is clearly merit in this suggestion. Indeed, it was because a case could reach the Judicial Committee that the Chairman of Committees had reservations about the Leader of the House ever consulting the Law Lords in respect of a relaxation of the *sub judice* rule.[49]

CONCLUSION

This saga demonstrates that here, as in many other areas of parliamentary procedure, Parliament is inclined not to update its rules and procedures to conform with developments elsewhere. The Lords, by failing to take account of the relaxation of the rule in the Commons in 1972, found itself some twenty-two years later with a procedure that did not allow it to debate a matter that involved individual liberty and the exercise of ministerial powers. The Commons has not

[47] N. 43 above.
[48] *Ibid.*
[49] *Ibid.*

really looked again at its *sub judice* rule since 1972, despite the changes in approach to judicial review that have occurred since then. The House of Lords is now more in step with judicial developments than the House of Commons. Both Houses are inclined to be reactive rather than proactive when it comes to procedural reform. Neither House has looked at whether there is a need for a further liberalisation of the *sub judice* rules in the light of the Contempt of Court Act 1981 and the changed judicial attitude to when proceedings may be prejudiced by media comment.[50] It is probably the case that members of both House are more restricted in what they can say on certain cases that are before the courts than are the media. Finally, the House of Lords had to accept, with reluctance, that if it is to be able to take a more active role in raising issues of ministerial responsibility that come before the courts, then the Leader of the House had to be given a new role akin to one of the roles of the Speaker of the Commons. It remains to be seen if this is the thin end of the wedge or another example of the adaptability of the Lords.

APPENDIX: TEXT OF *SUB JUDICE* RESOLUTIONS OF THE HOUSE OF COMMONS

## (1)  23 July 1963

Procedure (Debate on Matters awaiting Judicial Decision)—
*Resolved*: That subject always to the discretion of the Chair and to the right of the House to legislate on any matter,

(1)  matters awaiting or under adjudication in all courts exercising a criminal jurisdiction and in courts martial should not be referred to—
    (a)  in any motion (including a motion for leave to bring in a bill), or
    (b)  in debate, or
    (c)  in any question to a Minister including a supplementary question;
(2)  matters awaiting or under adjudication in a civil court should not be referred to—
    (a)  in any motion (including a motion for leave to bring in a bill), or
    (b)  in debate, or
    (c)  in any question to a Minister including a supplementary question;
from the time that the case has been set down for trial or otherwise brought before the court, as for example by notice of motion for an injunction; such matters may be referred to before such date unless it appears to the Chair that there is a real and substantial danger of prejudice to the trial of the case.
(3)  Paragraphs (1) and (2) of this Resolution should have effect

---

[50] See further my essay at n. 28 above. In my evidence to the Joint Committee on Parliamentary Privilege I suggested that the reform of the *sub judice* was something that the committee should consider as part of its general review of parliamentary privilege: H.L. Paper 50–viii/H.C. 401–viii (1997–8).

   (a)  in the case of a criminal case in courts of law, including courts martial, from the moment the law is set in motion by a charge being made;

   (b)  in the case of a civil case in courts of law, from the time that the case has been set down for trial or otherwise brought before the court, as for example by notice of motion for an injunction;

   (c)  in the case of any judicial body to which the House has expressly referred a specific matter for decision and report, from the time when the resolution of the House is passed.

(4)  Paragraphs (1) and (2) of this Resolution should cease to have effect

   (a)  in the case of courts of law, when the verdict and sentence have been announced or judgement given, but resumed when notice of appeal is given until the appeal has been decided;

   (b)  in the case of courts martial, when the sentence of the court has been confirmed and promulgated, but resumed when the convicted man petitions the Army Council, the Air Council or the Board of Admiralty;

   (c)  in the case of any judicial body to which the House has expressly referred a specific matter for decision and report, as soon as the report is laid before the House.

## (2)  28 June 1972

Procedure (Matters Awaiting Judicial Decision),—
*Resolved*: That—

(1)  Notwithstanding the Resolution of 23 July 1963 and subject to the discretion of the Chair reference may be made in Questions, Motions or debate to matters awaiting or under adjudication in all civil courts, including the National Industrial Relations Court, in so far as such matters relate to a Ministerial decision which cannot be challenged in court except on grounds of misdirection or bad faith, or concern issues of national importance such as the national economy, public order or the essentials of life.

### MATTERS *SUB JUDICE* IN THE HOUSE OF LORDS (1963)

A matter awaiting or under adjudication in any court exercising a criminal jurisdiction or in a court-martial should not be referred to in any Motion or debate on a motion or in any Question, including a supplementary question. A case which has been decided by a court, but is still open to appeal, is not considered *sub judice* until notice of appeal has been given.

    Matters awaiting or under adjudication in a civil court should not be referred to in any Motion or debate on a Motion or in any Question, including any supplementary question, from the time that the case has been set down for trial or otherwise brought before the court, as for example by notice of motion for an injunction: such matters may be referred to before such date unless it appears to the House that there is a real and substantial danger of prejudice to the trial of the case.

(Added 1995) This is subject to the proviso that, where a ministerial decision is in question, or a case concerns issues of national importance such as the national economy, public order or the essentials of life, reference may be made at the discretion of the Leader of the House, who must be satisfied that there is no real and substantial danger of prejudice to the proceedings. The Leader of the House should be given at least twenty-four hours' notice of any proposal to refer to a matter which is sub judice. It is undesirable that the exercise of his discretion should be challenged in the House.

(Added 1990) A case is deemed to be *sub judice* from the moment a petition for leave is presented to the House of Lords.

These rules do not apply to Bills or delegated legislation nor to matters being considered by departmental inquiries and the like; but it is recognised that it is often undesirable for Parliament to intervene in the settlement of matters upon which the decision has been delegated to others by Parliament itself. The House has agreed that the practice governing Motions and Questions relating to matters *sub judice* should be similar in both Houses of Parliament.

# PART TWO

# THE HOUSE AS A SUPREME COURT

# Introduction

ROBERT STEVENS

Academics looked seriously at the House of Lords as a judicial body for the first time in the mid-sixties. It was a period when the Lord Chancellor, Gerald Gardiner, had argued that the time had come to abolish the second appeal. The interests of litigants had to take priority over a court which no longer seemed to see a role for itself. To adapt Johnson, the prospect of its demise "powerfully concentrated the mind". Although Gardiner's plan proved of little interest to the profession itself, the proposed end of the judicial functions of the Lords stimulated three academic studies.

Louis Blom-Cooper and Gavin Drewry injected into what was then an intellectual vacuum the challenging *Final Appeal: A Study of the House of Lords in its Judicial Capacity (1972)*—a largely quantitative study, mainly about the judicial workings of the House during the previous twenty years. It was a trailblazing book. The authors argued that, on balance, the second appeal was justified. I then followed with *Law and Politics—The House of Lords as a Judicial Body (1978),* an attempt to write a politico-legal history of the House of Lords from 1800 to 1976, with emphasis on the law created and the *dramatis personae*. Finally, Alan Paterson's *The Lord Lords (1982)* was the first serious sociological study of the operation and mechanics of the House of Lords as a judicial body. From a social science perspective, if from no other, it was a highly significant book.

It would be pleasant to think that all three books had an important or at least useful impact. Except possibly within the rather closed ranks of legal history and socio-legal studies, they did not. Neither politicians nor lawyers—at least in the United Kingdom—seemed to think the ideas and issues raised about the role and workings of final appeal courts merited serious interest. Within academic law, the pedlars of legal philosophy, legal process and even introduction to law saw little of interest in any analysis of the judicial role of the House of Lords— an intellectual lacuna which was particularly unfortunate with respect to the interaction of legal philosophy and the study of the legal process.

At least one can understand the reasoning of leading lawyers and concerned politicians. In the 1960s and 1970s the House of Lords as a judicial body seemed of no great significance. Indeed, the judges' role in the British Constitution appeared as a marginal one. The Conservative position was that the English judges were the envy of the world—and that was because they were apolitical or non-political, by which was frequently meant they made no important decisions and were conservative (with a small "c") in their personal views. The official Conservative position was that they should be preserved in that blissful condition. Labour's view was rather different—judges' attitudes were innately conservative. They must therefore be given little power and discouraged from taking any but a highly formalistic view of the law within narrow confines of responsibility.

What has changed over the last twenty years can be explained in the politics of the 1980s. The era of consensus ended. Political consensus is never easy to define, but changing concepts of the market and the welfare state put the judges in a different political situation. After its defeat in 1979, Labour drifted for a while towards the "loony left"; then split. The Conservatives under Margaret Thatcher took on a Poujadiste spirit, which was alien to a judiciary which probably preferred—or at least had grown accustomed to—the consensus model. The strange Conservative urge on the one hand to claim great faith in the market and on the other to centralise and to weaken local government and then the civil service meant that the judges were increasingly exposed as one of the few power bases in government. They became a centre for independent decision-making, as well as independent thinking.

At the same time there was a change in the style of the judiciary. A new generation of judges was appearing who had been educated as lawyers (i.e. read law at the universities), had been exposed to a profession which was increasingly involved with commerce, and had operated in a profession which was less archaic in its structures and attitudes and more concerned with government decisions. As politics were fragmenting the judiciary was seen still to belong to consensus politics, which Mrs Thatcher was wont to categorize as "wet". In fact the backgrounds of the Law Lords were becoming more diverse. Many recruits to the Bench had studied in America; experience of European Union law was increasingly common. By the 1990s several of the Law Lords had been academics (Goff, Lloyd, Hoffmann) and almost all came from the specialised intellectual areas of the Bar—three from the same set of commercial chambers (Mustill, Lloyd, Steyn). Slynn came from Luxembourg; Steyn and Hoffmann were South African; Lowry from Northern Ireland; and the Scots (Mackay, Keith, Jauncey) had always been willing to take a broad approach. As an estate agent might say, the property was "ripe for development".

The linkage between the sixties and nineties is, however, vitally important and here the contribution by Louis Blom-Cooper and Gavin Drewry appears most significant (*"The Appellate Function"*; Chapter 6). The idea of Lord Gardiner's that the second appeal should be abolished went by the board in the following decades. Blom-Cooper and Drewry leave one in no doubt that the House of Lords has become vital (and better) in criminal cases; and in constitutional law, not surprisingly, the authors find the House has played a "leading part . . . consistent with its status". The significance of judicial review is accepted by all but the authors remind us that the House of Lords has "led the charge". In this context their analysis of the *Fire Brigades Union* case is particularly significant.[1]

[1] [1995] 2 AC 513.

The authors are understandably intrigued by the split between the judicial activists (Browne-Wilkinson, Lloyd and Nicholls) and those in favour of judicial restraint (Mustill and Keith) in the *Firemen's Case*. To Mustill, the decision to control the Home Secretary "pushes to the very boundaries of the distinction between court and Parliament established in, and recognised ever since, the Bill of Rights 1688". Lord Keith was more direct; the relief demanded would "represent an unwarrantable intrusion by the court into the political field and a usurpation of the function of Parliament". While Blom-Cooper and Drewry accept the view of the majority and agree that this might still be controversial, no-one could disagree with their conclusion that over the last thirty years the need for a Supreme Court has been firmly established.

The Blom-Cooper–Drewry thematic approach is neatly balanced by Brice Dickson's analysis of the Law Lords' work over the last thirty years ("*The Lords of Appeal and their Work 1967–1996*"; Chapter 7). It is vital to an understanding of the mechanics of running a final court of appeal—and the mechanics frequently help shape the outcomes. This chapter forces us to take account of the system of petitions for leave to appeal which now take such a significant part of the Law Lords' time. We are reminded that the Judicial Committee of the Privy Council is far from dead and forced to ponder why the leap-frog system never really worked. Dickson's analysis of the Northern Irish and Scottish judges reminds one that more work needs to be done on the role of the House of Lords with respect to these two jurisdictions, (although on Northern Ireland see also Blom-Cooper and Drewry). Finally, for those accustomed to looking at the Supreme Courts of Canada and the United States, the analysis of the Law Lords' terms reminds one of the relatively brief term of office of Law Lords. As the House has become more important as a final court of appeal and the mandatory retirement age has been imposed then lowered, Britain is going to have to appoint Law Lords in their early fifties if they are going to have the influence of a Frankfurter or a Warren, a Douglas or a Brennan.

Anthony Bradney's contribution ("*The Judicial Role of the Lord Chancellor*". Chapter 8) achieves far more than its title suggests. So frequently articles about the Lord Chancellor tend to be journalistic—the statement of the official position. This chapter is an important contribution to the much neglected, although frequently asserted, concept of the separation of powers. In addition to the analysis of the judicial contributions of the Lord Chancellor, Bradney offers a perceptive analysis of the types of case in which the Lord Chancellor, a number of the Cabinet, should sit. Is appropriate for him to sit in tax appeals, or was it appropriate for him to sit (and dissent) in *Pepper* v. *Hart*[2] where the use of legislative history was revolutionised? Lord Mackay's (and the same will be true for Lord Irvine) excursion into reforming and cutting the cost of legal aid is deftly analysed from a constitutional point of view. The conflict with Wood J, as President of the Employment Appeal Tribunal, is

---

[2] [1993] 1 All ER 42.

microscopically inspected, and Lord Mackay's assertion that the Lord Chancellor was acting as the senior judge and not as a member of the Executive is not easy to sustain. At the same time, Bradney unfortunately does not analyse the need on the part of the Executive to have some accountability from the judges. On the other hand his coverage of the discussion of the Green Papers on the legal profession in the House of Lords provides an analysis of that strange episode which may prove definitive.

As we look at the "new" role of the House of Lords, the practical, psychological and constitutional implications of the primacy of EU law cannot be underestimated. The implications of the European Union are elegantly and exhaustively analysed by Barry Fitzpatrick in *"A Dualist House of Lords in a Sea of Monist Community Law?"* (Chapter 9). With respect to the "Direct Effect" of the EU Treaty, relying especially on *Factortame*,[3] Fitzpatrick gives the House of Lords the same mark as the European Court—five out of ten—while for the monist approach to international obligations, Fitzpatrick gives the House six out of ten. "Given the enormous burdens of Diceyean insularity from which their Lordships have had to escape, it is a tribute to their adaptability and pragmatism that they can be accorded a status at least 'as monist as the ECJ', if not 'more monist that the ECJ'". Fitzpatrick also concludes that "the House has meticulously followed both the letter and the spirit of ECJ rulings on these constitutional questions and hence deserves at least nine out of ten for judicial solidarity". That is indeed a tribute to the House, although not a tribute that all politicians would be enthused about. To be more European than the European Court would be anathema to the Tory Right and New Labour's Left—or perhaps Old Labour itself.

One of the great changes is elegantly caught by Patricia Maxwell in her *"The House of Lords as a Constitutional Court—the implication of ex parte EOC"*; (Chapter 10). Over the last decade, the courts have been thrust into the limelight with continuous battles arising out of Britain's membership of the European Union. When the House decides that a British statute is inconsistent with a European directive, inevitably there is a clash of legal systems. In *Factortame* the House suspended an Act of Parliament while the politically unpopular European Court was consulted. That ruffled the feathers of the Eurosceptics. That was as nothing, however, compared with the *EOC Case*[4], where the Lords held that parts of the 1978 Employment Protection (Consolidation) Act were inconsistent with European employment law because they were inconsistent with European Community (as it was then) law. In particular, the Lords found that denying fringe benefits to part-time workers was tantamount to sexual discrimination, since 87% of part-time workers were women. The performance—both in striking down parliamentary legislation by reference to directives from the Commission, as well as the liberal interpretation of discrimination, based on its social and economic impact—was enough to cause *The Times'* leader writer to announce that Britain

³ [1991] 1 All ER 70.
⁴ [1994] 2 WLR 409.

"may now have, for the first time in its history a constitutional court". From whatever aspect one discusses the *EOC Case*, the change from the past is both obvious and dramatic. It is difficult to disagree with *The Times*' view that the traditional balance between Parliament and the judiciary had been changed.

The bold approach by the House of Lords to the automatic operation of EU law is paralleled by the new approach to statutory interpretation, dealt with by Kenny Mullan in his penetrating and detailed analysis in *"The Impact of Pepper v. Hart"* (Chapter 11). In so many ways, the decision is central to an understanding of the modern judicial process. The chief proponent of allowing legislative material to be used for interpreting statutes was Lord Browne-Wilkinson. His assumption that the criteria (and especially "where the promoter of the legislation has made a clear statement directed to that very issue") would mean that the new doctrine was rarely resorted to, has been easily evaded. His further emphasis on ambiguity has similarly receded as a requirement. Within the first three years, *Pepper* v. *Hart* had been referred to 140 times. As Mullan conclusively shows, the principle has been used in a wide range of situations, from reassuring doubting judges that their interpretation of the statutes was correct, to helping judges determine whether a phrase was in fact ambiguous. In short, the concerns of Lord Mackay, in his dissenting speech in *Pepper* v. *Hart*, have been more than borne out.

With that decision, no-one could now deny that a totally new approach to interpreting statutes—and thus inevitably to the relative balance between courts and legislature—has been accepted. It is true that in *Melluish (Inspector of Taxes)* v. *BMI (No 3) Limited*,[5] Lord Browne-Wilkinson endeavoured to put the genie back in the bottle, but too late. It may be that judges will be more circumspect about how they use the doctrine, and probably *Pepper* v. *Hart* will be cited less frequently, but the psychological Rubicon has been crossed and another important source of judicial power has been created.

There are, of course, various levels at which one can examine the new identity of the House of Lords. Partly, the willingness to open discussion to a wide range of concepts enabled it to "pierce the veil" of discrimination—as judges would have said twenty-five years earlier in the *EOC Case*. Simon Lee's powerful statement (*"Uneasy Cases"*; Chapter 12) takes a parallel issue, by examining the *Bland* case,[6] where the House allowed life support machines to be cut off for someone in a vegetative state as the result of the Hillsborough disaster. One has little doubt that a quarter of a century earlier the House would have found a way of finessing the issues and so avoiding the decision. Not so today. Only Lord Mustill seems to have thought publicly about the implications of judicial activism and judicial restraint and to have come down in favour of the latter. Mustill has advocated this position not only in *Bland*, but in a series of immigration cases and in *Brown*[7]—the homosexual sado-masochistic appeal.

---

[5] [1995] 4 All ER 453.
[6] *Airedale NHS Trust* v. *Bland* [1993] 1 All ER 821.
[7] *R.* v. *Brown* [1993] 2 All ER 75

The typical Law Lord is for forging ahead come what may. Lee does not believe that "the next generation of Law Lords will defer to Parliament as the right body to take the difficult moral decisions in a divided society". The presence of Lord Hoffmann and "the imminent arrival" of Laws and Sedley JJ will, in Lee's view, ensure this. After some scepticism about how they will go about their expansion and their general level of sophistication, he offers limited support: "What we need for the new millennium is a willingness to expand the horizons of arguments before the courts so as to respond to these challenges. This would recognise that our democracy is changing as Parliament shows itself to be ever less willing to come to terms with these dilemmas and the judges show an enthusiasm for greater involvement". In this sense, he would reject the Mustill and Browne-Wilkinson approach that the courts should tread water if possible while the legislature comes up with a principled decision. That he regards as dated.

These essays then provide an admirable guide to the changing nature of the final appeal court for the UK. The role of the judiciary has changed significantly—perhaps dramatically—over the last twenty-five years. Judicial review, *Pepper* v. *Hart*, the EU, a greater willingness to push forward the common law and tackle hard cases have changed substance and styles. The arrival of the New Labour government has brought new opportunities for expansion—the proposed judicial role in devolution and the incorporation of the European Convention on Human Rights. The judicial functions of the House of Lords are moving inexorably towards the centre of politics and public law.

It is beyond the jurisdiction of this introduction to discuss the merit of second chambers, but it is appropriate—in the light of what has gone before—to consider the role of the Law Lords. The second appeal and the link with a legislative body were saved by the Appellate Jurisdiction Act 1876—the work of a group of right-wing Tory MPs who cared nothing for law, the courts or litigants, but were anxious to prop up the hereditary principle by creating a group of judges who might balance the bishops. The move was opposed by those admirable reformers—Lord Cairns (Conservative) and Lord Selborne (Liberal).

Those two Lord Chancellors opposed a second level appeal court and in that they may well have been wrong. (They wanted second appeals to be heard by an expanded Court of Appeal.) They were, however, right to oppose this further blurring of the separation of powers. It may be that such blurring did not matter when judges rarely decided important—or at least politically sensitive—issues, but the rapid advances in judicial activism in the last twenty-five years make it essential that the separation be more clearly enforced. Removing the Law Lords from the House of Lords, it could be argued, would be an important first step. In that sense these comments provide a fresh opportunity to encourage a re-think not only of the judicial process, but of the concepts of separation of powers and the independence of the judiciary as part of the projected review of the Constitution.

# 6

# The Appellate Function

GAVIN DREWRY AND SIR LOUIS BLOM-COOPER

## INTRODUCTION

The curious location of the United Kingdom's final court of appeal in the second chamber of Parliament—and likewise the curious position within it of the Lord Chancellor, who trebles as its Speaker, as a leading government spokesman with a seat in the Cabinet, as well as chairing many Cabinet committees, and as a Law Lord[1]—have long been rich sources both of examination questions about the separation of powers and of wonderment to foreigners. The last time that legislators seriously looked at the House of Lords in its judicial capacity was in the 1870s, when the judicial function was abolished by the Judicature Act 1873, only to be restored by the Appellate Jurisdiction Act 1876.[2] Since then, by pragmatic and incremental stages rather than by grand design, there has been a growing separation between the legislative and judicial functions, to a point where the physical overlap between them has become largely ceremonial and symbolic.[3]

Hence the fact that, although there continues to be a great deal of discussion about the future of the second chamber itself, whose powers and composition have been considerably altered by the Parliament Acts of 1911 and 1949 and by the Life Peerages Act 1958 (and now look set to be changed more radically), the continuing survival and form of the judicial function has been treated very much as a secondary question. Two separate, but related issues have gone largely unaddressed by parliamentary and constitutional reformers. One is whether, in this day and age, the final appeal court should remain embedded in the second chamber of the legislature (a chamber whose own rationale has so often been questioned). One obvious possibility, last canvassed in the early years of this century, mainly in the context of debates about the handling of appeals from the

---

[1] See Chap. 8 below.

[2] Robert Stevens, "The Final Appeal: Reform of the House of Lords and Privy Council 1862–1876" [1964] *LQR* 343.

[3] Judgments (called "opinions" or "speeches") are still formally handed down in the Chamber of the House and the Law Lords, as judicial life peers, can, and sometimes do, participate in legislative debates. But appellate hearings are conducted in a committee room, away from the Chamber, often at times when the House itself is in deliberative session. Once a year the Law Lords sit in the Chamber to assert their right to hear appeals in the Chamber.

British Dominions,[4] is to merge its jurisdiction with that of the Judicial Committee of the Privy Council, which sits just across Parliament Square, in Downing Street, and which has substantially the same composition as the Appellate Committee of the House of Lords. The second issue is more fundamental. Given that we have perfectly respectable first-tier appeal courts, do we need a second appeal at all?

Now that we have acquired a new Labour government, committed to a programme of radical constitutional reform, including the elimination of the hereditary basis of the House of Lords, perhaps these issues will be reopened. House of Lords reform is the most obvious context in which this may happen. But, there are other elements in the reform package that may focus attention upon the future of the final appeal. Devolution, in particular, will change the geometry of the United Kingdom: under the provisions of the Scotland Act, the Judicial Committee of the Privy Council may be called upon to adjudicate upon matters relating to the legislative competence of the Scottish Parliament. Incorporation of the European Convention on Human Rights (and continuing development of the law of the European Union, and of the role of the European Court of Justice as an external Supreme Court in respect of national obligations under the Treaties) may prompt consideration whether the time has come to add a constitutional dimension to the jurisdiction of the final appeal court.

With constitutional change in the wind, these exciting, though admittedly highly speculative, thoughts serve as a topical backcloth to the present chapter.

### FINAL APPEAL REVISITED

In the late 1960s the present writers conducted a major study of the role and function of the House of Lords in its judicial capacity. The project was prompted mainly by two factors. First, a lingering sense of curiosity, which was shared probably by almost everyone who has ever looked at, or had dealings with, the courts of the United Kingdom about the rationale and practical implications of locating the final court of appeal within the upper chamber of Parliament whose own *raison d'être* has continually been subject to critical scrutiny. Secondly, the writers, who were curious about the nature of judicial appeal, wished to discover, in particular, whether there were any peculiarities about the cases that progressed to the House of Lords. Their curiosity extended to the manner in which the Law Lords handled these cases which distinguished—and perhaps justified—the retention of a second tier of appeal, over and above the English Court of Appeal, the Inner House of the Scottish Court of Session and the Northern Ireland Court of Appeal. Such questions gained additional salience from the Practice Direction of 1966, which empowered the

---

[4] R. Stevens, n. 2 above; and see Stevens, *The Independence of the Judiciary* (Oxford, Clarendon Press, 1993), at 18–19, 64.

House of Lords to relax the rule preventing it from reversing its own previous decisions.

The research for the study was based mainly on an exhaustive examination over the period 1952–66 of the documentary records of appeals and petitions for leave to appeal which came respectively from the Appellate and Appeals Committees of the House of Lords. It also involved a scrutiny of the relevant proceedings in the courts *a quo*. The findings were published in 1972 in a book entitled *Final Appeal*.[5] Twenty-six years later, while much is unchanging, much else has changed. Law Lords have come and gone. The era of the presidency of Lord Reid and then Lord Wilberforce, universally regarded as outstanding, has left its indelible mark. European law—a subject touched on only as an after-thought in *Final Appeal*—has permeated much of our municipal law. European administrative law, with its pronounced principle of proportionality, is creep-ing into the burgeoning public law of England. From *Ridge* v. *Baldwin*,[6] through to *O'Reilly* v. *Mackman*,[7] and on to the *GCHQ* case,[8] the House of Lords has led the march, almost a stampede, over the judicial control of ministers and administrators in central and local government. It is these, and other significant developments in the jurisprudence emanating from the Palace of Westminster, that have impelled the writers, in this chapter, to revisit their stamping ground to see how the final court of appeal appears today in the context of constitu-tional reform.

When we embarked in 1966 upon our research for *Final Appeal* we ques-tioned the value of a two-tier appellate system. Ultimately we came round to supporting the retention of the final court of appeal. Our conclusion was that, although there are significant costs in retaining a second appeal, in terms of expensive duplication of function and delay in the final resolution of disputes, the apparent duplication is not what it seems. Any delay, in the context of what is a minuscule number of cases proportionate to the total volume of litigation, is, we found, a modest price to pay for the special and valuable function served by the final appeal.

The main and obvious role of first-tier appellate courts is to resolve problems in particular cases. The function of the House of Lords is, however, the broader and deeper one of review and supervision rather than of appeal—giving in-depth attention to a small number of particularly important and difficult cases and enunciating authoritative legal principles for the guidance of the courts below and the general public. Our view (based on impression and reflection, rather than on any recent systematic research) is that the House of Lords con-tinues to justify its existence by the quality of its review function.

In our concluding chapter we flirted briefly with the idea that the jurisdiction of the House of Lords should be merged with that of the Judicial Committee of

---

[5] Blom-Cooper and Drewry, *Final Appeal* (Oxford, Clarendon Press, 1972).
[6] [1964] AC 40.
[7] [1983] 2 AC 237.
[8] *Council of Civil Service Unions* v. *Minister for the Civil Service* [1985] AC 374.

the Privy Council, to constitute "an all-purpose tribunal, combining an appellate and a constitutional role in respect both of the UK and of the Commonwealth"; but we conceded that such a proposal belonged "more to speculation than to reality". In any case, our own research scarcely touched upon the work of the Privy Council—an omission which we would rectify, were we to set about updating our book. Robert Stevens has given a fascinating account, in his book, *The Independence of the Judiciary*, of the debates about a possible merger that took place intermittently around the turn of the century, in the context of various schemes for establishing an imperial court of appeal. A post-imperial age provides a very different context for re-opening the debate about a possible merger; nevertheless the debate has relevance today.

We also—and more seriously—suggested that ways should be found of increasing the case-load of the House of Lords, to enhance the opportunities for their Lordships to exercise their supervisory jurisdiction and contribute to the development of coherent legal principles. We noted the tendency for appeals (tax cases were a qualified exception to this) to be thinly spread over the different legal subject categories, and for some troublesome areas of law to come up on appeal only spasmodically. It *appears*, however, that the number of cases heard annually by the Appellate Committee is much the same in the 1990s as it was in the 1960s—something in the region of fifty appeals.

When we tried, for the purpose of writing this chapter, to obtain up-to-date statistics about the volume of cases and the distribution of subject-matter and appeal-outcomes, we quickly re-discovered both the helpfulness of the judicial office of the House of Lords and the quirky, unhelpfulness of the official *Judicial Statistics*. To take one instance, the 1992 statistics show that the House disposed of fifty civil cases in that year, reversing the court below on twenty-six occasions. There were ten income tax cases—by far the biggest subject category—all reversed. On closer inspection, however, these ten revenue appeals turned out to be the consolidated appeals in a single case, *Pepper* v. *Hart*, a case significant for its constitutional impact, permitting their Lordships to study the debates in *Hansard* to resolve ambiguities in the words used by Parliament,[9] and for the Lord Chancellor's politically-motivated dissent. Even ignoring any other consolidated appeals, this dramatically alters the reversal rate from just over 50 per cent to about one third. Quite apart from our views about the final appeal, we wish to renew our plea of more than twenty-five years ago that something be done to rationalise the *Judicial Statistics*. Recent volumes are presentationally much more attractive and user-friendly than were their 1960s counterparts, but they are still virtually useless for purposes of serious analysis.

On the combined basis of the limited statistical information available and of our own impressionistic view from the reported cases, we can say with some confidence that our observations about the shift in the balance of court business are broadly correct. Revenue appeals no longer occupy much of the case-load.

---

[9] See Chap. 11 below.

There were only two such out of fifty-four appeals in 1997, while there were four cases involving social security legislation, demonstrating the significant growth in public law. Depending on the classification of appeals, we calculate that eight out of fifty-four were in the field of public law. And the criminal law attracted no fewer than nine appeals.

## REVENUE APPEALS AND CRIMINAL APPEALS

In the period covered by *Final Appeal*, appeals in revenue matters bulked large in the case-load, so large in fact that the Law Lords might on occasions almost have been mistaken for an ennobled extension of the Special Commissioners for Income Tax; and where the Revenue fell foul of the highest judiciary, the legislature in its annual implementation of Budget proposals was quick to change the law. In this area of law we have a clear illustration of the complementarity of the judicial and legislative process—perhaps the merest hint of a justification for maintaining the link between the final court of appeal and the legislature. Revenue appeals accounted for thirty per cent of English appeals and for twenty per cent of Scottish appeals (these are figures that we compiled ourselves, rather than relying on the official statistics). This marked predominance of appeals in a single area of law—of public significance because of the vast amounts of public money in dispute—had important implications in terms of the spread of subject-matter brought to the highest court in the land.

Activity in criminal appeals, by contrast, was small but beginning to grow. The jurisdiction in criminal cases had only recently received a filip from the Administration of Justice Act 1960, whereby the procedure of the Attorney-General's fiat was superseded by a double-track system under which the aspiring appellant had first to obtain a certificate that the case raised a point of law of general importance and, only then, could seek leave to appeal. In the period immediately following the procedural change, the House of Lords found few friends in a trilogy of decisions—first, *DPP* v. *Smith*,[10] and then two subsequent decisions, *Shaw* v. *DPP*[11] and *Sykes* v. *DPP*.[12] They did nothing to enhance the House of Lords' reputation for sound exposition of the criminal law.

While the case-load has increased, the jurisprudential output continues to give less than satisfaction to practitioners, who complain that too little expertise in criminal law is evident among their Lordships. Lords Mustill and Steyn have proved the exceptions to the rule. There has been a rash of cases demonstrating the inability of the Law Lords to remedy a defective law of murder. Lord Mustill, in *Attorney-General's Reference No 3 of 1994*,[13] said that "the

---

[10] [1961] AC 290.

[11] [1962] AC 220.

[12] [1962] AC 528. See R Pattenden, *English Criminal Appeals, 1844–1994* (Oxford, Clarendon Press, 1996), at 333–8.

[13] [1997] 3 All ER 936.

English law of homicide is permeated by anomaly, fiction, misnomer and obsolete reasoning". An impressive juristic contribution recently came from Lord Lowry in C *(a minor)* v. *DPP*,[14] explaining why the Divisional Court was wrong to sweep away the presumption that a child between the ages of ten and fourteen cannot be criminally responsible unless it is rebutted by evidence that the child knew that his or her act was seriously wrong.[15]

## LEAPFROGGING APPEALS

The force of the argument in favour of abolishing the appellate hierarchy and of meeting litigant-satisfaction by providing for only one appeal, was prospectively weakened by the introduction of leap-frogging. The Administration of Justice Act 1969 permits—critics complain that it came belatedly, since it was proposed by Lord Greene MR during the 1940s and adapted by the Evershed Committee on Supreme Court Practice and Procedure in 1953[16]—certain categories of appeal to "leapfrog" over the backs of the Lords Justices, but only where there is a binding precedent in the Court of Appeal or in a case of statutory construction. The practice has been used very sparingly in the twenty-five years of its existence, for the reasons given by Megarry J. in *IRC* v. *Church Commissioners for England*.[17] Recently, the practice was given a boost in a homeless persons case, *R.* v. *London Borough of Wandsworth, ex p. Coggins*,[18] where the certifying trial judge explained that cases of judicial review, where the primary facts on affidavit evidence are already found rather than having to be determined by the trial judge and potentially to be canvassed at the first appellate stage, are peculiarly apt for leap-frogging. Unfortunately, the Law Lords declined to accept the "leap-frog", and the case later went to the Court of Appeal. In recent years, the number of leap-frog cases reaching the Lords seems to have averaged, at most, about one *per annum*. There may be a case for a fresh impetus to leap-frog in public law cases, to which we now turn.

## PUBLIC LAW CASES IN THE LORDS

The growth in the development of judicial review is perhaps the most compelling illustration of the virtues of the three-tier system. When we wrote *Final Appeal*, the supervisory jurisdiction by the courts of administrative action was only just beginning to burgeon. A trilogy of cases, all decided by the House of

---

[14] [1996] AC 1.
[15] The doctrine of *doli incapax* is to be swept away in the Crime and Disorder Act 1998.
[16] London, HMSO, Cmnd 8878, 1953.
[17] [1975] 1 WLR 251.
[18] [1996] unreported.

Lords—*Ridge* v. *Baldwin*,[19] *Padfield* v. *Minister of Agriculture*[20] and *Anisminic Ltd* v. *Foreign Compensation Commission*[21]—laid the foundation for a modern system of public law. Under the leadership of Lord Reid, the House of Lords, as Lord Browne-Wilkinson observed in his Foreword to the Supperstone-Goudie book on *Judicial Review*:[22]

> "cultivated the perhaps unpromising seed of the prerogative writs (and orders) into a wide-ranging system of public law which for the most part ensures that statutory (and prerogative) powers are exercised only for the purpose and in the manner in which Parliament intended."

In recent years the House of Lords has addressed issues that go to the very heart of executive power—in a period when the apparatus of government and the role of the state have been undergoing a period of revolutionary change and reappraisal. New trends in public management have been matched by new trends in public law (though it is arguable that the matching still has a long way to go). The House of Lords has played a leading part in the process, consistent with its special status as the final court of review and supervision. One has only to think of such landmark cases as *GCHQ*,[23] *M* v. *Home Office*[24] and *R.* v. *Secretary of State for the Home Department, ex p. Fire Brigades Union*[25] to realise the extent to which the courts in general, and the House of Lords in particular, have begun to exercise a measure of control, not just over bureaucrats but also over elected ministers of the Crown. It is to the instructive example of the Fire Brigades Union case that we now turn.

THE FIRE BRIGADES UNION CASE

The period since publication of *Final Appeal* has appropriately culminated in the decision in this case, which focused on the fate of the Criminal Injuries Compensation Board (CICB). Since 1964 the Board had administered the non-statutory, *ex gratia* scheme of compensation for victims of crimes of violence. The constitutional issue in the case formed part of the on-going debate about the relationship between Parliament, ministers, the courts and the private citizen. Unlike the contemporary judicial activity to ensure legality of ministerial and administrative implementation of statutory powers to which we have already alluded, the CICB decision uniquely interpreted the parliamentary process of law-making and the relationship between the legislature and the judiciary.

---

[19] [1964] AC 40.
[20] [1968] AC 997.
[21] [1969] 2 AC 147.
[22] London, Butterworths, 1997.
[23] [1985] AC 374.
[24] [1994] 1 AC 377.
[25] [1995] 2 AC 513.

For all of its thirty years of life, the CICB had administered a scheme, established under prerogative powers and awarding compensation on the common law rules for assessing damages. The Board was composed of a leading Queen's Counsel as chairman and a panel of silks and top solicitors, providing a financial bonanza for the top echelons of the legal profession. In 1988 Parliament determined to put the scheme on a statutory footing, by a fasciculus of sections—sections 108 to 117, together with dependent Schedules 6 and 7 in Part VII of a ten-part statute effecting major changes to criminal justice.[26] Section 171 of the Act provided: "(i) Subject to the following provisions of this section, this Act shall come into force on such day as the Secretary of State may by order made by statutory instrument appoint . . . ". In 1992 the then Home Secretary, Mr Kenneth Clarke, gave notice of his intention to replace the existing scheme with a new tariff scheme, with effect from 1994. The statutory scheme of 1988 was to be treated as redundant, to be obliterated from the statute book by Parliament as and when convenient to the dictates of the government's legislative programme. Meanwhile the tariff scheme was put into place by resort to prerogative powers, the new Home Secretary, Mr Michael Howard, crucially (and fatally) publicly declaring himself unwilling to exercise the power under section 171(1) of the 1988 Act. Had he reserved his decision, he might at least have escaped judicial opprobrium.

No issue at all focused on the merits either of the old scheme or of the new tariff scheme, although the public controversy that drove the trade unions to take up the cudgels on behalf of claimants for compensation was quintessentially about the government's apparent parsimony towards the victims of violent crime. *Victim Support* had proposed a compromise of a basic tariff scheme, with an additional ingredient of monetary award for loss of earnings; the legal profession clung to its system of common law damages which generally supplied more generous awards. The Home Secretary ignored all protestations and ploughed on, mindless of growing impatience at his unpreparedness to halt a while and listen to the public debate about the rights of victims. On 11 May 1996, the government announced its adherence to the tariff scheme, but made some notable concessions, principally in relation to loss of earnings after twenty-eight weeks. The Opposition in Parliament had switched its attention to the manner in which the Home Secretary had approached his statutory power to bring the old scheme into force.

By three judicial votes to two, the Home Secretary was told by the House of Lords that his decision to introduce the tariff scheme, at a time when the statutory process and his powers under section 171(1) were still on the statute book, was unlawful and an abuse of prerogative powers. The majority opinions—of Lords Browne-Wilkinson, Lloyd of Berwick and Nicholls of Birkenhead—deserve close reading for their individual ratiocination. For present purposes we desire to concentrate on the two dissents, more particularly the intellectually persuasive reasoning of Lord Mustill.

---

[26] Criminal Justice Act 1988.

Lord Keith of Kinkel was dismissive of the case for judicial control of the ministerial power to activate statutory provisions "on such day as the Secretary of State" may determine. To grant relief to the trade union applicants would, he said, "represent an unwarrantable intrusion by the court into the political field and a usurpation of the function of Parliament". He had prefaced that challenging statement by concluding, primarily, that section 171(1) was inapt "to create any duty in the Secretary of State owed to members of the public". That conclusion sounds ill in the ears of a citizen in a democratic society who would conclude that, whatever duty ministers owe to Parliament, their constant obligation is to the electorate. It is the precise scope of the public duty (or, more properly, the exercise of power) that is potentially up for judicial scrutiny.

Lord Mustill excites the constitutionalist in a system of government which draws no explicit lines of demarcation between judicial and elective power.[27] The key to his holding back from intervention in the instant process of law-making by the legislature is to be found in his peroration. He said:

> "Some of the arguments addressed would have the court push to the very boundaries of the distinction between court and Parliament established in, and recognised ever since, the Bill of Rights 1688. Three hundred years have passed since then, and the political and social landscape has changed beyond recognition. But the boundaries remain; they are of crucial significance to our private and public lives; and the courts should, I believe, make sure that they are not overstepped."

If we are inclined to applaud those remarks, it is nevertheless not the case that boundary lines are immutable. (Devolution brings in its trail new boundary lines.) The impact of a boundary which marks out the functions of those who operate on either side depends on where the playing surface—the pitch—is sited in relation to the spectators. For a Test Match, the pitch will be neatly placed in centre-stage; the wickets will be equiparate and equidistant from the boundary. On another day the pitch will be nearer one side of the ground than the other, any slope in the ground (as at Lords, the Mecca of cricket) being emphasised. Some spectators will be nearer the scene of play then others in another part of the ground. Analogously, the boundary line of parliamentary activity that must not be intruded upon will depend on the siting of the pitch.

Section 171(1) of the Criminal Justice Act 1988 was, moreover, essentially a procedural matter; it did not arouse any issue as to merit. In this sense it was a microcosm of the traditional grounds for judicial review. It could only be a case of procedural irregularity. No *Wednesbury* unreasonableness of the decision to introduce the tariff scheme came over the judicial horizon. But, more still, the meaning of a statutory provision is always, as a last resort, a matter for judicial interpretation. Parliament is sovereign, but the courts have their constitutional duty.[28] Section 171(1) was ambiguous. Did Parliament intend, by the use of its statutory language, to permit the Home Secretary to render its effect nugatory?

---

[27] See too the stimulating article by Sir John Laws, "Law and Democracy" [1995] *PL* 72.
[28] See Lord Simon of Glaisdale in *Farrell* v. *Alexander* [1977] AC 59.

Or was it reasonable to suppose that Parliament would expect to have the opportunity to say whether the old scheme, which it had determined to put on a statutory footing, should be superseded legislatively, and not by resort to the outmodish prerogative power of the Crown? The upsetting of the Home Secretary's diversionary tactics over a statutory power was properly brought under judicial scrutiny.

PUBLIC LAW CASES FROM NORTHERN IRELAND

The House of Lords is the final court of appeal for the United Kingdom; it performs an important function in co-ordinating legal development throughout the nation, crucially so in a devolved nation. Its jurisdiction extends to Scotland, and of course to Northern Ireland. Appeals from Northern Irish cases have been few in number—about one a year on average—but they have not been lacking qualitatively. Inevitably, arising from the troubles of the last twenty-five years or so, many of the cases that have come up for adjudication have touched on delicate socio-political issues. Duress in aiding and abetting murder—*Lynch* v. *DPP*;[29] criminal homicide by members of armed forces using excessive force—*Attorney-General's Reference No 1*[30] and *R* v. *Clegg*,[31] interpretation of the limitations on the right to silence—*Murray* v. *DPP*,[32] and the extent of a police officer's power of arrest—*O'Hara* v. *Chief Constable of RUC*;[33] these and many allied issues have exercised the minds of the highest judiciary.

The Northern Irish contribution to the membership of the Appellate Committee has been disproportionate to the meagre case load from the Province. Lord MacDermott was the first Ulsterman to be appointed a Lord of Appeal in Ordinary since partition. He sat for four years, from 1947–51, until his appointment as Lord Chief Justice of Northern Ireland (in which role he served until 1971, when he was succeeded by Sir Robert (later Lord) Lowry). Thereafter he sat spasmodically as a Law Lord. Robert Stevens in *Law and Politics: The House of Lords as a Judicial Body, 1800–1976*, wrote of Lord MacDermott:

> "[He] did not see the role of the final appeal court as one of further refining the previously refined. Instead he sought to construe statutes with legislative intent in mind, to restate common law principles broadly, and to protect the law from deviating too noticeably from common sense or the current political and social developments of modern Britain. [His] greatest contribution to the law was that he was always aware of the realities of the situation and the practical result of his decisions. He refused to sit down complacently and merely extol the virtues of the existing legal system."[34]

[29] [1975] AC 753.
[30] [1977] AC 105.
[31] [1995] 1 AC 482.
[32] [1994] 1 WLR 1.
[33] [1997] AC 286.
[34] At 380–4.

That much, and a good deal more, could be said of the short period of Lord Lowry's membership of the House of Lords. From 1988 to 1994—he had sat occasionally on becoming a peer in 1980—he was a distinct judicial voice, ever-challenging traditional modes of thought. Notable among his judgments are his recent assessment of public policy in ousting established principles of liability (*Spring* v. *Guardian Assurance plc*[35]) and an impressive exegesis on the evidentiary law relating to the criminal responsibility of children between the ages of ten and fourteen (*C (a minor)* v. *DPP*).[36]

The future constitutional status of the province, with its devolved Assembly and cross-border agencies, is unlikely to disturb the judicial link with the House of Lords. Indeed, it may cement the link. Just as tradition has consistently ordained that there shall always be two Scots on the Appellate Committee, so it seems equally important that there should always be one representative from the province of Northern Ireland. After a lapse of a couple of years, the Lord Chief Justice of Northern Ireland (Sir Brian Hutton) was made a Lord of Appeal in Ordinary as Lord Hutton in 1997.

### LINKS WITH THE LEGISLATURE

Those who have called for reform or abolition of the second legislative chamber seldom give more than a passing thought (if that) to the judicial function that resides so incongruously in the House of Lords. It seems tacitly to be assumed that arguments concerning the possible disappearance or metamorphosis of the Lords as a part of the legislature can be conducted with little reference to the judicial function.

It is certainly true that the final appellate court could be transferred—whether the House of Lords itself survives or not—to an ordinary court building (one probably more convenient for the conduct of judicial business). The severing of the Parliamentary link would mean that some of the ceremonial paraphernalia would go (including the archaic rigmarole of handing down judgments in the Chamber, in the form of printed opinions, formerly speeches); some footnotes in constitutional textbooks would need to be rewritten. But, for most practical purposes, the process could surely be effected without much upheaval.

One issue that would need to be considered, however, is the impact of reform on the present legislative role of the Law Lords, as members of the second chamber of Parliament.[37] There has been a long-standing perception that the Law Lords—whose writ of summons to the Lords takes exactly the same form as that of other categories of peer—have a valuable legislative role to play as (to quote the 1968 White Paper on House of Lords Reform) "resident legal experts".[38]

---

[35] [1995] 2 AC 296.
[36] [1996] AC 1.
[37] See Chap. 10 of *Final Appeal*, n. 5 above.
[38] London, HMSO, Cmnd 3799, 1968.

This applies particularly to the consideration of technical law reform Bills, which usually start in the Lords, and scrutiny of European draft directives, statutory instruments and consolidation Bills (which always start in the Lords). The implicit argument is that it is much better for the judicial members of the House, acting as legislators, to assist the government to get its Bills right from the outset, than for them to find fault with the Act several years later, sitting as the Appellate Committee on a particular case raising interpretation of the statutory provision. We are not aware of any instances of a Law Lord pouring scorn on the obscurity of a statutory provision, only to recall afterwards, and too late, that he had played a part, even *sub silentio*, in fashioning it.

There is a convention that Law Lords should avoid political controversy (and they invariably sit on the crossbenches). There have been, however, quite a number of instances over the years of Lords of Appeal moving amendments to government Bills: in 1978, Lord Kilbrandon, Lord Diplock and Viscount Dilhorne each moved amendments to the Scotland Bill; in 1984, Lord Scarman moved amendments to the Police and Criminal Evidence Bill, and defeated the government on two occasions; Lord Ackner (an active participant in debate, particularly since his retirement as a Lord of Appeal in 1993) acted as a teller against the government in a division that resulted in the second defeat of the War Crimes Bill in 1991, and in 1998 he successfully promoted an amendment to the Crime and Disorder Bill setting up a Standing Advisory Council on Criminal Justice and the Penal System.[39] It is possible that the acrimonious debates to which several of the Law Lords, notably Lord Lane CJ, made angry contributions on the 1989 Green Papers on reform of legal services, and on the Courts and Legal Services Bill the following year, marked a modification of this self-denying convention, as the judges found themselves faced with the administration of justice being subjected to economic disciplines similar to those being applied in other areas of public administration by an uncompromising Lord Chancellor. More recently, some Law Lords displayed hostility to the Home Secretary's refusal to abolish the mandatory penalty for murder.

Interventions by serving Lords of Appeal are quite rare—though retired judges take part in debate quite frequently. Thus, looking at the index to *Hansard* for the 1993–4 session, eleven Law Lords (all of them retired from judicial office) spoke at various stages of the Criminal Justice and Public Order Bill, and seven on the Police and Magistrates' Courts Bill—of whom Lord Slynn of Hadley, who intervened at report stage and third reading, is a serving Lord of Appeal. Altogether, the index to *Hansard* shows that Law Lords contributed to proceedings on nineteen Bills. Most of the contributions were brief. Only four Bills received any input from serving Lords of Appeal. The Law Lords made a notable contribution to the government's Human Rights Bill in 1997–8.

We see considerable value in retaining the facility for contributions to legislative scrutiny by peers with judicial experience. Presumably, if the voting

---

[39]   H.L. Deb., vol. 588, col. 170 (31 Mar. 1998).

rights of hereditary peers were to be abolished, the Law Lords would remain fully participant members of the House, as Life Peers.

Ultimately, the worth of any public institution depends on the quality of its output, and that in turn depends on its membership, particularly where collegiality is fostered, as it is with the House of Lords through the compactness of the court and, where appropriate, the practice of individual Law Lords delivering separate assenting or dissenting judgments. When we wrote *Final Appeal* the Appellate Committee was dominated by two judicial colossi—Lords Reid and Wilberforce. For a period their departure left a gap. By the middle of the 1990s it had regained its earlier reputation as an outstanding court.

If we were to engage in a second edition of *Final Appeal*, we would not, as we did in 1966, start from a position of agnosticism but would tend towards endorsement of the enduring value of the House of Lords in its judicial capacity. As and when reform comes to the House of Lords itself, there will be no reversion to the onslaught of 1873 on a second tier of appellate court. On the contrary, there will indubitably be an enduring place for the final court of appeal, whether in the Palace of Westminster or elsewhere.

# 7

# *The Lords of Appeal and their Work 1967–1996*

BRICE DICKSON*

## INTRODUCTION

Lords of Appeal in Ordinary are the top judges in the United Kingdom. Appointed under the Appellate Jurisdiction Act 1876, they serve in the country's two most important courts, the Appellate Committee of the House of Lords and the Judicial Committee of the Privy Council. The rulings they issue are therefore amongst the most influential emanating from any judicial body in the world. In addition, they have the opportunity, as Life Peers,[1] to contribute to debates both on policy and on draft legislation whenever the House of Lords is sitting as a parliamentary chamber.

Despite their pivotal role as law makers, Lords of Appeal have been surprisingly under-studied. As noted in Robert Stevens' *Introduction* to this part of the book and in the preceding chapter, they have been the object of only three major works. The first of these covers their activities from 1954 to 1968,[2] the second takes a longer historical look over the period 1800 to 1976[3] and the third examines the period 1957 to 1973.[4] Nothing of real substance has been published since 1982.[5] The present chapter seeks to fill part of the vacuum by looking

---

* I am grateful to Sir Louis Blom-Cooper Q.C. for comments made on a draft of this chapter and to Patricia McKee for her help with the graphs. Errors remaining are mine alone.

[1] Under the Appellate Jurisdiction Act 1887, s. 2, Lords of Appeal are entitled to vote and sit in the House of Lords for life, not just during their tenure of office (which had been the original position under the 1876 Act): see Lord Macmillan, "The Lords of Appeal in Ordinary" (1947) 98 *LJ* 541.

[2] Louis Blom-Cooper and Gavin Drewry, *Final Appeal: A Study of the House of Lords in its Judicial Capacity* (Oxford, Clarendon Press, 1972).

[3] Robert Stevens, *Law and Politics: The House of Lords as a Judicial Body, 1800–1976* (Oxford, Clarendon Press, 1979).

[4] Alan Paterson, *The Law Lords* (London, Macmillan Press, 1982).

[5] Though there have of course been many illuminating journal articles, not least those of A. Bradney, "The Changing Face of the House of Lords" (1985) *Juridical Review* 178 (which analyses decisions between 1974 and 1984); T. Murphy and R. Rawlings, "After the Ancien Regime: The Writing of Judgments in the House of Lords, 1979–80" (1981) 44 *MLR* 617 and (1982) 45 *MLR* 34; and S. Livingstone, "The House of Lords and the Northern Ireland Conflict" (1994) 57 *MLR* 333 (which examines the "troubles-related" cases which went to the House of Lords from Northern Ireland between 1969 and 1994). For a very good textbook treatment, see T. Ingman, *The English Legal Process* (7th edn., London, Blackstone Press, 1998), at 4–11.

primarily at statistical information on the Lords of Appeal and their work over a recent thirty-year period. Blom-Cooper and Drewry, in Chapter 6, point to inadequacies in the way some of these statistics are currently presented by the Lord Chancellor's Department; for present purposes the published figures have been accepted at their face value.[6]

The period chosen for scrutiny is that between 1967, the first full year in which the Lords were able to apply the right they proclaimed for themselves in July 1966 to overrule previous decisions of the House,[7] and 1996, the last year for which full statistics were available at the time of writing. This is a long enough period to enable patterns and trends to be identified, if there are any. After first examining the individuals who served as Lords of Appeal during these years, together with their educational and professional backgrounds, the chapter looks at the work they have undertaken in dealing with petitions for leave to appeal to the House of Lords, with actual appeals in that House, and with appeals in the Judicial Committee of the Privy Council.

## THE PERSONS WHO SERVED AS LORDS OF APPEAL

During most of the period under review, to be appointed as a Lord of Appeal a person must already have held "high judicial office" for two years or have been a practising barrister for fifteen years. "High judicial office" means being the Lord Chancellor or a judge of one of Her Majesty's superior courts in Great Britain or Northern Ireland. Since the coming into force of the Courts and Legal Services Act 1990, a person in England and Wales is eligible for appointment if he or she has been in possession of a "Supreme Court qualification" for at least fifteen years.[8] A "Supreme Court qualification" means having the right of audience in relation to all proceedings in the Supreme Court of England and Wales.[9] Practice for fifteen years as an advocate in Scotland, or as a solicitor entitled to appear in the Court of Session and High Court of Justiciary, is also enough.

Appointment as a Lord of Appeal is made in the name of the Queen,[10] but in practice by the Prime Minister after consultations with the Lord Chancellor. The Prime Minister and Lord Chancellor, when considering whom to appoint, will bear in mind the need to have an array of different legal expertise on the court, such as in chancery matters, the commercial field or criminal law.[11] If appointed after 31 March 1995 Lords of Appeal must retire at the age of sev-

---

[6] Before 1975 these were known as the *Civil Judicial Statistics*. As far as the House of Lords is concerned the reports include information on the cases originating from Scotland and Northern Ireland, as well as all criminal cases.

[7] *Practice Statement* [1966] 1 WLR 1234, [1966] 3 All ER 77.

[8] Appellate Jurisdiction Act 1876, s. 6 (as amended).

[9] Courts and Legal Services Act 1990, s. 71(3)(a).

[10] Appellate Jurisdiction Act 1876, s. 6.

[11] To deal with Admiralty actions the Lords of Appeal may call in the aid of one or more specially qualified assessors: Supreme Court of Judicature Act 1891, s. 3.

enty,[12] but if appointed before that date they can continue in office "during good behaviour", i.e. until they wish to retire.[13] However no-one can sit to hear an appeal, or a petition for leave to appeal, after he or she attains the age of seventy-five.[14]

In the period in question, as Table 7.1 indicates, 44 individuals served as Lords of Appeal. They swelled the total of those ever appointed to the role to 96.[15] Every single one of them was a male. In 1967 the number who could hold office at any one time was nine,[16] and there were indeed nine in post throughout that year. By the Administration of Justice Act 1968,[17] the maximum permitted number was raised to eleven. This led to the appointment of an additional Lord of Appeal (Lord Diplock) in September 1968, and from then until January 1975, when Lord Reid and Morris both retired, there were ten Lords of Appeal in office. Strangely, but quite lawfully,[18] from January 1975 until September 1979 the House reverted to making do with just nine Lords of Appeal (it was not until the appointment of Lord Lane that the earlier judicial strength was restored) and barely a year later the number had again been reduced to nine, where it stayed until May 1985 (with the appointment of Lord Griffiths), even reaching just eight during the summer of 1982. The number fell to nine once more between June 1987 and August 1988, when Lord Lowry was appointed (and for a five month spell during that period was again at eight). The first occasion on which there were eleven Lords of Appeal in post was when Lord Slynn was appointed in March 1992. Then, by the Maximum Number of Judges Order

---

[12] Judicial Pensions and Retirement Act 1993, s. 26, which was brought into force on 31 Mar. 1995.

[13] Appellate Jurisdiction Act 1876, s. 6. In Apr. 1997 Lord Mustill retired just a month short of his sixty-sixth birthday. R. Walker and R. Ward, in *Walker and Walker's English Legal System* (7th edn., London, Butterworths, 1994) appear inaccurate at 182 in saying that Lords of Appeal, unless appointed before 1959, must retire at seventy.

[14] Judicial Pensions and Retirement Act 1993, s. 26(7)(b).

[15] The 97th appointee was Lord Hutton (from 6 January 1997, aged 65), the 98th Lord Saville (from 28 July 1997, aged 61). The other 52 Lords of Appeal (in order of appointment) were: Lords Blackburn (1876–87), Gordon (1876–9), Watson (1880–99), Fitzgerald (1882–9), Macnaghten (1887–1913), Morris (1889–99), Hannen (1891–3), Bowen (1893–4), Russell (1894), Davey (1894–1907), Lindley (1899–1905), Robertson (1899–1909), Atkinson (1905–28), Collins (1907–10), Shaw (1909–29), Robson (1910–12), Moulton (1912–21), Parker (1913–18), Dunedin (1913–32), Sumner (1913–30), Cave (1919–22), Carson (1921–9), Blanesburgh (1923–37), Atkin (1928–44), Tomlin (1929–35), Thankerton (1929–48), Russell (1929–46), Macmillan (1930–9 and 1941–7), Wright (1932–5 and 1937–47), Maugham (1935–8 and 1939–41), Roche (1935–41), Romer (1938–44), Porter (1938–54), Simonds (1944–51 and 1954–62), Goddard (1944–6), Uthwatt (1946–9), Du Parcq (1946–9), Normand (1947–53), Oaksey (1947–57), Morton (1947–59), MacDermott (1947–51), Greene (1949–50), Radcliffe (1949–64), Tucker (1950–61), Asquith (1951–4), Cohen (1951–60), Keith (1953–61), Somervell (1954–60), Denning (1957–62), Jenkins (1959–63), Devlin (1961–4) and Evershed (1962–5). Sources: Lord Macmillan, n. 1 above, and Blom-Cooper and Drewry, n. 2 above, at 160–3.

[16] The maximum number was increased from seven to nine by the Appellate Jurisdiction Act 1947, s. 1(1).

[17] S. 1(1)(a).

[18] By the Appellate Jurisdiction Act 1947, s. 1(1) the Queen may not be advised to make an appointment to fill any vacancy as a Lord of Appeal (except where the number in office falls below seven) unless the Lord Chancellor, with the concurrence of the Minister for the Civil Service (the Prime Minister) is satisfied that the state of business requires that the vacancy should be filled.

1994,[19] the number of posts available was further raised to twelve, and this figure was realised soon after when Lord Hoffmann was appointed in February 1995. By the end of 1996 the number had again fallen to eleven, since Lord Woolf was appointed to be Master of the Rolls in June 1996.[20]

Of the thirty Lords of Appeal who, during the period under scrutiny, retired or died in office, as opposed to being moved to another judicial role such as that of Lord Chancellor, Lord Chief Justice or Master of the Rolls, the average period served as a Lord of Appeal was nine years and eleven months. Easily the longest serving Lord of Appeal was Lord Reid, who spanned the period September 1948 to January 1975, and another Scottish judge, Lord Keith, has the second longest period of service at nineteen years and ten months; two other Lords of Appeal, Lords Wilberforce and Diplock, were each in office for more than seventeen years. To some extent these very long periods cause the average period served by each of the Law Lords to be skewed: if they are discounted, the average period served by the other twenty-six Lords of Appeal falls to eight years and four months. The shortest serving Lord of Appeal was Lord Cross, but even he was in office for four years and seven months. It is safe to say that, with the introduction of retirement at seventy, we will never again see a Lord of Appeal in office for as long a period as that served by Lord Reid: the youngest Lords of Appeal ever appointed have been Lord Radcliffe, who was fifty, and Lord MacDermott, who was fifty-one; for someone to serve longer than Lord Reid he or she would now have to be appointed at the age of forty-three.

In addition to the Lords of Appeal *per se*, there are five individuals, again all male, who were appointed as Lord Chancellor during this thirty-year period.[21] Only one of them, Lord Mackay, had first been appointed as a Lord of Appeal.[22] All of the Lord Chancellors sat from time to time in the Appellate Committee of the House.[23] Other judges entitled to sit were retired Lords of Appeal (e.g. Lord Devlin, who retired in 1964 aged fifty-eight, but lived until 1992[24]) and serving or retired Lord Chief Justices and Masters of the Rolls (e.g. Lords Widgery,

---

[19] SI 3217, made under Administration of Justice Act 1968, s. 1(2), and coming into force on 15 Dec. 1994. It is interesting that the maximum number of Court of Appeal judges was set, by the Administration of Justice Act 1968, at thirteen, just two more than that for Lords of Appeal; by 1995 this maximum had risen to thirty-two (and was raised again to thirty-five by the Maximum Number of Judges Order 1996, SI 1142). Clearly the work of the Court of Appeal has expanded at a much more dramatic rate than that of the House of Lords.

[20] Lord Hutton was appointed to the vacancy created by this move, but not until Jan. 1997. He was John Major's twelfth and last appointee. Tony Blair's first appointee was Lord Saville, who took up the post on 28 July 1997.

[21] Lord Gardiner (appointed by Wilson 17 Oct. 1964, resigned 22 June 1970); Lord Hailsham (appointed by Heath 22 June 1970, resigned 5 Mar. 1974; appointed again by Thatcher 5 May 1979, resigned 13 June 1987); Lord Elwyn-Jones (appointed by Wilson 5 Mar. 1974, resigned 5 May 1979); Lord Havers (appointed by Thatcher 13 June 1987, resigned 26 Oct. 1987); Lord Mackay (appointed by Thatcher 27 Oct. 1987).

[22] Lord Mackay resigned on 2 May 1997 and was replaced the following day by Prime Minister Blair's nominee, Lord Irvine.

[23] For some further details, see Chap. 8 below.

[24] He once said that he had found life as a Law Lord "utterly boring" (*The Times*, 11 June 1985, quoted by Ingman, n. 5 above, 62).

Taylor and Denning). In practice, and unlike some of their predecessors,[25] it seems that these judges did not sit at all, or only very rarely, in the House of Lords or in the Privy Council.[26]

The average age at which the Law Lords were appointed to their office during the period was sixty-three. The youngest appointee was Lord Keith, at fifty-four,[27] the oldest was Lord Brightman, at seventy-one. If we look at the appointments per decade we see that for the ten Lords of Appeal appointed during the 1960s the average age was sixty-two, for the ten appointed in the 1970s it was sixty-four and for the twelve appointed in the 1980s it was again sixty-four. Only in the 1990s has a slightly younger breed been appointed, the average age of the eleven listed in Table 7.2 being just sixty-one.[28] As new appointments now have to retire at the age of seventy, it is likely that we will see a continuing drop in the average age of those appointed; this will permit them to develop several years' of experience in the House of Lords before having to retire.

Table 7.2 also reveals what little shift there has been in the social background of the judiciary at this level during the past thirty years. Over the whole period, thirty-seven of the forty-four Law Lords were educated at a public school, twelve of them at just three establishments, namely, Edinburgh Academy (four), Eton (four) or Winchester (four). As many as forty-one of the Law Lords studied for a time at either Oxford (twenty) or Cambridge (twenty-one), the two best represented colleges being St John's, Cambridge (five) and Trinity, Cambridge (five). Only Lord Woolf went to another University (London), while Lords Donovan and Bridge did not go to University at all. While Lords Steyn and Hoffmann are *immigrés* from South Africa (both Rhodes Scholars at Oxford), it appears that only one other Law Lord (Lord Morris) studied at a University outside England or Scotland.

The standard qualification for the job of Law Lord appears indeed to be previous judicial experience. Of the thirty-four Law Lords appointed from England and Wales during the period, thirty-one had already served as a judge in the High Court *and* in the Court of Appeal. The exceptions are Lord Wilberforce, who was promoted directly from the High Court (after just three years as a Chancery judge), Lord Dilhorne, who had previously served as Lord Chancellor before being appointed a Law Lord, and Lord Slynn, who had moved to

---

[25] Lord MacDermott, who was a Lord of Appeal from 1947 to 1951, served as Lord Chief Justice of Northern Ireland from 1951 to 1971. During those years he sat in several cases in the House of Lords.

[26] In 1996 a former Chief Justice of New Zealand, Lord Cooke of Thorndon, sat in some appeals: see e.g. *R. v. Bedwelty Justices, ex p. Williams* [1996] 3 WLR 361, where he gave the only judgment.

[27] In general, Scottish Lords of Appeal are appointed at a younger age than their English counterparts.

[28] With the appointment of Lord Hutton in 1997 (aged sixty-five) and Lord Saville in 1997 (aged sixty-one) the average age for appointments in the 1990s has risen to sixty-two.

*Table 7.1: The periods served by the Lords of Appeal in office, 1967–96*[a]

| No | Law Lord | Date appointed | Date leaving office | Reason for leaving office | Period served |
|----|----------|----------------|---------------------|---------------------------|---------------|
| 1 | Reid | 16.09.48 | 10.01.75 | retired | 26yrs 4mths |
| 2 | Morris | 07.01.60 | 10.01.75 | retired | 15yrs |
| 3 | Hodson | 01.10.60 | 07.04.71 | retired | 10yrs 6mths |
| 4 | Guest | 20.01.61 | 30.09.71 | retired | 10yrs 7mths |
| 5 | Pearce | 19.04.62 | 02.06.69 | retired | 7yrs 1mth |
| 6 | Upjohn | 26.11.63 | 27.01.71 | died[b] | 7yrs 2mths |
| 7 | Donovan | 11.01.64 | 12.12.71 | died | 7yrs 11mths |
| 8 | Wilberforce | 01.10.64 | 10.03.83 | retired | 18yrs 5mths |
| 9 | Pearson | 18.02.65 | 30.09.74 | retired | 9yrs 7mths |
| 10 | Diplock | 30.09.68 | 14.10.85 | died | 17yrs 1mth |
| 11 | Dilhorne[c] | 09.06.69 | 01.08.80 | retired | 11yrs 2mths |
| 12 | Cross | 12.03.71 | 30.09.75 | retired | 4yrs 7mths |
| 13 | Simon | 19.04.71 | 30.09.77 | retired | 6yrs 5mths |
| 14 | Kilbrandon | 04.10.71 | 31.12.76 | retired | 5yrs 3mths |
| 15 | Salmon | 10.01.72 | 30.09.80 | retired | 8yrs 9mths |
| 16 | Edmund Davies | 01.10.74 | 30.09.81 | retired | 7yrs |
| 17 | Fraser | 13.01.75 | 30.09.85 | retired | 10yrs 10mths |
| 18 | Russell | 30.09.75 | 27.06.82 | retired | 6yrs 10mths |
| 19 | Keith | 10.01.77 | 30.09.96 | retired | 19yrs 10mths |
| 20 | Scarman | 30.09.77 | 12.01.86 | retired | 9yrs |
| 21 | Lane | 28.09.79 | 15.04.80 | appointed LCJ | 8mths |
| 22 | Roskill | 15.04.80 | 12.01.86 | retired | 5yrs 9mths |
| 23 | Bridge | 29.09.80 | 26.02.92 | retired | 11yrs 5mths |
| 24 | Brandon | 24.09.81 | 30.09.91 | retired | 10yrs |
| 25 | Brightman | 12.03.82 | 19.06.87 | retired | 5yrs 3mths |
| 26 | Templeman | 30.09.82 | 30.09.94 | retired | 12yrs |
| 27 | Griffiths | 23.05.85 | 30.09.93 | retired | 8yrs 4mths |
| 28 | Mackay | 01.10.85 | 27.10.87 | appointed LC | 2yrs 1mth |
| 29 | Ackner | 30.01.86 | 30.09.92 | retired | 6yrs 8mths |
| 30 | Oliver | 31.01.86 | 31.12.91 | retired | 5yrs 11mths |
| 31 | Goff | 06.02.86 | | | |
| 32 | Jauncey | 09.02.88 | 30.09.96 | retired | 8yrs 8mths |
| 33 | Lowry | 05.08.88 | 07.01.94 | retired | 5yrs 5mths |
| 34 | Browne-Wilkinson | 01.10.91 | | | |
| 35 | Mustill | 10.01.92 | 07.04.97 | retired | 5yrs 3mths |
| 36 | Slynn | 11.03.92 | | | |
| 37 | Woolf | 01.10.92 | 04.06.96 | appointed MR | 3yrs 8mths |
| 38 | Lloyd | 01.10.93 | | | |
| 39 | Nolan | 07.01.94 | | | |
| 40 | Nicholls | 03.10.94 | | | |
| 41 | Steyn | 11.01.95 | | | |
| 42 | Hoffmann | 21.02.95 | | | |
| 43 | Clyde | 01.10.96 | | | |
| 44 | Hope | 01.10.96 | | | |

a—Source: Preliminary pages to the volumes of the All ER, 1967–95 and various editions of *Who's Who*. The information in this Table may be compared with that in Table 13 in *Final Appeal*, n. 2 above, at 160–3.

b—Lord Upjohn died between the hearing of the appeal and the delivery of the judgments in *Kennedy* v. *Spratt* [1972] AC 99. He had indicated before his death that he would dismiss the appeal, but his vote was ignored; the remaining votes were two for and two against, so the appeal was dismissed anyway.

c—Viscount Dilhorne had previously served as a Conservative Lord Chancellor from 16.07.62 to 17.10.64.

*Table 7.2: The backgrounds of the Lords of Appeal in office, 1967–96*[a]

| No | Law Lord | Age appointed | School attended | University attended | Previous judicial or political experience |
|----|----------|---------------|-----------------|---------------------|-------------------------------------------|
| 1  | Reid     | 58 | Edinburgh Academy | Jesus, Cambridge | Sol Gen Scotland 1936–41; Lord Advocate 1941–5 |
| 2  | Morris   | 64 | Liverpool Institute | Trinity Hall, Cambridge and Harvard | JA IoM 1938–45; KB 1945–51; CA 1951–60 |
| 3  | Hodson   | 65 | Cheltenham College | Wadham, Oxford | PDA 1937–51; CA 1951–60 |
| 4  | Guest    | 60 | Merchiston Castle | Cambridge and Edinburgh | Sheriff 1952–5; College of Justice 1957–61 |
| 5  | Pearce   | 61 | Charterhouse | Corpus Christi, Oxford | PDA 1948–54; QB 1954–7; CA 1957–62 |
| 6  | Upjohn   | 60 | Eton | Trinity, Cambridge | Ch 1951–60; CA 1960–3 |
| 7  | Donovan  | 65 | n/a | – | KB 1950–9; CA 1960–3 |
| 8  | Wilberforce | 57 | Winchester | New, Oxford | Ch 1961–4 |
| 9  | Pearson  | 66 | St Paul's | Balliol, Oxford | Recorder 1937–51; QB 1951–61; CA 1961–5 |
| 10 | Diplock  | 61 | Whitgift | University College, Oxford | QB 1956–61; CA 1961–8 |
| 11 | Dilhorne | 64 | Eton | Magdalen, Oxford | Sol Gen 1951–4; Att Gen 1954–62; LC 1962–4 |
| 12 | Cross    | 66 | Westminster | Trinity, Cambridge | Ch 1960–9; CA 1969–71 |
| 13 | Simon    | 60 | Gresham's School, Holt | Trinity Hall, Cambridge | Sol Gen 1959–62; PDA 1962–71; CA 1971–2 |
| 14 | Kilbrandon | 65 | Charterhouse | Balliol, Oxford and Edinburgh | Sheriff 1954–57; College of Justice 1959–71 |
| 15 | Salmon   | 68 | Mill Hill | Pembroke, Cambridge | QB 1957–64; CA 1964–72 |
| 16 | Edmund Davies | 68 | Mountain Ash Grammar | King's, London and Exeter, Oxford | QB 1958–66; CA 1966–74 |

a—Source: Preliminary pages to the volumes of the All ER, 1967–95 and *Who's Who*. The information in this Table may be compared with that in Table 13 in *Final Appeal*, n. 2 above, at 160–3. Abbreviations in the Table are as follows: JA IoM: Judge of Appeal in the Isle of Man, CAs Jer & Guern: Court of Appeals of Jersey and Guernsey, KB/QB: King's/Queen's Bench Division of the High Court, PDA: Probate, Divorce and Admiralty Division of the High Court, Ch: Chancery Division of the High Court, Fam: Family Division of the High Court, CA: Court of Appeal, Sol/Att Gen: Solicitor/Attorney General, VC: Vice-Chancellor of the Supreme Court, LC: Lord Chancellor, LCJ: Lord Chief Justice, HC of NI: High Court of Northern Ireland, ECJ: European Court of Justice, Adv Gen: Advocate General of the ECJ, LJ Gen: Lord Justice General, Pres Ct: President of the Court, n/a: not available.

*Table 7.2: cont.*

| No | Law Lord | Age appointed | School attended | University attended | Previous judicial or political experience |
|---|---|---|---|---|---|
| 17 | Fraser | 63 | Repton | Balliol, Oxford | College of Justice 1964–74 |
| 18 | Russell | 67 | Beaumont | Oriel, Oxford | Ch 1960–2; CA 1962–75 |
| 19 | Keith | 54 | Edinburgh Academy | Magdalen, Oxford and Edinburgh | Sheriff Principal 1970–1; College of Justice 1971–7 |
| 20 | Scarman | 66 | Radley College | Brasenose, Oxford | PDA/Fam 1961–73; CA 1973–7 |
| 21 | Lane | 61 | Shrewsbury | Trinity, Cambridge | Recorder 1963–6; QB 1966–74; CA 1974–9 |
| 22 | Roskill | 69 | Winchester | Exeter, Oxford | QB 1962–71; CA 1971–80 |
| 23 | Bridge | 63 | Marlborough | – | QB 1968–75; CA 1975–80 |
| 24 | Brandon | 61 | Winchester | King's, Cambridge | PDA/Fam 1966–78; CA 1978–81 |
| 25 | Brightman | 71 | Marlborough | St John's, Cambridge | Ch 1970–9; CA 1979–82 |
| 26 | Templeman | 62 | Southall Grammar School | St John's, Cambridge | Ch 1972–8; CA 1978–82 |
| 27 | Griffiths | 61 | Charterhouse | St John's, Cambridge | Recorder 1962–70; QB 1971–80; CA 1980–5 |
| 28 | Mackay | 58 | George Heriot's, Edinburgh | Edinburgh and Trinity, Cambridge | Sheriff Principal 1972–4; Lord Advocate 1979–84; College of Justice 1984–5 |
| 29 | Ackner | 65 | Highgate | Clare, Cambridge | Recorder 1962–71; CAs Jer & Guern 1967–71; QB 1971–80; CA 1980–6 |
| 30 | Oliver | 64 | The Leys, Cambridge | Trinity Hall, Cambridge | Ch 1974–80; CA 1980–6 |
| 31 | Goff | 59 | Eton | New, Oxford | Recorder 1974–5; QB 1975–82; CA 1982–6 |
| 32 | Jauncey | 62 | Radley | Christ Church, Oxford and Glasgow | Sheriff Principal 1971–4; CAs Jer & Guern 1972–9; College of Justice 1979–88 |
| 33 | Lowry | 69 | Royal Belfast Academical Institution | Jesus, Cambridge | HC of NI 1964–71; LCJ of NI 1971–88 |
| 34 | Browne-Wilkinson | 61 | Lancing | Magdalen, Oxford | CAs Jer & Guern 1976–7; Ch 1977–83; CA 1983–85; VC 1985–91 |

| No | Law Lord | Age appointed | School attended | University attended | Previous judicial or political experience |
|----|----------|---------------|-----------------|---------------------|-------------------------------------------|
| 35 | Mustill | 60 | Oundle | St John's, Cambridge | Recorder 1972–8; QB 1978–85; CA 1985–92 |
| 36 | Slynn | 62 | Sandbach | Goldsmiths', London and Trinity, Cambridge | Recorder 1972–6; QB 1976–81; Adv Gen 1981–8; ECJ 1988–92 |
| 37 | Woolf | 59 | Fettes College | University College, London | Recorder 1972–9; QB 1979–86; CA 1986–92 |
| 38 | Lloyd | 64 | Eton | Trinity, Cambridge | QB 1978–84; CA 1984–93 |
| 39 | Nolan | 65 | Ampleforth | Wadham, Oxford | Recorder 1975–82; QB 1982–91; CA 1991–3 |
| 40 | Nicholls | 61 | Birkenhead | Liverpool and Trinity Hall, Cambridge | Ch 1983–6; CA 1986–91; VC 1991–4 |
| 41 | Steyn | 62 | Jan van Riebeek School, Cape Town | Stellenbosch and University College, Oxford | QB 1985–91; CA 1992–5 |
| 42 | Hoffmann | 60 | South African College School, Cape Town | Cape Town and Queen's, Oxford | CAs Jer & Guern 1980–5; Ch 1985–92; CA 1992–5 |
| 43 | Clyde | 64 | Edinburgh Academy | Corpus Christi, Oxford and Edinburgh | CAs Jer & Guern 1979–85; College of Justice 1985–96 |
| 44 | Hope | 58 | Edinburgh Academy and Rugby | St John's, Cambridge | LJ Gen Scotland and Lord Pres Ct of Session 1989–96 |

Luxembourg from the High Court. The average period spent in the High Court was 8.1 years and the average spent in the Court of Appeal was 5.3 years. Given the compression caused by the introduction of earlier retirement ages, it is no surprise that the average period of previous High Court service has fallen from 8.9 years for those Law Lords appointed in the 1960s to 7.5 years for those appointed in the 1990s; similarly, the average period of previous Court of Appeal service has fallen from 5.7 years to 4.6 years between the same four decades. Of the ten Law Lords appointed from Scotland, all but one had previous judicial experience, as did the sole Northern Irish appointee, Lord Lowry. Today a Law Lord can be expected to be appointed after an average of 12.1 years of previous judicial experience, whereas in the 1960s the average was 14.6 years. It is remarkable, too, how many of the Law Lords have served in the

Court of Appeals of Jersey and Guernsey—no fewer than five of the last sixteen appointed have had that distinction in their *curriculum vitae*.

What has also changed has been the prior involvement of Law Lords in political work. Lord Reid was a Unionist MP in Scotland for a total of fifteen years before being appointed to the Lords in 1948, having never previously served as a judge. Lord Guest unsuccessfully contested another Scottish seat for the Unionists in the 1945 election. Terence Donovan was a Labour MP for East Leicester from 1945 to 1950 and was appointed to the High Court when he lost his seat. Lord Dilhorne was a Conservative MP from 1943 to 1962 before being elevated to the Lords and appointed Lord Chancellor and, later a Lord of Appeal. And Lord Simon was Conservative MP for Middlesborough West from 1951 to 1962, when he too was appointed to the High Court. But, with the exception of Lord Fraser from Scotland,[29] no Law Lord appointed since 1971 has previously served as an MP.[30] Whatever may have been the position in the past,[31] it would appear that patronage of this nature has died out. It is not likely to reappear, given the moves afoot to make the appointment of judges a less secretive exercise.[32]

*Table 7.3: Who succeeded whom, 1967–96*

| No | First holder | Second holder | Third holder | Fourth holder | Fifth holder |
|----|-------------|---------------|--------------|---------------|--------------|
| 1 | Reid | Fraser | Mackay | Jauncey | Hope |
| 2 | Morris | Lane | Roskill | Goff | |
| 3 | Hodson | Simon | Scarman | Oliver | Mustill |
| 4 | Guest | Kilbrandon | Keith | Clyde | |
| 5 | Pearce | Dilhorne | Griffiths | Lloyd | |
| 6 | Upjohn | Cross | Russell | Templeman | Nicholls |
| 7 | Donovan | Salmon | Bridge | Steyn | |
| 8 | Wilberforce | Brightman | Lowry | Nolan | |
| 9 | Pearson | Edmund Davies | Brandon | Browne-Wilkinson | |
| 10 | Diplock | Ackner | Woolf | | |
| 11 | Slynn | | | | |
| 12 | Hoffmann | | | | |

Table 7.3 attempts to show who replaced whom during the thirty-year period. It must be stressed that vacancies were sometimes left unfilled for some time, so it is not always possible to say that a person eventually appointed was filling a particular judge's shoes. For example, after Lord Morris's retirement in 1975 one of the ten posts then available was left unfilled until Lord Lane joined his nine colleagues in 1979; in no sense was the baton handed directly by Lord Morris to Lord Lane.

[29] Who stood unsuccessfully for the Unionist Party in East Edinburgh in the 1955 election.

[30] The tradition of former Attorney-Generals being elevated to the Bench seems to be dying.

[31] See J. A. G. Griffith, *The Politics of the Judiciary* (5th edn., London, Fontana Press, 1997), at 13–18.

[32] See C. Thomas and K. Malleson, "Judicial Appointment Commissions", Lord Chancellor's Department's Research Series 6/97 (Dec. 1997).

Within the House of Lords itself (when serving as a court) the Lords of Appeal perform two main functions: as the Appeal Committee they deal with petitions for leave to appeal and as the Appellate Committee they deal with the appeals themselves.[33] The first of these roles needs to be played whenever the court appealed against has not itself granted leave to appeal. The requirement for leave in a civil case is laid down by section 1(1) of the Administration of Justice (Appeals) Act 1934, though it does not apply in cases appealed from Scotland. The requirement for leave in a criminal case is laid down by section 33(2) of the Criminal Appeal Act 1968, which as a prerequisite to the granting of leave also demands that the Court of Appeal certify that a point of law of general public importance is involved.[34] In 1993 the Royal Commission on Criminal Justice recommended abolition of this latter requirement, which it designated as "unduly restrictive".[35] There is no need for formal leave to appeal to be granted by any court in a case dealing with a reference by the Attorney-General after an acquittal (which in any event is not an appeal *stricto sensu*): the Court of Appeal has power to refer the case to the Lords "if it appears to the court that the point ought to be considered by that House".[36]

A party who loses in the Court of Appeal, whether in a civil case or a criminal case, can thus make two attempts to get leave to appeal to the House of Lords: if the Court of Appeal refuses leave, the Appeal Committee of the House of Lords can be approached. It seems that all petitions for leave considered by the Appeal Committee are, in this sense, second bites of the cherry. Section 34(1) of the Criminal Appeal Act 1968 presupposes this for criminal cases because it stipulates that an appellant has fourteen days from the original court decision in which to apply to the Court of Appeal for leave to appeal to the House and then, if leave is refused, a further fourteen days from the date of the refusal to petition for leave from the House itself. "Leapfrog" appeals from the High Court, which are allowed under sections twelve and thirteen of the Administration of Justice Act 1969, also require an application for leave to be made to the House itself (this time within one month of the decision being appealed): the House may grant leave only if "it appears . . . to be expedient to do so".[37]

---

[33] They also by convention help to constitute the House's Committee of Privileges when dealing with disputes over entitlements to peerages, but there are few of these. The Judicial Statistics list just eight in the thirty-year period (though the Statistics for 1974 and 1975 give no informnation on this point). For reported examples, see the *Ampthill Peerage Case* [1977] AC 547 (where four of the nine Lords were Lords of Appeal) and the *Annandale and Hartfell Peerage Claim* [1986] AC 319 (where four of the eight Lords were Lords of Appeal).

[34] A note to the relevant Procedure Direction [1988] 2 All ER 831 at 832, indicates that, even in civil cases, leave to appeal is liable to be refused if the petition does not raise an arguable point of law of general public importance.

[35] (London, HMSO, 1993, Cm 2263), chap. 10, para. 79.

[36] Criminal Justice Act 1972, s. 36(3).

[37] S. 13(2).

The Appeal Committee of the House of Lords comprises three Lords of Appeal and they will usually take their decision on the basis of written submissions from the parties. Until 1988 it was the custom to allow an oral hearing for many of the petitions for appeal, but in that year Procedure Directions were issued which reversed this trend both in civil and in criminal cases.[38] The position today is that if the three Lords of Appeal are unanimously of the view that the petition should be rejected, that is the end of the matter. If they unanimously agree that it should be allowed, this is notified as a "provisional" view to the respondents, who are given fourteen days to lodge objections to the petition. If the Lords of Appeal, having considered those objections (if there are any), remain unanimously of the view that the petition should be allowed, then it is. In all cases where the Lords of Appeal cannot agree whether to reject or allow the petition, an oral hearing will be arranged (except in applications for leapfrog appeals from the High Court[39]).

Petitions for leave to appeal tend not to attract much attention beyond that given to them by the particular parties and lawyers involved. This is because the decisions taken on them are not reported. Some are now noted in the law reports,[40] with the names of the judges who sat in the Appeal Committee being listed, but reasons for the decisions are never made public, even in summary form. This is surely unfortunate, even though the European Commission of Human Rights, no less, has said that, in appropriate circumstances, it sees nothing wrong with the practice.[41] If reasons were made public it would help lawyers to know what legal points might be ones which the Lords would want to examine in future. But of course the granting or refusing of leave cannot in any event set a binding precedent.

Despite its low-profile status, the work which has to be done by Lords of Appeal in Appeal Committees is substantial. Two statistical indicators provide evidence of this. The first is the number of petitions disposed of by an Appeal Committee year by year; the second is the number of days on which an Appeal Committee sits every year (i.e. days on which an oral hearing takes place). By comparing these, as Figures 7.1 and 7.2 do, with the number of actual appeals disposed of by the Appellate Committee every year and with the number of days on which an Appellate Committee sits, we gain some idea of the proportion of time which Lords of Appeal spend on their filtering function.

[38] [1988] 2 All ER 819 and 831.

[39] Administration of Justice Act 1969, s. 13(3).

[40] E.g. the WLR now note all those Appeal Committee decisions in cases which have already been reported, at a lower level, by that series of reports. For a note of a successful petition see *R. v. Home Secretary, ex p. Pierson* [1996] 3 WLR 547 at 562; for a note of an unsuccessful petition see *Coca-Cola Financial Corp. v. Finsat Ltd* [1996] 3 WLR 849 at 859. The bound volumes of the All ER adopt a similar practice.

[41] *Webb v. UK* (1997) 24 EHRR CD 73, a case involving an appeal from the Supreme Court of Bermuda to the Privy Council. Citing *Monnell and Morris v. UK* (1988) 10 EHRR 205 at para. 58, where one of the issues was whether the absence of an oral hearing made an application for leave to appeal unfair under Art. 6(1) of the European Convention on Human Rights, the Commission said "in the case of leave to appeal proceedings, the nature of those proceedings and their significance in the context of the proceedings as a whole must be considered, together with the powers of the appellate jurisdiction and the manner in which the proceedings are actually conducted" (at CD 74).

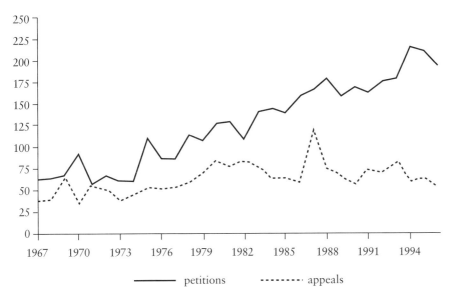

*Figure 7.1: Petitions and appeals disposed of, 1967–96*[a]

a—Source: n. 6 above. The Civil Judicial Statistics for 1974 differ in layout from every other year, supposedly in light of recommendations made by the Adams Committee on Civil Judicial Statistics (Cmnd 3684) and an inter-departmental working party. In 1976 the Statistics reverted to their pre-1974 format.

It is obvious that, in terms of the number of cases considered, the workload of the Appeal Committee has increased dramatically during the thirty-year period under review: by 1996 there were over three times as many petitions being considered *per annum* as there were in 1967 (196 compared with 62). There was an increase, too, in the number of appeals actually heard in a year, but this was of a much smaller order: only about half as many appeals were being heard in 1996 as in 1967 (fifty-eight compared with thirty-nine). The number of Law Lords available to hear cases also rose between 1967 and 1996, but only by one-third, from nine to twelve, and this should not have impacted any more significantly on petitions than on appeals. The rise in the number of petitions must be partly explained by the rise in the number of lower court decisions eligible to be appealed against.

Of course the average amount of time required for the disposal of an appeal is much greater than that required for the disposal of a petition, and five or even seven Lords of Appeal will be involved in the disposing of an appeal, whereas only three will be involved in the disposing of a petition, so the statistics above do not prove that the proportion of the Law Lords' collective time spent on petitions is increasing. In fact, when the figures on days sat in the Appeal and Appellate Committees are considered it seems clear that the proportion of time spent on petitions is diminishing. As reflected in Figure 7.2, in the first third of our period (1967–76) the days sat in the Appeal Committee represented fourteen

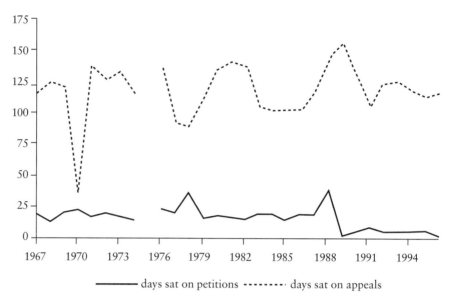

*Figure 7.2: Days sat in the Appeal and Appellate Committees of the House of Lords, 1967–96*[a]

a—Source: n. 6 above. The figures for days sat in 1975 are unavailable.

per cent of all the days sat by the Lords of Appeal; in the next ten-year period the figure was fifteen per cent; but in the last third of the period (1987–96) the figure dropped to eight per cent and in the last five years it was just five per cent. As "days sat" are those days on which an oral hearing takes place, the effect of the 1988 Procedure Directions mentioned above is quite apparent in the statistics. The question which cannot be answered definitively from the statistics is whether the time taken to deal with the increased number of petitions now being considered each year outweighs the time saved through the reduction in the number of oral hearings. Given that the documents which have to be submitted for a petition are not at all as voluminous as those required for an actual appeal, it is likely that the answer would be in the negative.

Figure 7.3 provides information on the success rate of petitions for leave to appeal (whatever the eventual outcome of the appeal itself), although the published statistics are not always consistently presented from year to year.[42] By the end of our period the success rate had reverted to more or less what it was at the start, about one in four (36 out of 196 in 1996 compared with fifteen out of sixty-

[42] Some of the annual (Civil) Judicial Statistics record only the number of petitions emanating from England and Wales; others include Northern Ireland but still exclude Scotland. Moreover, it is not always clear whether petitions in respect of "leapfrog" appeals, or in cases being appealed from the Divisional Court, are included in the figures.

two in 1967). In the early 1980s, however, the success rate rose noticeably, to about one in three of the petitions disposed of. It is difficult to identify any reason for this other than that the Lords of Appeal in question must have been willing to see importance in the points of law brought before them in the petitions. To that extent the Lords of Appeal of that era could be said to have been more judicially activist than their brethren at other times.

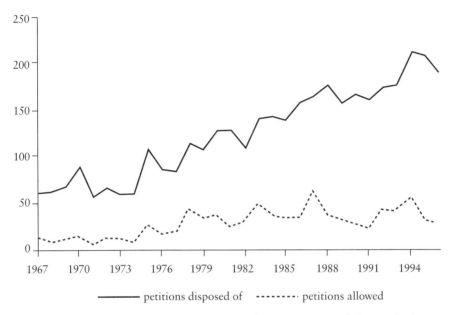

*Figure 7.3: The success rate of petitions for leave to appeal disposed of,*
*1967–96[a]*

Figures 7.4, 7.5 and 7.6 break down the petition statistics for the period of the study in order to assess whether the success rate for petitions in civil cases was higher or lower than that for petitions in criminal cases. The statistics for petitions in civil cases include cases where leave to appeal was sought to go directly from the High Court to the House of Lords under the so-called leapfrog procedure allowed by the Administration of Justice Act 1969.[43] The statistics for petitions in criminal cases include cases where leave to appeal was sought to go from the Divisional Court of the Queen's Bench Division to the House of Lords in a criminal cause or matter (including judicial review cases in that category). Figure 7.6 shows that over the whole period the success rate in criminal cases was one-and-a-half times higher than that for civil cases, though obviously there

---

[43] Ss. 12–15. The number of petitions in respect of leapfrog appeals is listed separately in the statistics only from 1977 onwards. In the twenty years from 1977 to 1996 there were eighty-eight such petitions to the Lords, an average of four or five; sixty-seven (seventy-six per cent) of them were allowed.

*Figure 7.4: The proportion of successful petitions for leave to appeal in civil cases, 1967–96*[a]

a—Source: n. 6 above and n. a to Fig. 7.1.

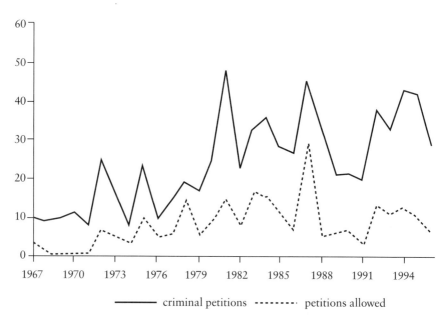

*Figure 7.5: The proportion of successful petitions for leave to appeal in criminal cases, 1967–96*[a]

a—Source: n. 6 above and n. a to Fig. 7.1.

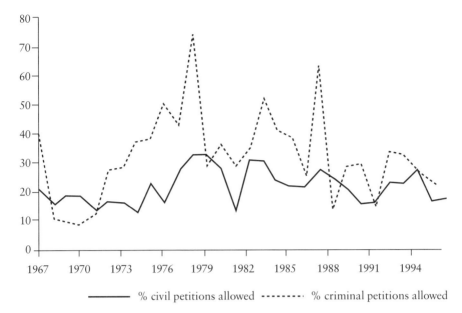

*Figure 7.6: A comparison of the success rate for petitions for leave to appeal in civil and criminal cases, 1967–96[a]*

a—Source: n. 6 above and n. a to Fig. 7.1.

were fluctuations from year to year. It is perhaps surprising that as many as one-third of all petitions to the Lords in criminal cases are successful, but no doubt this reflects the fact that when a person's liberty is at stake the Lords are prone to err on the side of caution by allowing the appeal to go to a full hearing.

THE WORK OF THE LORDS OF APPEAL IN THE APPELLATE COMMITTEE

**What Proportion of Appeals Follow a Successful Petition for Leave?**

We know the number of appeals which are heard by the Appellate Committee after having first been the subject of a successful petition for leave to appeal, and also the number which are heard in total, so we can calculate the number which reach the Appellate Committee directly from lower courts. Figure 7.7 summarises the position for the period in question, although it should be remembered that the year in which a petition is allowed is not necessarily the same as the one in which the appeal comes on for hearing. The Figure demonstrates that there has been a dramatic fall in the proportion of appeals being presented to the Appellate Committee directly, down from a substantial majority of all appeals presented to a definite minority. The turning point seems to have been 1977 and the fall seems to be even greater when the figures for years prior to 1967 are considered.[44] This trend demonstrates a growing unwillingness on the part of the Court of Appeal in England and Wales, and in Northern Ireland, and of the Court of Session in Scotland in civil cases, to grant leave to appeal, since they are the only courts apart from the House of Lords itself with power to grant leave to appeal to the Appellate Committee. Of course this unwillingness may in some instances reflect a desire on the part of the lower courts to allow the Lords of Appeal to determine their own workload: it is not uncommon, for instance, for the Court of Appeal to refuse leave to appeal but to intimate that the case might still be suitable for consideration by the House of Lords if the Lords of Appeal felt so inclined.

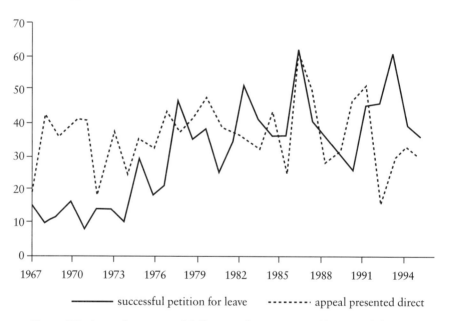

——— successful petition for leave     ····· appeal presented direct

*Figure 7.7: Appeals presented following the granting of leave and directly from lower courts, 1967–96*

### From Which Courts do Appeals Originate?

Table 7.4 provides information on which of the United Kingdom's courts gave rise to the appeals disposed of by the Appellate Committee in each of the years in question.

[44] In *The Law Lords*, n. 4 above, Alan Paterson says, "[e]ighty per cent of the [House's] civil caseload and sixty percent of its criminal caseload during the period of my study [1957–73] came to the House as of right or by leave of a lower court" (at 87).

*Table 7.4: The origin of appeals disposed of, 1967–96[a]*

| Year | England and Wales | | | | | Scotland | N.Ireland | Total |
|---|---|---|---|---|---|---|---|---|
| | CA Civ | CA Cr | Div Ct | H Ct | All | | | |
| 1967 | 23 | 1 | 2 | 0 | 26 | 13 | 0 | 39 |
| 1968 | 28 | 5[b] | 4 | 0 | 36 | 4 | 0 | 40 |
| 1969 | 37 | 1 | 9 | 0 | 47 | 13 | 4 | 64 |
| 1970 | 27 | 3 | 1 | 0 | 31 | 6 | 1 | 38 |
| 1971 | 37 | 3 | 4 | 0 | 44 | 12 | 1 | 57 |
| 1972 | 29 | 7 | 8 | 0 | 44 | 8 | 0 | 52 |
| 1973 | 18 | 12 | 6 | 0 | 36 | 3 | 1 | 40 |
| 1974 | 29 | 7 | 4 | 0 | 40 | 6 | 0 | 46 |
| 1975 | 35 | 7 | 8 | 0 | 50 | 4 | 1 | 55 |
| 1976 | 37 | 7 | 4 | 0 | 48 | 3 | 2 | 53 |
| 1977 | 46 | 4 | 3 | 0 | 53 | 2 | 0 | 55 |
| 1978 | 39 | 7 | 3 | 4 | 53 | 5 | 2 | 60 |
| 1979 | 43 | 4 | 4 | 14 | 65 | 5 | 1 | 71 |
| 1980 | 63 | 7 | 3 | 2 | 75 | 9 | 1 | 85 |
| 1981 | 50 | 5 | 7 | 4 | 66 | 12 | 2 | 80 |
| 1982 | 49 | 11 | 14 | 2 | 76 | 10 | 0 | 86 |
| 1983 | 45 | 11 | 7 | 2 | 65 | 11 | 3 | 79 |
| 1984 | 39 | 6 | 8 | 3 | 56 | 7 | 3 | 66 |
| 1985 | 46 | 8 | 5 | 1 | 60 | 6 | 0 | 66 |
| 1986 | 37 | 10 | 4 | 2 | 53 | 8 | 0 | 61 |
| 1987 | 64 | 10 | 31 | 0 | 105 | 12 | 2 | 119 |
| 1988 | 57 | 3 | 6 | 4 | 70 | 4 | 4 | 78 |
| 1989 | 53 | 1 | 2 | 2 | 58 | 10 | 1 | 69 |
| 1990 | 44 | 2 | 4 | 4 | 54 | 3 | 2 | 59 |
| 1991 | 60 | 5 | 3 | 4 | 72 | 4 | 1 | 77 |
| 1992 | 47 | 5 | 6 | 0 | 58 | 10 | 5 | 73 |
| 1993 | 56 | 12 | 6 | 2 | 76 | 7 | 1 | 84 |
| 1994 | 42 | 6 | 7 | 1 | 56 | 7 | 1 | 64 |
| 1995 | 47 | 4 | 3 | 2 | 56 | 10 | 2 | 67 |
| 1996 | 39 | 9 | 1 | 1 | 50 | 7 | 1 | 58 |
| Total | 1266 | 181 | 177 | 54 | 1678 | 221 | 42 | 1941 |

a—Source: n. 6 above.
b—This includes one appeal from the Courts-Martial Appeal Court.

Clearly it is the English and Welsh courts which supply the vast majority of the appeals—eighty-six per cent over the thirty-year period. The Civil Division of the Court of Appeal is responsible for most of these (sixty-five per cent), and from the mid-1970s there has been a noticeable increase in the annual number reaching the House of Lords from that source. The cases coming from the Criminal Division, on the other hand, are barely more numerous today than they were in the late 1960s. There has been a rise in the number of appeals coming from the Divisional Court, no doubt partly reflecting the increasing popularity of applications for judicial review.

Of course "leapfrog" appeals have developed since they were first permitted by the Administration of Justice Act 1969. Even so, throughout the thirty-year period there were only fifty-four of these appeals. In the past ten years there have, on average, been only two such appeals per year. Clearly this fast-track facility for appeals has not done much to alleviate the burden on the Court of Appeal, since even in the last twenty years leapfrog appeals represent less than five per cent of the combined total of these civil appeals.

The figures for Scotland (twelve per cent of appeals, all from the Court of Session) are by no means negligible, especially given that no criminal case can reach the House from that jurisdiction. They are roughly in line with the population proportions of the two land masses. The number seems to justify the convention whereby at any one time at least two of the Law Lords must have an expertise in Scottish law. With Lord Mackay appointed as Lord Chancellor from 1987, succeeded as a Lord of Appeal by Lord Jauncey, there was even the possibility that three Scottish judges might sit in an appeal.

In all of the thirty years there were only forty-two appeals to the House of Lords from Northern Ireland. The annual Judicial Statistics, when aggregated, reveal that thirty of these were in civil cases and twelve in criminal cases, including two in judicial review appeals from the Divisional Court.[45] For all but five years and five months of the thirty-year period (the time served by Lord Lowry as a Lord of Appeal), there was no Lord of Appeal who had a special expertise in Northern Irish law. The former Lord of Appeal, Lord MacDermott (who had been appointed Lord Chief Justice of Northern Ireland in 1951), continued to sit occasionally in the House until 1971, but *ex officio*, not as a Lord of Appeal. Interestingly, it was not long after Lord Lowry retired that another Northern Irish Lord of Appeal was appointed, but this occurred outside the period covered by this review.[46]

## How Many of the Appeals are in Criminal Matters and How Many in Civil?

Figure 7.8 provides information on what is known of the division of labour between criminal and civil law appeals in the Appellate Committee. It aggregates the cases coming from all three jurisdictions within the United Kingdom. The figures for appeals from the Divisional Court in England and Wales have been included in the criminal totals and leapfrog appeals from the High Court have been included in the civil totals. The statistics show that the throughput of

[45]  In Northern Ireland appeals from magistrates' courts in criminal cases go first to the Court of Appeal, not the Divisional Court. Appeals to the House of Lords relating to the "troubles" are analysed by S. Livingstone in "The House of Lords and the Northern Ireland Conflict" (1994) fifty-seven *MLR* 333.

[46]  Lord Hutton, on 6 Jan. 1997. There thus seems to be a convention developing whereby Lord Chief Justices of Northern Ireland become Lords of Appeal during the last few years of their working lives. The current Lord Chief Justice of Northern Ireland, Sir Robert Carswell, was sixty-two when appointed to that position in succession to Sir Brian Hutton in 1997.

criminal appeals has remained fairly constant, certainly over the last twenty years, while the number of civil appeals has increased significantly—by sixty-six per cent between the first ten-year period and the last, when there were nearly five times as many civil appeals as criminal (622 as opposed to 131). The reason for this is not that the success rate for petitions for leave in civil cases has risen, since Figure 7.4 above shows this to be untrue.

It is not possible to summarise the subject-matter of the criminal or civil appeals heard in the Appellate Committee because the annually published Judicial Statistics do not provide any information about the former, and for the latter they use different categories almost each year to classify the appeals. These are not always very helpful, e.g. the 1996 statistics reveal that in that year there were seven appeals dealing with "process of law".[47]

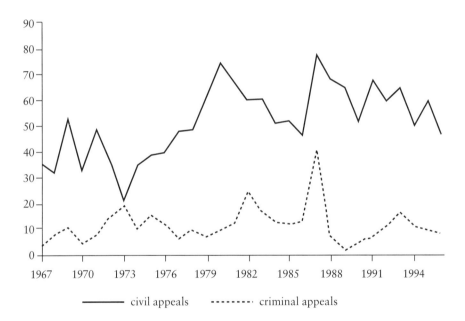

*Figure 7.8: Numbers of civil and criminal appeals disposed of, 1967–96*[a]
a—Source: n. 6 above.

## What Has Been the Outcome of Appeals?

In the Appellate Committee most appeals are heard by five Lords of Appeal. Occasionally seven will sit, but this has been a rare event in the period under

[47] Cmnd 3716, Table 1.5. See too Chap. 6 above.

consideration.[48] The Judicial Statistics provide information on the number of appeals which are disposed of without a judgment (presumably because they have been withdrawn or declared incompetent) as well as on the outcome of those disposed of with a judgment, the latter being categorised as "allowed", "allowed in part/varied" or "dismissed". Table 7.5 aggregates these statistics over the thirty-year period. They indicate a remarkable degree of consistency in the success rate for appeals, especially when averaged over a five-year or ten-year period. The trend has been very slightly upwards. Today, between four and five out of every ten appeals—or at any rate those disposed of by judgment—result in the appeal being wholly or partly (but mainly wholly) allowed. The appeals disposed of by judgment each year represent approximately eighty-five per cent of those presented to the House each year, so even if the rate of success is measured against the latter base it is still very significant, at around forty per cent.

It is not possible from the published statistics to calculate whether the success rate is higher in those cases where leave to appeal has been granted by the House itself rather than by a lower court. But it is possible to compare the success rate in civil cases with that in criminal cases, just as we were able to do in Figure 7.6 with regard to petitions for leave to appeal. This comparison is provided in Figures 7.9 and 7.10. They show that over the thirty-year period, but especially

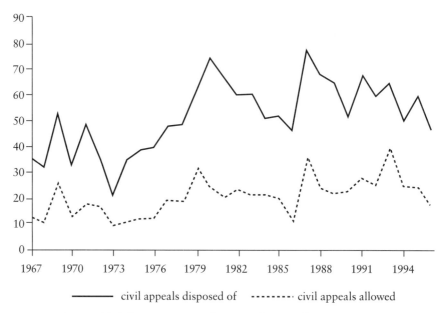

civil appeals disposed of  ·······civil appeals allowed

*Figure 7.9: The success rate for appeals in civil cases, 1967–96*

[48] Examples are *Pepper (Inspector of Taxes)* v. *Hart* [1993] 1 All ER 42 and *Murphy* v. *Brentwood District Council* [1990] 2 All ER 908. Lord Mackay, the Lord Chancellor, sat in both cases.

*Table 7.5: The outcome of appeals disposed of, 1967–96*[a]

| Year | Appeals disposed of | Without judgment[b] | Appeals allowed[c] | Appeals dismissed | Success rate[d] |
|------|------|------|------|------|------|
| 1967 | 39 | 6 | 11 (2) | 20 | 39% |
| 1968 | 40 | 7 | 13 (0) | 20 | 39% |
| 1969 | 64 | 6 | 25 (6) | 27 | 53% |
| 1970 | 38 | 3 | 13 (0) | 22 | 37% |
| 1971 | 57 | 10 | 18 (2) | 27 | 43% |
| 1972 | 52 | 2 | 23 (8) | 19 | 62% |
| 1973 | 40 | 4 | 15 (2) | 19 | 47% |
| 1974 | 46 | 10 | 11 (1) | 24 | 38% |
| 1975 | 55 | 8 | 13 (2) | 32 | 32% |
| 1976 | 53 | 11 | 8 (8) | 26 | 38% |
| 1977 | 55 | 8 | 22 (0) | 25 | 47% |
| 1978 | 60 | 8 | 22 (6) | 24 | 54% |
| 1979 | 71 | 2 | 35 (1) | 33 | 52% |
| 1980 | 85 | 16 | 32 (0) | 37 | 46% |
| 1981 | 80 | 8 | 25 (0) | 47 | 35% |
| 1982 | 86 | 8 | 33 (0) | 45 | 42% |
| 1983 | 79 | 3 | 31 (0) | 45 | 41% |
| 1984 | 66 | 4 | 28 (1) | 33 | 47% |
| 1985 | 66 | 8 | 24 (2) | 32 | 45% |
| 1986 | 61 | 11 | 16 (1) | 33 | 34% |
| 1987 | 119 | 10 | 61 (5) | 43 | 61% |
| 1988 | 78 | 4 | 23 (6) | 45 | 39% |
| 1989 | 69 | 5 | 23 (0) | 41 | 36% |
| 1990 | 59 | 7 | 23 (3) | 26 | 50% |
| 1991 | 77 | 15 | 30 (3) | 29 | 53% |
| 1992 | 73 | 10 | 34 (0) | 29 | 54% |
| 1993 | 84 | 9 | 23 (1) | 51 | 32% |
| 1994 | 64 | 1 | 30 (1) | 32 | 49% |
| 1995 | 67 | 8 | 23 (5) | 31 | 48% |
| 1996 | 58 | 5 | 22 (0) | 31 | 42% |
| Average | | | | | |
| 1967–76 | 48 | 7 | 15 (3) | 24 | 43% |
| 1977–86 | 71 | 8 | 27 (1) | 35 | 44% |
| 1987–96 | 75 | 7 | 29 (2) | 36 | 46% |

a—Source: n. 6 above and n. a to Fig. 7.1. Before 1993 some appeals were listed each year as "Otherwise disposed"; an example of this would be where the appeal was declared incompetent. The Civil Judicial Statistics for 1974 (Cmnd. 6361) give a figure of twenty-nine appeals disposed of, but the Judicial Statistics for 1975 (Cmnd. 6634) say it was forty-six. In cases of such disparity the figure in the later report has been preferred, since it is likely to have adjusted earlier inaccuracies.

b—This includes appeals categorised as "otherwise disposed of"; the Judicial Statistics do not explain the difference between this and "disposed of without a judgment".

c—The numbers in brackets represent those appeals which were allowed in part.

d—This is the number of appeals allowed, in whole or in part, as a percentage of the number of appeals disposed of *with* a judgment.

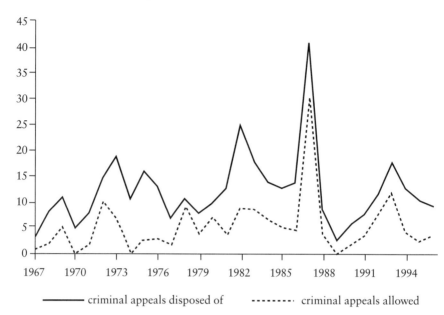

*Figure 7.10: The success rate for appeals in criminal cases, 1967–96*

over the most recent twenty years, the success rate in criminal cases has been higher than that in civil cases, but not significantly so. The difference does not mirror that which arises when the success rates of petitions for leave to appeal in the two types of case are compared. The number of criminal appeals each year is in any event relatively small, so the fluctuations in percentage success rates can be great.

## THE WORK OF THE LORDS OF APPEAL IN THE PRIVY COUNCIL[49]

It is often assumed that the bulk of the workload of Lords of Appeal is under-taken within the Appeal and Appellate Committees of the House of Lords, if not within the Appellate Committee alone, and that the case-load within the Judicial Committee of the Privy Council is comparatively light. In fact, the pic-ture is not at all as stark as one might think. Figure 7.11 shows that a consider-able amount of work is undertaken within the Judicial Committee of the Privy Council. Even this is an under-representation because it does not take account of the applications for special leave to appeal.[50] When measured in terms of the

[49] No attempt is made here to analyse the work of the Privy Council in any detail. It is hoped to make that the basis of a future article.

[50] Appeals to the Privy Council are admitted only with the leave of the court appealed from or with the "special leave" of the Judicial Committee itself. Special leave will not be granted in a crim-inal case unless there has been a grave violation of the principles of natural justice.

appeals *presented* each year, the number of Privy Council cases is eighty-one per cent of the number of House of Lords cases; when measured in terms of the appeals *disposed of* after a hearing each year, the proportion still remains very high, at seventy per cent. A higher fraction of the appeals entered in the Privy Council fall by the wayside on the road to a hearing than is the case for appeals presented to the House of Lords.

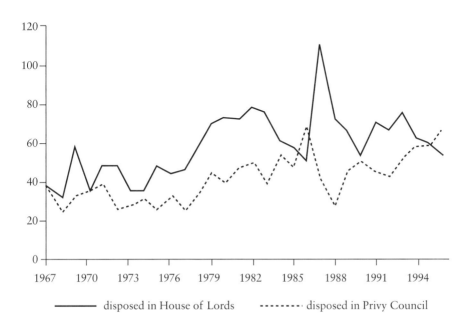

Figure 7.11: *Appeals disposed of in the House of Lords and Privy Council,*
*1967–96*[a]

a—Source: *Judicial Statistics for England and Wales*, Annual Reports (Lord Chancellor's Department), issued as Command Papers. The figures for 1996 are sixty-five appeals presented in the House of Lords and eighty entered in the Privy Council: Cm 3716 (Tables 1.1 and 1.3).

Of course the size of the case-load is not necessarily a reliable indicator of the amount of work involved in handling the cases. It has to be borne in mind, for instance, that cases in the Judicial Committee are sometimes heard by fewer than five judges,[51] and in the Privy Council Lords of Appeal are frequently assisted in their work by senior judges from other Commonwealth jurisdictions or by retired Lords Justices of Appeal.[52] Moreover it is customary for the Privy Council to issue one single judgment; although this will have been read, and per-

---

[51] E.g., only four Lords of Appeal sat in *Ng Enterprises Ltd* v. *Urban Council* [1996] 3 WLR 751, an appeal from the Court of Appeal of Hong Kong.
[52] E.g., Ralph Gibson L.J. sat in *Moses* v. *The State* [1996] 3 WLR 534, an appeal from Trinidad and Tobago.

haps altered in places, by the other judges, those judges will not have had to go to the trouble of preparing their own judgments; dissenting judgments, moreover, permitted only since 1966,[53] are still rare.

Nevertheless, the workload of the Lords of Appeal in Privy Council cases is far from negligible. This is substantiated by the figures for "days sat" by the Lords of Appeal. As far as the House of Lords is concerned, these figures have for long been supplied in the Judicial Statistics, but only in the last few years have figures also been included for days sat in the Privy Council. As Figure 7.12 shows, there is not a great deal of difference between the two sets of figures: the average number of days sat in the Privy Council per year in the five years from 1992 to 1996 was 85 per cent of that in the House of Lords.[54]

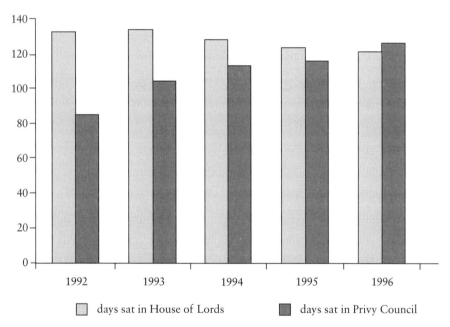

*Figure 7.12: Days sat by Lords of Appeal in the House of Lords and Privy Council, 1967–96*[a]

a—Source: n. 6 above.

The size of the workload of the Lords of Appeal in the Judicial Committee raises the issue of whether, when the House of Lords as a parliamentary chamber is reformed, as it is due to be, the opportunity should not be taken to redistribute the function of the Lords of Appeal as Privy Councillors to some other body (whether in the United Kingdom or elsewhere). In 1996, the Privy Council

[53] By the Judicial Committee (Dissenting Opinions) Order 1966.
[54] It is assumed that there is no double-counting in these figures, i.e. that Lords of Appeal do not in the one day sit both in a House of Lords case and in a Privy Council case.

disposed of seventy-one appeals from fourteen different jurisdictions,[55] sixty-five of them from Hong Kong, Jamaica and New Zealand. With the appeal route from Hong Kong having terminated at the end of June 1997, the workload in the Privy Council is likely to diminish in the immediate future, but no doubt cases, including death row cases, will continue to proliferate from the Caribbean states (in the absence of any regional Court of Appeal for that area) and Jersey, Guernsey and the Isle of Man may well provide more work than heretofore. Predictions of the Judicial Committee's demise in the past, such as when appeals ceased to be sent from Ceylon, have proved incorrect. Meanwhile care will have to be taken that the time of Lords of Appeal is not devoted disproportionately to the laws and legal systems of very small jurisdictions.[56]

CONCLUSION

This foray into the statistics concerning the Lords of Appeal in office during a thirty-year period has shown that forty-four men have fulfilled the role. The average age of the persons appointed has been sixty-three and the average period served has been almost ten years. Nearly all of the Law Lords have been educated at public school and at Oxford or Cambridge. They have not, however, worn their politics on their sleeves. As regards their workload, in 1996 they were dealing with more than three times as many petitions for leave to appeal as their predecessors in 1967, although the number of days on which they sat to deal with oral hearings arising out of these petitions had fallen to just a twentieth of the number of days on which they sat to hear actual appeals. This appears to be a direct result of Procedure Directions issued in 1988. About a quarter of all petitions for leave to appeal are successful, the success rate in criminal cases being half as good again as that in civil cases.

These days only a minority of appeals are heard by the Law Lords without their first having granted leave themselves. Some sixty-five per cent of the appeals disposed of emanate from the Civil Division of the Court of Appeal in England and Wales, only nine per cent from the Criminal Division of that court, nine per cent from the Divisional Court and three per cent from the High Court by way of leapfrog. The Scottish civil courts provide twelve per cent of the appeals to the Lords and two per cent come from Northern Ireland. The number of criminal appeals has remained fairly even over each of the last thirty years but the number of civil appeals has risen dramatically. Between forty per cent and fifty per cent of appeals are allowed each year, with a higher proportion of criminal appeals being allowed than civil appeals, especially in the late 1980s and early 1990s.

[55] Antigua, Bahamas, Barbados, Belize, Brunei, Gambia, Hong Kong, Jamaica, Mauritius, New Zealand, Singapore, St Vincent and the Grenadines, Trinidad and Tobago and the Virgin Islands. The Judicial Committee also dealt with twelve appeals under the Medical Act 1984, and one each under the Dentists Act 1984 and the Opticians Act 1989.

[56] Cf. Alan Paterson, n. 4 above: "A balance has to be struck to ensure that junior Law Lords are not relegated to the Privy Council for more than fifty per cent of the year" (at 88).

The Law Lords have also been busy in the Privy Council. For every ten appeals disposed of after a hearing in the Appellate Committee of the House, a further seven or so are disposed of after a hearing in the Judicial Committee of the Council. Many of the Privy Council cases involve small jurisdictions, and it is therefore questionable whether the time of the Law Lords is being well spent in this regard.

# 8

# *The Judicial Role of the Lord Chancellor*

ANTHONY BRADNEY

## INTRODUCTION

The office of Lord Chancellor has always caused problems for those who have sought to apply the constitutional theory of the separation of powers to the United Kingdom.[1] The triple task of the Lord Chancellor, judge, Cabinet Minister and Speaker of the House of Lords, seems to mock the simple verities of Montesquieu's thesis that a division and balance of power is necessary for the preservation of liberty. The new question, which has become apparent in the mid and late 1990s, is does the judicial role of the Lord Chancellor now cause problems for application of the concept of the independence of the judiciary to the United Kingdom? As judiciary, government and Lord Chancellor politely collide with ever-increasing frequency and fury, can the judicial part of the Lord Chancellor's triple task survive?

The judicial role of the Lord Chancellor can be divided into four parts. First, the Lord Chancellor is a judge. Under section 5 of the Appellate Jurisdiction Act 1876 the Lord Chancellor is empowered to sit in the House of Lords when it hears cases on appeal alongside the Lords of Appeal in Ordinary and peers who have held high judicial office. The Lord Chancellor is also President of the Chancery Division of the High Court.[2] Secondly, the Lord Chancellor advises on the appointment of High Court judges, circuit judges, recorders and stipendiary magistrates who are appointed by the Crown.[3] The Lord Chancellor also appoints district judges, lay magistrates and tribunal chairs. Thirdly, the Lord Chancellor exercises a disciplinary function with respect to part of the judiciary, having the right to dismiss some judges for misbehaviour or incapacity. Fourthly and finally, the Lord Chancellor, as Speaker of the House of Lords and a government Minister in the Cabinet, has a position which "gives him a voice both in the legislature and the executive which enables the claims of the

---

[1] See, e.g., D. Shell, *The House of Lords* (Hemel Hempstead, Harvester Wheatsheaf, 1992), at 112.

[2] Supreme Court Act 1981, s. 5(1)(a).

[3] Supreme Court Act 1981, s. 10.

administration of justice to be clearly articulated, particularly in the Cabinet and its committees".[4] Amongst these claims is that of the independence of the judiciary. Lord Hailsham has written that "[t]he most important constitutional function of the Lord Chancellor in the twentieth century remains to preserve the integrity and impartiality of the judiciary against all comers".[5]

The size of the Lord Chancellor's job inevitably brings with it problems. No Lord Chancellor has the time assiduously to pursue all the various parts of the office. Each individual Lord Chancellor decides what priority is going to be given to each aspect.[6] Thus, for example, Lord Gardiner took his duties as Speaker of the House of Lords so seriously that he made special arrangements for providing a presiding judge in the House of Lords when he himself was unable to sit.[7] On the other hand, Lord Hailsham gave precedence to his duty to sit as a judge, creating twenty-six deputy speakers to take over from him in the House of Lords.[8] Because of this individual element to the Lord Chancellor's job, generalisations about the Lord Chancellor's position can be suspect. No Lord Chancellor is ever the same in background, experience or performance as any other Lord Chancellor. Some Lord Chancellors, like Lord Hailsham, come to the position with the experience of long and central involvement in the political conflicts of their times. Others have had a more marginal political role or, like Lord Mackay, come to the office having previously held senior judicial office. Nevertheless, certain questions persist which relate not to the quality of the work of individual Lord Chancellors but to an inherent dysfunction in the idea of a Lord Chancellor.

THE LORD CHANCELLOR AS JUDGE

Amongst commentators and judges there are broadly three reactions to the fact that a Lord Chancellor has the statutory right to sit as a judge. The first is to argue that this is no more than a formal right. Thus Bradley and Ewing state that "the Lord Chancellor rarely sits for judicial business".[9] This position of denial is difficult to sustain when looking at the history of the Lord Chancellors and is particularly difficult to accept in the case of two out of the last three Lord Chancellors, Lord Hailsham and Lord Mackay.

---

[4] Lord Mackay, *The Administration of Justice* (London, Sweet and Maxwell, 1994), at 18.

[5] Lord Hailsham, *A Sparrow's Flight* (London, Fontana, 1990), at 385. Similarly, *The Times'* obituary for Lord Dilhorne reports him as having said that "the Lord Chancellor's chief job in life . . . was to preserve the independence of the judiciary" (*The Times*, 10 Sept. 1980).

[6] "It has to be remembered that our constitution is a conventional one and therefore the role to be played [by the Lord Chancellor] is determined by each holder of the office" (Sir Francis Purchas, "The Constitution in the Market Place" (1993) 143 *NLJ* 1604).

[7] R. Stevens, *Law and Politics* (London, Weidenfeld and Nicolson, 1979), at 436.

[8] Hailsham, n. 5 above, at 380.

[9] A. W. Bradley and K. D. Ewing, *Constitutional and Administrative Law* (11th edn., Longman, London, 1993), at 371. For a similar view see Shell, n. 1 above.

All Lord Chancellors since the end of the Second World War have exercised their right to sit in the House of Lords.[10] It is true to say that they have shown a very great range of interest in their work as judges. Thus, whilst Lord Gardiner sat in seven cases and Lord Simonds sat in eight cases, Lord Hailsham sat in forty-five.[11] Lord Mackay continued Lord Hailsham's practice of taking a great interest in the judicial work of the House of Lords, sitting in seventy-two cases.[12] This is perhaps unsurprising, given that Lord Mackay was, until his appointment as Lord Chancellor, a salaried Law Lord in the House of Lords. Lord Irvine has continued to exercise this aspect of the Lord Chancellor's role.[13] Moreover, it is not possible to argue that the cases that Lord Chancellors have sat in have been minor in their nature or that the Lord Chancellor's participation has been peripheral to the case taken as a whole. Apart from the difficulty of arguing that any case heard in the House of Lords is minor in nature, recent cases heard by Lord Mackay have included *Pepper* v. *Hart*[14] and *Murphy* v. *Brentwood District Council*,[15] both cases which have occasioned considerable comment in academic legal literature and both cases in which Lord Mackay gave a judgment which has been the subject of academic analysis.[16] Similarly, previous Lord Chancellors have also been heavily involved in cases which have had a high profile. Lord Hailsham, for example, gave one of the leading judgments in both *Richards* v. *Richards* and *Re W*, and Lord Kilmuir gave the sole judgement in *Wigley* v. *British Vinegars Ltd*.[17]

An alternative analysis to that typified by Bradley and Ewing is to argue that sitting as a judge is in fact vital to the Lord Chancellor's performance. This is the view of Lord Hailsham who, in describing the judicial functions of the Lord Chancellor, has argued that "their regular discharge is the only factor ensuring that a politically motivated prime minister does not give the office to a no-good lawyer".[18] Lord Mackay has also stressed the importance of the Lord Chancellor being respected as a judge by other members of Cabinet and the value that there is in the person who is responsible "for administering the important boundary between the executive and the judiciary" having actual experience of the judicial task.[19] In this view the judicial

---

[10] A. Bradney, "The Judicial Activity of the Lord Chancellor 1946–87: A Pellet" (1989) 16 *Journal of Law and Society* 360.

[11] *Ibid.*, at 367.

[12] This information is taken from the LEXIS database.

[13] His first judgment is to be found in *Boddington* v. *British Transport Police*, *The Times*, 3 Apr. 1998.

[14] [1993] AC 593.

[15] [1991] 1 AC 398.

[16] [1993] AC 593 and [1990] 2 All ER 908. For comments, see D. Miers, "Taxing Perks and Interpreting Statutes: *Pepper* v. *Hart*" (1993) 56 *MLR* 695 at 699, 700, 703, 704 and 705 and I Duncan Wallace, "*Anns* Beyond Repair" (1991) 107 *LQR* 228 at 233. See too Chap. 11 below.

[17] [1984] 1 AC 174, [1971] AC 682 and [1964] AC 307 respectively. The extent of the judicial activity of Lord Chancellors and ex-Lord Chancellors between 1947 and 1987 is examined at greater length in Bradney, n. 10 above, *passim*.

[18] Hailsham, n. 5 above, at 379.

[19] Mackay, n. 4 above, at 18 and 24.

role of the Lord Chancellor is central to the Lord Chancellor's job taken as a whole.

Against this approach, although again accepting the reality of the Lord Chancellor's role as a judge, is the view that "[The Lord Chancellor's] judicial functions . . . are clearly contrary to the concept of judicial independence: when sitting as a judge he cannot be independent of the Government since he is part of it".[20] This view vaunts the separateness of the judiciary, values its otherness in society, and thus finds the Lord Chancellor's triple allegiance to judiciary, Cabinet and legislature an anathema.

Deciding between these latter two approaches involves measuring competing advantages and disadvantages. On any view the Lord Chancellor's place in Cabinet causes difficulties for his duties as a judge. If he or she is to be seen to be independent, no judge can sit in a case in which he or she has a personal interest. The Lord Chancellor's position in Cabinet is adjudged to give an institutional link with government which restricts the cases that can be heard. Lord Mackay phrases the restrictions as being that:

> "The Lord Chancellor would not sit in a case involving decisions of his own nor of members of the government in their executive capacity. . . . It has also been customary for the Lord Chancellor to sit in cases involving important questions of law, even if Government agencies are involved, where the decisions are not those of ministers but of independent persons appointed for that purpose".[21]

Although, in essence, this is no more than an application of the maxim *nemo debet esse judex in propria causa* (no man shall be a judge in his own cause) to the rather special circumstances of the Lord Chancellor's position, the difficulty is that the breadth of the Lord Chancellor's task arguably makes this application near impossible if the Lord Chancellor is to have a continuing judicial role. The Lord Chancellor is responsible for the administration of justice as a whole—for the development and reform of law. As Lord Mackay himself has noted, there is "no clear statement in statute of the overall functions of the Lord Chancellor".[22] It is thus difficult to say at what point the Lord Chancellor's role with respect to legislation is at an end or at what point the Lord Chancellor can properly be said to be independent of an issue in court.

The difficulty of determining the limits of the Lord Chancellor's Executive role, and thus the permissible limits of the exercise of the judicial function, can be seen in the work of the last Lord Chancellor. Lord Mackay's formulation of the *nemo debet* maxim meant that he felt able to take part in the important tax case, *Pepper* v. *Hart*, since he regarded the Inland Revenue as, for this purpose, entirely divorced from government.[23] This argument has not proved attractive to everybody. Oliver has commented that:

---

[20]  T. C. Hartley and J. A. G. Griffith, *Government and Law* (London, Weidenfeld and Nicolson, 1975), at 180.

[21]  Mackay, n. 4 above, at 24–5.

[22]  Lord Mackay, "The Lord Chancellor's Role within Government" (1995) 146 *NLJ* 1650 at 1650.

[23]  Lord Mackay took part in a number of cases involving the Inland Revenue whilst Lord

"The participation of a member of the Cabinet in a decision about the powers of the courts to take into consideration ministerial statements to Parliament necessarily raises issues of conflict of interest, and it does not engender confidence in the independence of the judiciary and the immunity of the system from pressures emanating from government. The problem was particularly acute in *Pepper* v. *Hart* because the budget of the Lord Chancellor's Department was likely to be affected by the decision if, as he feared, it would result in increased costs in litigation. Indeed, this was the consideration which led the Lord Chancellor to dissent from the other members of the panel".[24]

The salient point made by Oliver is that the Lord Chancellor's participation in the case "does not engender confidence". Whilst the apparent coincidence of interest and decision in *Pepper* v. *Hart* may heighten concerns about conflicts between the Lord Chancellor's various tasks, those concerns arise before and irrespective of the actual judgment. At issue is not simply the reality of the effect of the other tasks of the Lord Chancellor on the judicial activity of the Lord Chancellor. The appearance of the effect, whatever the reality, is sufficient to cause worries. Judges, including Lord Chancellors who are judges, have to appear to be unbiased as well as be unbiased. They have to appear to be unbiased whilst taking part in a case, not appear to be unbiased in the light of their subsequent decision. Moreover, they have to appear to be unbiased to a lay, not a professional, audience. The question thus is, which are the legal cases in which a government minister, responsible for the administration of justice and law reform, can clearly be said, by those outside the legal system as well as those within, to have no particular interest? The allegation need not be of potential, direct, corrupt interest but merely of the possibility of the insidious, unconscious influences that come from seeing issues from a single perspective generated by the political posture that one's job forces one to adopt. The question is, does there appear to be a possibility of interest? It is not enough for judgments to be ones which can be justified *ex post facto* as being ones which a reasonable judge could have made. The questions are precisely matters of confidence: the confidence of those who know nothing about the probity of the individuals concerned or the technicalities of the decisions being made. The questions are about the legitimacy of the legal system and are therefore, in turn, about perception.

---

Chancellor. In *Marshall* v. *Kerr* Lord Mackay notes that he had drafted a judgment but, having read the drafts of the judgments of the other Lords, "find myself readily in agreement with . . . Lord Browne-Wilkinson's approach to this case . . . but for the fact that I have had the help of . . . Lord Browne-Wilkinson's opinion I should have been persuaded by the taxpayer's argument" (*Marshall* v. *Kerr* [1995] AC 148 at 153). In *IRC* v. *Herd* [1993] 3 All ER 56 he gave the sole judgment of substance and allowed the Revenue's appeal. In *R.* v. *IRC and Another* [1991] 2 AC 283 he gave a short judgment following the majority in allowing an appeal by the Inland Revenue. In *Bray (Inspector of Taxes)* v. *Best* [1989] 1 All ER 969 Lord Mackay followed the majority in rejecting an appeal by the Revenue.

[24] D. Oliver, "*Pepper* v. *Hart*: A Suitable Case for Reference to *Hansard*?" [1993] *PL* 5 at 5–6.

THE LORD CHANCELLOR AND LEGAL AID

Conflict between the Lord Chancellor's ministerial role and his participation in the work of the Appellate Committee of the House of Lords is not limited to a connection with the work of the Inland Revenue. Questions of perception and confidence are put in an even starker light when examining the presentation of the Lord Chancellor's role in the management of legal aid.

In a series of news stories in the media during the 1990s Lord Mackay, then Lord Chancellor, was associated with plans to reduce the legal aid budget. For example, in 1994 *The Guardian* contained one item headed "Ministers use reshuffle for sneak orders".[25] The story concerned "forty-three announcements and decisions" which had been released by government ministers "under the cover of . . . a reshuffle". These included the abolition of the Agricultural Wages Council, Great Britain's withdrawal from two International Labour Organisation Conventions and the Lord Chancellor's announcement of the intended abolition of the Legal Aid Advisory Committee. Whether or not there was an attempt "to sneak out" potentially unpopular measures, as is suggested in the article, or whether these government releases were mere coincidence is not at issue, nor is the political legitimacy of news management. What matters is the plausible association of the Lord Chancellor with what are clearly political concerns. This story and many others like it portray a Lord Chancellor as just one more government Minister engaged in a Conservative Party agenda of cutting the costs of publicly-funded activities. In this context one might then ask whether it is appropriate for the Lord Chancellor to take part in cases where the interpretation of legal aid legislation plays a central part in the judgment, as Lord Mackay did in *O'Sullivan* v. *Herdman Ltd (No. 2)*.[26] As with *Pepper* v. *Hart*, the problem with the Lord Chancellor's participation in this case is not one of a suggestion of bias, unconscious or otherwise, in the decision. Lord Mackay's short judgment in *O'Sullivan* v. *Herdman Ltd (No. 2)* agrees with that of Lord Bridge, reaffirming an order for payment out of the legal aid fund, thus adding to legal aid costs. But, whatever the outcome of any individual case, it is difficult to see how the Lord Chancellor can be said not to have an interest in an issue which enmeshes him in so much press coverage. It is the possibility of bias, that bias might be suggested, that a Lord Chancellor might even unconsciously seek to avoid the suggestion of bias by giving a judgment which is contrary to government interests, which is important.[27]

---

[25] *Guardian*, 21 July 1994.

[26] [1988] 1 WLR 1373.

[27] Other areas of activity give rise to similar grounds for concern. E.g., Lord Mackay has described domestic violence as being one area where the Lord Chancellor has particular responsibility for policy, and yet Lord Hailsham took part in *Richards* v. *Richards* ([1984] 1 AC 174), a case of especial importance in this area (Mackay, n. 22 above, at 1652).

THE LORD CHANCELLOR AND THE MANAGEMENT OF COURTS

The 1980s and 1990s have seen a rising tide of judicial comments about financial constraints on the work of the judiciary and the management of courts. A number of judges have suggested that new fiscal imperatives threaten the judiciary's ability to act independently. The number of these complaints about these controls does not of itself necessarily indicate any increase in the size of the problem. There has always been some monetary control of the courts. In part the apparent rise in the number of these complaints may simply reflect Lord Mackay's abolition of the Kilmuir Rules, which prohibited public comment by members of the judiciary unless they had the prior sanction of the Lord Chancellor.[28] Nevertheless, to some extent the work of the judiciary has been affected by the general decrease in the amount of money devoted to the public sector. This has led some judges to argue that a "threat [to judicial independence] arises by reason of the executive's control of finance and administration".[29]

Judges have seen themselves as being more and more beset by civil service control which has its roots first in the Lord Chancellor's Department and secondly in the Treasury. Thus, for example, one County Court judge has written of the County Court:

"The new system involves four tiers of civil service management. Local court staffs are answerable to a wholly deracinated central administration which is organised on a regional basis and is in turn answerable to a higher layer at circuit level. And then all these tiers are answerable to the Lord Chancellor's Department in Westminster."[30]

In more general terms the argument has been that:

"Judges are sitting in an environment wholly determined by executive decisions in the Lord Chancellor's Department, which in turn is operating under the constraints and pressures imposed by the Treasury."[31]

In the context of this conflict the Lord Chancellor's position has been difficult. On the one hand, he is the government Minister in charge of the government department responsible for imposing financial limitations on the work of the courts. That department has stated that its "fundamental aim" is "to ensure the efficient and effective administration of justice *at an affordable price*" and that its "strategic priority . . . [i]n support of the Government's objective of controlling public expenditure" is "to control legal aid costs and *contain expenditure*

---

[28]  Mackay, n. 4 above, at 26. Lord Kilmuir, the Lord Lord Chancellor who had introduced these restrictions, believed that "[s]o long as a Judge keeps silent his reputation for wisdom and impartiality remains unassailable" (A. Bradley, "Judges and the Media—the Kilmuir Rules" [1986] *PL* 383 at 385).

[29]  Sir Nicolas Browne-Wilkinson, "The Independence of the Judiciary in the 1980s" [1988] *PL* 44 at 44.

[30]  H. Wilson, "The County Court Judge in Limbo" (1994) 144 *NLJ* 1453.

[31]  Browne-Wilkinson, n. 29 above, at 50.

*on court services*, while maintaining proper standards of service by means consistent with this priority".[32] On the other hand, the previous Lord Chancellor, Lord Mackay, accepted not just a general responsibility for protecting the independence of the judiciary but also the point that:

> "in order to preserve their independence the judges must have some control or influence over the administrative penumbra immediately surrounding the judicial process."[33]

The multi-faceted nature of the Lord Chancellor's office has meant that the Lord Chancellor is both the person who should represent to government the judiciary's legitimate concerns about the preservation of their integrity and also the person who has final political responsibility for managing the new systems which the judges believe damage that integrity. Lord Irivine has indicated that he will attempt to maintain these two roles stating, in a speech to the London Common Law and Commercial Bar Association, that his:

> "objective is to leave a valuable legacy to the future—an efficient, affordable, flexible civil justice system which commands people's confidence. A civil justice system which all the people know exists to gaurantee their rights and which delivers."[34]

What is now at issue is whether the judiciary, let alone the population at large, will accept that one person can focus on both the costs of the legal system and its integrity at the same time.

THE LORD CHANCELLOR AND THE EMPLOYMENT APPEAL TRIBUNAL

The relationship between the Lord Chancellor, financial imperatives and the judiciary has taken on a particular edge in connection with the work of the Employment Appeal Tribunal. In December 1992 Lord Mackay wrote to Wood J., the then President of the Employment Appeal Tribunal, expressing concern about the backlog of cases that had built up in the Tribunal. He sought assurances that Rule 3 of the Employment Appeal Tribunal Rules, which provided for cases to be struck out where the Notice of Appeal raised no arguable point of law, would be applied. Lord Mackay's concern was the "waste" of public money where there was a preliminary hearing in cases that had no chance of success and the financial consequences of having to appoint more High Court judges to deal with the backlog, a course which he said he was unwilling to undertake. He asserted "procedural rules which allow for cheap and efficient disposal of unmeritorious cases might be used to much greater effect". Following this letter Lord Mackay and Wood J. held a meeting. Wood J.,

---

[32] Emphasis added. Quoted from the Lord Chancellor's entry on the Government Home Page on the internet (http://www.open.gov.uk).

[33] Lord Mackay, "The Lord Chancellor in the 1990s" (1991) 44 *CLP* 241 at 247.

[34] A copy of the speech is to be found on the Lord Chancellor's Department's Home Page on the internet.

having consulted colleagues, then wrote a response to Lord Mackay. The interpretation of this response has been a matter of dispute. Lord Mackay has said that Wood J.'s response was a refusal to apply Rule 3.[35] Others have taken the view that Wood J. was setting out the situations with which the Employment Appeal Tribunal was regularly faced and, in so doing, indicating that Rule 3 would rarely, if ever, apply to those factual circumstances. A further correspondence ensued during which Lord Mackay sent a letter once again asking for an assurance that Rule 3 would be applied more regularly, concluding "[i]f you do not feel you can give me that assurance, I must ask you to consider your position".[36] In his reply Wood J. wrote:

> "I have, of course, given the most serious consideration to my position as you required of me. You have demanded that I exercise my judicial function in a way which you regard as best suited to your Executive purposes, but I have to say that in all the circumstances that present themselves to me and in the light of the existing law, I cannot regard compliance with your demand as conducive to justice.
>
> You express disappointment. I express profound regret that it has ever been the uncomfortable duty of a judge in this country in compliance with his Judicial Oath, to write to a Lord Chancellor refusing a demand such as the one which you have made of me."

In a Press Release about this exchange the Lord Chancellor's Office state that in the correspondence:

> "The Lord Chancellor was acting in his capacity as the most senior judge, not as a member of the Executive or Cabinet. Essentially, they were discussing the application of existing rules, as to how the EAT should operate."[37]

The Lord Chancellor's position was thus that this was no more than an exchange of views between judges where he was seeking an assurance that the law as it was would be applied.[38]

In his article on the exchange between the Lord Chancellor and Wood J. Sir Francis Purchas, a retired Lord Justice of the Court of Appeal, has written:

> "Taken at its lowest the letter was an attempt to force a High Court Judge to follow a legal course which to his, the Lord Chancellor's, knowledge that Judge thought was contrary to his judicial oath."[39]

Taken at its highest Lord Mackay's letter can be seen as a threat to remove Wood J. from the Presidency of the Employment Appeal Tribunal if he, Wood

---

[35] H.L. Deb., vol. 554, cols. 793–6.

[36] The correspondence is discussed in D. Rose, "Revealed: How Lord Mackay misled Parliament", *Observer*, 3 Apr. 1994; Sir Francis Purchas, "Lord Mackay and the Judiciary" (1994) 144 *NLJ* 527, and in a debate in the House of Lords at H.L. Deb., vol. 554, cols. 751–804. The relevant text of this letter and other letters is found in these sources. Lord Mackay placed all the correspondence in the library of the House of Lords prior to debate.

[37] *Ibid.*

[38] H.L. Deb., vol. 554, col. 800.

[39] Purchas, n. 36 above.

J., did not interpret and apply the law in the way that the Executive wanted. As Sir Francis Purchas goes on to observe in his article:

> "[W]hat he [the Lord Chancellor] intended is not so important as what meaning the reasonable reader would give to the purpose and intent of the letter in the overall context. On any view an attempt to influence a Judge backed up with a threat, whatever the precise form it may have taken, was almost certainly an unconstitutional act."[40]

In a House of Lords debate, subsequent upon this exchange of letters becoming public knowledge, a number of senior judicial figures, Lord Ackner, Lord Oliver and Lord Donaldson, together with other members of the House of Lords, commented adversely on the Lord Chancellor's actions.[41] Although Lord Mackay continued to argue that his position was correct, and although he received some support in the House of Lords, the affair is both illustrative of and reinforces the argument that there has been a failure by the Lord Chancellor to preserve, if not judicial independence, at least judicial integrity. As Lord Oliver argued, the clash between Lord Mackay and Wood J. suggested a degree of Executive interference which sapped confidence in the integrity of the system, suggested the interest of citizens in pursuing their cases was less important than a narrowly conceived idea of "value for money" and put new judges on notice that they might be pressurised, not protected, when they made decisions about the nature of the law.[42]

### THE LORD CHANCELLOR, THE JUDICIARY AND NEW LEGISLATION

The clash over Rule 3 highlights, and is a particularly dramatic example of, the concern that some judges have about the relationship between the Lord Chancellor and the Treasury agenda. However, concern about the Lord Chancellor's role in protecting and representing the judiciary has gone further than the fiscal field.

Sir Francis Purchas has asserted the introduction by the Lord Chancellor of the Judicial Pensions and Retirement Act 1993, which worsened the pension terms for the judiciary, "was a strange thing for the person charged with protecting their independence and integrity".[43] Judicial concern was voiced about a number of matters in the legislation. It was argued that worsening pension arrangements might make it difficult to attract appropriately experienced judges. However, the strongest objections to the legislation on grounds of constitutional principle were raised in relation to those provisions which gave the

---

[40] Purchas, n. 36 above.

[41] For comments by Lords Ackner, Oliver and Donaldson, see H.L. Deb., vol. 554, cols. 766–70, 777–82 and 759–61. The matter had first been the subject of a question by Lord Lester to Lord Mackay before the correspondence had been made publicly available (H.L. Deb., vol. 553, cols. 497–500).

[42] H.L. Deb., vol. 554, cols. 781–2.

[43] Sir Francis Purchas, "The Constitution in the Market Place" (1993) 143 *NLJ* 1604.

Lord Chancellor power to permit a judge to continue working for periods of one year at a time after reaching the normal retirement age of seventy.[44] Under the proposed provisions the Lord Chancellor would have to decide on an annual basis whether to allow a judge to continue in office. The judge whose job was the subject of such annual review might be one who had taken part in a case where government interests were central to the decision.[45] The most common example of this would be cases involving judicial review of ministerial decisions. Ministers have been severely critical of some such decisions in the past. In debate in the House of Lords Lord Ackner stated that:

> "it is constitutionally unacceptable that the security of a judge should depend upon a decision of an appropriate Minister—the Lord Chancellor of the day—as to whether or not he should continue in office."[46]

Lord Ackner's arguments were supported by both Lord Donaldson and Lord Taylor.[47] Despite the potential difficulties caused by giving one Cabinet member the power to determine the job security of a judge who may have caused difficulties either for himself or for other Cabinet colleagues, the legislation was passed.

Sir Francis Purchas has also asserted that Lord Mackay has failed to consult with senior judicial figures when the government were considering legislation which would have a widespread effect on the legal system.[48] The most obvious example of this alleged failure to consult was the publication of the Green Paper on the organisation of the legal profession, which eventually resulted in the Courts and Legal Services Act 1990.[49] In its published response to this Green Paper the judiciary argued that:

> "The Government is proposing that in future the Lord Chancellor should make a final decision on standards of education and training for advocates, prescribe the principles to be embodied in codes of conduct for advocates, and be empowered to make decisions on rights of audience in the High Court and Court of Appeal by means of subordinate legislation. *These proposals represent a grave breach of the doctrine of separation of powers.*"[50]

---

[44] Judicial Pensions and Retirement Act 1993, s. 26(5).

[45] The Lord Chancellor's disciplinary role with respect to judges is limited to those lower levels of judges who would not be involved in cases such as these.

[46] H.L. Deb., vol. 538, col. 737.

[47] H.L. Deb., vol. 538, cols. 738 and 740.

[48] N. 43 above.

[49] "The Work and Organisation of the Legal Professions", (London, HMSO,Cm 570). Lord Mackay has been reported as having said that he did offer to consult the judiciary before publishing the Green Paper but that it preferred to remain "at arm's length" (*Guardian*, 8 Apr. 1989). However, both Sir Francis Purchas and Lord Lane have said that there was no consultation (Purchas, n. 43 above; *Guardian*, 17 Feb. 1989). The publication of the Green Paper and the history of the subsequent debate about it, including the response of the judiciary, is discussed in F. Cownie, "The Reform of the Legal Profession or the End of Civilization as We Know It" in F. Patfield and R. White, *The Changing Law* (Leicester, Leicester University Press, 1990).

[50] Judges' Response, "Summary", para. 3. Emphasis in the original.

The judiciary has long seen its own independence as being protected in part by the fact that the Bar, the body of people arguing before it, is itself independent of outside control. The Bar, with its notion of professional responsibility and duty towards the court, can be seen as a *cordon sanitaire*. By providing for outside control of the Bar, and by potentially weakening the Bar by allowing others to argue before the courts, the government could be seen as threatening the judiciary. That the judiciary should suggest that government proposals involve a breach of the doctrine of the separation of powers is grave enough; that it should suggest that the Lord Chancellor had allowed himself to be directly implicated in that breach makes the matter still worse. During subsequent debate about the Green Paper Lord Mackay sought to refute the arguments of the judiciary but failed to convince it that the government's position was correct.[51] The eventual legislation, the Courts and Legal Services Act 1990, created the Lord Chancellor's Advisory Committee on Legal Education.[52] The Advisory Committee, whose members are appointed by the Lord Chancellor, has a statutory duty to review the education and training of those who provide "legal services".[53] The Act also gave the Lord Chancellor power to authorise bodies to have rights of audience or to conduct litigation.[54]

Articulating the claims of the administration of justice in Cabinet is, as was observed at the beginning of this chapter, one of the tasks of the Lord Chancellor. It is not unreasonable for the judiciary to feel that its views on matters germane to its task might be sought by the Lord Chancellor and conveyed to the government; that this might be one way in which its independence and integrity might be preserved, one way in which public quarrels between judiciary and government might be avoided or, at least, reduced. The apparent failure of the then Lord Chancellor to accept this, together with the adding of further Executive duties to the Lord Chancellor's portfolio, duties which are in conflict with the Lord Chancellor's responsibility to the judiciary, indicate a further weakening of the relationship between the Lord Chancellor and the judiciary. Even if Lord Mackay is right in saying that he did offer to consult the judiciary about his proposed reforms prior to their publication in the Green Paper, the fact that it wished to distance itself and refused that offer suggests that it had little belief that its views, expressed privately, would have any effect.

THE LORD CHANCELLOR'S DEPARTMENT

Whilst the potential conflict between the Lord Chancellor's judicial activity and the Lord Chancellor's Executive functions is a long-standing matter to be seen in the work of many Lord Chancellors, the conflict between the Lord

---

[51] See Cownie, n. 49 above, at 221.
[52] Courts and Legal Services Act 1990, s. 19.
[53] Courts and Legal Services Act 1990, s. 19 and Sch. 2, para. 1(1).
[54] Courts and Legal Services Act 1990, s. 29.

Chancellor's duty to protect judicial independence and the wider responsibilities of the office is something that has become very much more acute during Lord Mackay's period of office as Lord Chancellor. Since, as was said at the beginning of this chapter, the Lord Chancellor's office is to some extent a personal one, where the holder's subjective interpretation of the balance of responsibilities affects the way in which he or she works, it might therefore be thought that the problems described above simply reflect the existence of a particularly Executive-minded Lord Chancellor; that they will not necessarily continue in the work of Lord Irvine or subsequent Lord Chancellors. If this is so, such problems would not, of themselves, suggest any deep-rooted difficulties in the nature of the office itself. There are, however, grounds for thinking such an argument is implausible.

It would be strange, although not psychologically impossible, for a Lord Chancellor who is himself a former Lord of Appeal in Ordinary and who has no great political experience to become an Executive-minded Lord Chancellor. Before accepting this idea, however, it is worthwhile considering an alternative explanation. Until 1972 the Lord Chancellor's Department was not staffed by normal civil servants; instead the Department was staffed by lawyers.[55] Until 1990 the Permanent Secretary of the Lord Chancellor's Department had to be a barrister.[56] The administrative arrangements under which the Lord Chancellor's Office was originally set up largely resisted the meritocratic reforms of the Northcote–Trevelyan reforms to the civil service in the nineteenth century.[57] Unlike other civil service departments there was a predominance of senior appointments in the department and the Permanent Secretary was appointed from within the department.

> "One of the results has been that the department has seen its role not as one primarily of managing the areas for which it was responsible but rather as that of a lobbyist for quasi-independent activities, like the judges or the court."[58]

In the nineteenth and early twentieth centuries the Lord Chancellor's Office was a small semi-independent empire. As late as 1988 it was being argued that:

> "the centre of gravity of the British civil service has always been the generalist administrator, with specialists (such as scientists, lawyers, accountants and economists) playing a supportive and subordinate role. *There are some exceptions (e.g. the lawyers who occupy the strategic posts in the Lord Chancellor's Department . . . )*."[59]

---

[55] R. Stevens, *The Independence of the Judiciary: The View from the Lord Chancellor's Office* (Oxford, Clarendon Press, 1993), at 7.

[56] *Ibid.*

[57] The reforms were designed to make sure entry into the civil service was based upon ability. See E. Cohen, *The Growth of the British Civil Service 1780–1939* (London, George Allen and Unwin) chaps.VI–VIII.

[58] N. 55 above, at 9.

[59] Emphasis added. G. Drewry and T. Butcher, *The Civil Service Today* (Oxford, Basil Blackwell, 1988), at 25–6.

The latter part of the twentieth century has, however, brought great changes to the Lord Chancellor's Department. The Courts Act 1971, for example, resulted in the financial management of many courts coming under the control of the Lord Chancellor's Department. Legal aid, involving the spending of considerable sums of public money, has been administered by the Lord Chancellor's Department since 1980, in the case of criminal legal aid, and since 1989, in the case of civil legal aid. In 1992 the Lord Chancellor became responsible for magistrates' courts which had, before then, been the responsibility of the Home Secretary.[60] "The requirements of judicial independence make the Lord Chancellor's Department wholly different from any other department of state", the then Vice-Chancellor, Sir Nicolas Browne-Wilkinson, argued in the late 1980s.[61] In the past the Department had been "wholly different", but by the end of the twentieth century it has become "the largest of the medium sized Departments", with 11,000 staff in 500 buildings and in, 1990–1, an expenditure of £1,078 million.[62]

The structural changes in the Lord Chancellor's Department and the consequent effect they have had on the work of the Lord Chancellor seem to be at least as plausible an explanation for the more Executive-minded approach of Lord Mackay as any personal inclinations on his part. The Lord Chancellor has myriad tasks and a billion pound budget. The needs of the judiciary are just one small part of this. A genuine but abstract belief in the importance of the independence of the judiciary might not prevent one's attention from being diverted by seemingly more pressing immediate needs or problems on a grander scale. The nature of the office may have become such as to drive a Lord Chancellor to be largely Executive-minded. If this is so, it strengthens the case for asking the question, can the office of Lord Chancellor continue to protect the independence of the judiciary in the way that it once did?

### CONCLUSION

Disentangling the various aspects of the Lord Chancellor's office is a complicated matter and falls outside the scope of this chapter. The judicial role is more limited, and how appropriate it is for the Lord Chancellor to carry on the different tasks contained within it can be assessed without detailed consideration of the other parts of the office.

If it is accepted that the Lord Chancellor's Department will continue at its present size, it is now difficult to justify the continuing role of the Lord Chancellor as a judge. The number of areas for which the Lord Chancellor has

---

[60] The growing tasks of the Lord Chancellor's Department are discussed in Stevens, n. 55 above, at 181 and Mackay, n. 22 above, at 1651 and in Mackay, n. 33 above, at 243–7.

[61] Sir Nicolas Browne-Wilkinson, "The Independence of the Judiciary in the 1980s" [1989] *PL* 44 at 48.

[62] Mackay, n. 22 above; Mackay, n. 33 above, at 245.

Executive responsibility grows apace. As it does, so the importance of the Lord Chancellor's Executive actions for other Cabinet colleagues also increases.[63] Inevitably the Lord Chancellor becomes more and more a member of the government and less and less a semi-detached figure. This further heightens the tension between the Lord Chancellor's position as a judge and that as a member of the Cabinet. Even if there is an advantage in the Minister who has responsibility for judges taking part in the work of the judges, and thus experiencing their difficulties at first hand, this advantage is outweighed by the damage of the spectacle of a political appointee who need have no judicial training taking part in the deliberations of the highest court at a time when there is considerable conflict between the courts and the government.

The Lord Chancellor's role as judge is dispensable. For the Lord Chancellor not to sit as a judge does not significantly alter the nature of the office. Lord Gardiner was not less of a Lord Chancellor by virtue of the comparative rarity of his appearances in the Appellate Committee of the House of Lords. The Lord Chancellor's role as being especially concerned with protecting the independence and integrity of the judiciary seems already to have been dispensed with. This is not to say that there is any evidence that either the present Lord Chancellor or the government in general has resiled from a belief in the desirability of these matters. Indeed one of Lord Irvine's earliest actions was to support the senior judiciary in their attempt to refuse to say whether or not they were Freemasons.[64] But the history of the last few years does not suggest that for either the present or past Lord Chancellor or for the present or past government the principles of judicial independence or integrity have been regarded as of paramount importance or have been at the forefront of their thinking. Independence sits uneasily with the current passion for accountability. A Lord Chancellor who has given "[o]ne of the most forceful warnings against the alleged vice of an assertive judiciary" may not be seen as the most forceful protector of that judiciary.[65] The judiciary is not the only institution which has had its traditional position questioned. Universities, which also claim autonomy and independence, have been put under similar, somewhat less gentle, pressure. In resisting this pressure the judiciary seems increasingly to have relied on its efforts rather than on any protection by the Lord Chancellor. When a serving Lord of Appeal in Ordinary, Lord Steyn, is reported as saying that the "[t]he proposition that a cabinet minister must be head of our judiciary in England is no longer sustainable on either constitutional or pragmatic grounds" the continued existence of the role mut be put in doubt.[66]

If the Lord Chancellor's role as a judge *should be* dispensed with, and if the Lord Chancellor's role as being especially concerned with the protection of the

---

[63] See, e.g., Lord Lawson's comments about Lord Mackay in N. Lawson, *The View From No. 11* (London, Bantam Press, 1992), at 620–4.

[64] *Observer*, 15 Nov. 1997; *Guardian*, 25 Nov. 1997.

[65] I. Loveland, "The War Against the Judges" (1997) 68 *Pol Q* 162 at 170.

[66] *Guardian*, 3 Dec. 1996.

judiciary *has been* dispensed with, there remains for consideration the Lord Chancellor's role in appointing and disciplining judges. There no longer remains any particular reason why this role should be retained in the hands of the Lord Chancellor. Senior judges are already amenable to discipline only by way of being dismissed through address by both Houses of Parliament.[67] There is no reason in principle why less senior judges should not be subject to being disciplined by other judges higher in the hierarchy rather than by a government minister. Similarly, the judiciary is in a better position to recommend or to make appointments to the Bench than is any Cabinet minister. The strongest objection to this arrangement would be the danger of the judiciary becoming a self-perpetuating oligarchy appointed without attention to merit. Independence always brings with it the danger of isolation and insularity. However, the Lord Chancellor's role in judicial appointments has not, to date, resulted in a judiciary notable for its width of social background or its representativeness of society in terms of gender or ethnic mix. There are no clear grounds for thinking that a judiciary selected by, or on the recommendation of, a judiciary would be any worse.

The fusion of judicial and executive role in the Lord Chancellor may once have served to provide a convenient means by which two organs of power in the state could communicate and co-operate. The evolution of the Lord Chancellor's role has meant that this is no longer the case. In 1975 Lord Hailsham observed that "[i]t is clear that the pressure on the independence of the judiciary is increasingly great".[68] Continuance of the Lord Chancellor's judicial role serves only to give rise to potential embarrassment and to prevent the establishment of new and more secure arrangements to preserve this independence in the future.

---

[67] Supreme Court Act 1981, s. 11(3).

[68] Lord Hailsham, *The Door Wherein I Went* (London, Collins, 1975), at 246.

# 9

# A Dualist House of Lords in a Sea of Monist Community Law?

## BARRY FITZPATRICK

### INTRODUCTION

This chapter will analyse the development of case law in the House of Lords on questions concerning the constitutional relationship between Community law and national law. First, some points on the traditional role of international law in United Kingdom law will be outlined. Secondly, the response of the European Court of Justice (ECJ) will be examined within the context of broad principles of monism and dualism. This will be followed by consideration of the case law of the House of Lords as the highest court in a common law system of law based upon dualism, but dealing with the legal principles of a Community legal system which has civilian roots and which has, through the ECJ's concept of Community law supremacy, adopted a partly monist approach towards the relationship between Community and national law.

### THE PAST: MONISM AND DUALISM IN UNITED KINGDOM LAW

Without entering into a detailed survey of these concepts, it is clear that the English legal system stands out as a primarily dualist system, although European influences may be gradually modifying the rigidity of this approach. By dualist, we mean a system of law in which international law and national are two separate systems. International treaty obligations can normally only become part of national law by means of transformation of the international obligation into national law by ordinary legislative procedures.[1] By contrast, a monist system treats international and national law as one system.[2] Hence international obligations which satisfy tests of "justiciability" may be invoked in national courts and may take precedence over conflicting national law.

---

[1] R. M. Wallace, *International Law* (3rd edn., London, Sweet and Maxwell, 1997), at 36.
[2] *Ibid.*

## Traditional Principles

The attitude of the English courts towards the significance of international obligations is focused upon the principle of legislative supremacy. Only Parliament can enact laws and the courts are bound to interpret but not override them. A classic statement of this approach can be found in the extraordinary case of *Madzimbamuto* v. *Lardner-Burke*, in which Madzimbamuto sought, before the Privy Council, to assert the applicability of the Southern Rhodesia Act 1965 in face of a unilateral declaration of independence by a Rhodesian government including Lardner-Burke.[3] Lord Reid said in this case:

> "It is often said that it would be unconstitutional for the United Kingdom Parliament to do certain things, meaning that the moral, political and other reasons against doing them are so strong that most people would regard it as highly improper if Parliament did these things. But that does not mean that it is beyond the power of Parliament to do these things. If Parliament chose to do any of them, the courts could not hold the Act of Parliament invalid."

It is therefore consistent with such an approach for *customary* rules of international law to be recognised in the *common* law,[4] but such common law recognition is overriden by a UK statute. A classic statement of this position can be found, ironically perhaps, given the civilian origins of the Scottish legal system, in the judgment of the High Court of Justiciary in *Mortensen* v. *Peters*.[5] A Norwegian sea captain was prosecuted for fishing in UK territorial waters. Mortensen claimed that the stretch of the Moray Firth at issue was, by way of customary principles, in international waters. Lord Kyllachy, in deciding that the UK Act was unambiguous, concluded:

> "A legislature may quite conceivably, by oversight or even design, exceed what an international tribunal (if such existed) might hold to be its international rights. Still, there is always a presumption against its intending to do so. . . . But then it is only a presumption; and, as such, it must always give way to the language used if it is clear, and also to all counter presumptions which may legitimately be had in view in determining, on ordinary principles, the true meaning and intent of the legislation. Express words will, of course, be conclusive, and so will plain implication."

As far as treaty-making is concerned, the Crown can enter into international obligations and is liable in international law for breaches of them, but it cannot by means of its treaty-making power create legislative measures binding upon English courts.[6] It naturally follows that, if Parliament should wish to legislate

---

[3] [1969] 1 AC 645 (PC), *per* Lord Reid. Examples of precedents for these constitutional principles are taken from M. Allen and B. Thompson, *Cases and Materials on Constitutional and Administrative Law* (4th edn., London, Blackstone Press, 1996).

[4] Wallace, n. 1 above, at 39.

[5] (1906) 14 SLT 227.

[6] "A treaty to which Her Majesty's Government is a party does not alter the laws of the United Kingdom. A treaty may be incorporated into and alter the laws of the United Kingdom by means of

contrary to a pre-existing international obligation, nothing, even in the statute which transformed the obligation in UK law, could stand in the way of the primacy of the later Act.[7]

Another facet of the dominance of legislative supremacy is reflected in the literal rule of statutory interpretation.[8] Most international obligations rarely impinge upon British litigation. However, it can be seen that a national law which transforms an international obligation may, in cases of ambiguity, be interpreted in the light of the international obligation.[9] Indeed, the European Convention of Human Rights appears to have taken on a special status, despite its lack of transformation.[10] With this possible exception, British law still adheres to a Diceyean view of legislative supremacy[11] in the face of international obligations. Indeed, given the status of the House of Lords as both a judicial and a legislative institution, this is hardly a surprising outcome.

THE PRESENT: HOW MONIST IS EUROPEAN COMMUNITY LAW?

## The Basic Structure of the Community Legal System

It cannot be said that the initial structure of the Community legal system was based upon a potentially monist relationship between Community law and national law. Certainly, the Treaty of Rome provided that regulations should be "directly applicable",[12] an indication that the provisions of regulations should

---

legislation. Except to the extent that a treaty becomes incorporated into the laws of the United Kingdom by statute, the courts of the United Kingdom have no power to enforce treaty rights and obligations at the behest of a sovereign government or at the behest of a private individual": *J. H. Rayner (Mincing Lane) Ltd* v. *Department of Trade and Industry (International Tin Council Case)* [1990] 2 AC 418 at 476 (HL), *per* Lord Templeman.

[7] "Once the Government has legislated, which it may do in anticipation of the coming into effect of the treaty . . . the court must in the first instance construe the legislation, for that is what the court has to apply. If the terms of legislation are clear and unambiguous they must be given effect to, whether they carry out Her Majesty's treaty obligations, for the sovereign power of the Queen in Parliament extends to breaking treaties": *Saloman* v. *Commissioners of Customs and Excise* [1967] 2 QB 116 (CA), *per* Diplock L.J. See also *Ellen Street Estates Limited* v. *Minister of Health* [1934] 1 KB 590 (CA).

[8] See Chap. 11 below.

[9] "But if the terms of the legislation are not clear but are reasonably capable of more than one meaning, the treaty itself becomes relevant, for there is a prima facie presumption that Parliament does not intend to act in breach of international law, including therein specific treaty obligations; and if one of the meanings which can be reasonably ascribed to the legislation is consonant with the treaty obligations and another or others are not, the meaning which is consonant will be preferred": *Saloman v Commissioners of Customs and Excise* [1967] 2 QB 116 (CA), *per* Diplock L.J.

[10] This proposition is accepted in *R.* v. *Secretary of State for the Home Department, ex p. Brind* [1991] 1 AC 696 (HL), *per* Lord Bridge, but then limited both in its substance to a "mere canon of construction" and in its scope to ambiguities in legislation rather than an implicit fetter upon administrative discretion.

[11] See generally J. McEldowney, *Public Law* (London, Sweet and Maxwell, 1994), at 23.

[12] Art. 189 EC (to become Art. 249 if the Treaty of Amsterdam is ratified) provides that "[a] regulation shall have general application. It shall be binding in its entirety and directly applicable in all Member States".

be automatically incorporated into national law. Perhaps, in 1957, the regulation was seen as the primary Community law instrument, and hence our assessment of monism within the system undervalues this perspective. But within the substantive provisions of the Treaty, only the provision of Article 85(2) that anti-competitive agreements should be "void" indicated that Treaty Articles might be directly applicable also. Other Treaty provisions are largely addressed to the Member States, indicating that these obligations were to be incorporated into national law in dualist fashion. This impression is strongly reinforced by the nature of directives, whereby a binding obligation is placed upon a Member State to legislate within a given period of time.[13] Both in relation to directives and also Treaty articles, it would appear that the Community obligations reside merely upon the shoulders of the Member States but that the effect of these obligations is felt only indirectly through national legislation. The enforcement of these obligations is then achieved through another strictly dualist mechanism, namely the action by the Commission under Article 169 (to become Article 226) against an allegedly recalcitrant Member State before the Court of Justice, which could only result in a declaration of no binding force against the Member State.[14] The basis upon which the ECJ could identify a breach of Community obligations can be traced back to Article 5 EC, which states:

> "Member States shall take all appropriate measures, whether general or particular, to ensure fulfilment of the obligations arising out of this Treaty or resulting from action taken by the institutions of the Community. They shall facilitate the achievement of the Community's tasks.
>
>   They shall abstain from any measure which could jeopardise the attainment of the objectives of this Treaty."

Hence, a cursory examination of the original Treaty would indicate a predominantly dualist relationship between Community and national law, subject to national constitutional traditions, some of which may be of a more monist nature[15]—but with elements of a more universal monist approach, in particular through the nature of regulations.

### The Direct Effect of Treaty Articles

The past 30 years have seen an intensification of these monist tendencies through the jurisprudence of the ECJ, although much of the original dualism remains intact, albeit with monist overtones. The starting point for this process

---

[13] Art. 189 EC also provides that "[a] directive shall be binding, as to the result to be achieved, upon each Member State to which it is addressed, but shall leave to the national authorities the choice of form and methods".

[14] Although such a declaration can now be augmented by a fine, imposed by the ECJ at the behest of the Commission, against a Member State which fails to abide by it (Art. 171(2), to become Art. 228(2) EC).

[15] See, e.g., Art. 25 of the German Constitution and Arts. 65 and 66 of the Dutch Constitution.

was, of course, the seminal judgment of the ECJ in Case 26/62 *van Gend en Loos*,[16] in which the Court identified as "directly effective" Article 12 of the Treaty, which prohibited increases in custom duties after the entry into force of the Treaty, what is known as a "standstill" provision. A directly effective provision of Community law is one which creates individual rights which national courts must protect. The implications of *van Gend en Loos*, reinforced the following year by Case 6/64 *Costa* v. *ENEL*,[17] were profound. Not only was this standstill provision sufficiently precise (today we would say "justiciable"[18]) to be enforced in national law, hence bestowing upon this, and then many other Treaty Articles, the equivalent effect to that of at least a regulation. The Court also declared that a limitation of national sovereignty had occurred through the Treaty and that directly effective Treaty norms took precedence over conflicting national provisions. In *van Gend en Loos*, the Court stated:

> "the Community constitutes a new legal order of international law for the benefit of which the states have limited their sovereign rights, albeit within limited fields, and the subjects of which comprise not only Member States but also their nationals. Independently of the legislation of Member States, Community law therefore not only imposes obligations on individuals but is also intended to confer upon them rights which become part of their legal heritage. These rights arise not only where they are expressly granted by the Treaty, but also by reason of obligations which the Treaty imposes in a clearly defined way upon individuals as well as upon the Member States and upon the institutions of the Community."

Indeed, the approach in *Costa*, concerning the compatibility with Community law, of Italian law nationalising the electricity supply industry, was more dogmatic:

> "The integration into the laws of each Member State of provisions which derive from the Community . . . make it impossible for the States, as a corollary, to accord precedence to a unilateral and subsequent measure over a legal system accepted by them on a basis of reciprocity. . . . The executive force of Community law cannot vary from one State to another in deference to subsequent domestic laws, without jeopardising the attainment of the objectives of the Treaty set out in Article 5(2)."

The focus of this strongly monist approach to the relationship between Community and national law was therefore Article 5 EC. The national courts, as a part of the Member State, were under an equal duty with that of other elements of the State to ensure that Community obligations were satisfied. This was stated most forcefully by the Court in *Simmenthal*,[19] concerning the obligation upon an Italian judge to refer apparently unconstitutional statutes to the Constitutional Court:

---

[16] *van Gend en Loos* v. *Nederlands Administratie der Belastingen* [1963] ECR 1. Amongst many texts on the development of Community constitutional law, see J Shaw, *Law of the European Union* (2nd edn., Basingstoke, Macmillan, 1996).

[17] [1964] ECR 585.

[18] P. Pescatore, "The Doctrine of 'Direct Effect': An Infant Disease of Community Law" (1983) 8 *ELR* 155.

[19] Case 106/77 *Amministrazione delle Finanze dello Stato* v. *Simmenthal* [1978] ECR 629.

"any provision of a national legal system and any legislative, administrative, or judicial practice which might impair the effectiveness of Community law by withholding from the national court having jurisdiction to apply such law the power to do everything necessary at the moment of its application to set aside national provisions which might prevent Community rules from having full force and effect are incompatible with those requirements which are the very essence of Community law."

On a spectrum between dualism and monism, the direct effect of Treaty Articles therefore reflected an appreciably more monist approach. It also commenced a process which has elevated the status of the Treaty, as amended, into the realms of a purported "Constitution for Europe"[20] and established an exclusive relationship between supremacy and direct effect which has only recently been modified. Given its central role and also its largely determined nature, a monist approach to the enforcement of the Treaty in national law has not proved to be a source of profound controversy.[21]

## The Direct Effect of Directives

However, to finesse an element of monism into the effect of the strictly dualist instrument of the directive has been a very different exercise. Whether on the technical ground that a directive leaves discretion to Member States, at least as to its outcome, or upon the more ideological ground that a directive, by its nature and unlike a regulation, requires national legislation, it would seem to follow from the structure of the Community legal system that directives are immune from direct effect.

Such considerations did not deter the ECJ from declaring in cases such as *van Duyn*[22] that a sufficiently precise provision of a directive could, after the deadline in a directive had passed, create "similar effects" to those of a regulation, namely individual rights which overrode conflicting national provisions. Given what was by then taken to be the inherently monist nature of a regulation and given the direct effect of many fundamental Treaty Articles, the potential direct

---

[20] F. Mancini, "The Making of a Constitution for Europe" (1989) 26 *CMLRev*. 595.

[21] At least outside the scope of fundamental rights in the German, and also the Italian, Constitutions. See Case 11/70 *Internationale Handelsgesellschaft mbH* v. *Einfuhr- und Vorratsstelle für Getreide und Futtermittel* [1970] ECR 1125 and Case 106/77 *Simmenthal*. See, however, H. Rasmussen, *On Law and Policy in the European Court of Justice* (Dordrecht, Martinus Nijhoff, 1986).

[22] Case 41/74 *Van Duyn* v. *Home Office* [1974] ECR 1337: "If, however, by virtue of the provisions of Article 189 regulations are directly applicable and, consequently, may by their very nature have direct effects, it does not follow from this that other categories of acts mentioned in that Article can never have similar effects. It would be incompatible with the binding effect attributed to a directive by Article 189 to exclude, in principle, the possibility that the obligation which it imposes may be invoked by those concerned. In particular, where the Community authorities have, by directive, imposed on Member States the obligation to pursue a particular course of conduct, the useful effect of such an act would be weakened if individuals were prevented from relying on it before their national courts and if the latter were prevented from taking it into consideration as an element of Community law."

effect of some provisions in directives appeared to accelerate the process of imposing monist principles upon the Community/national law relationship even within the apparently dualist realm of the enforcement of directives. Here the Court's advances met serious resistance.[23] While some controversies over Community law supremacy have received an unequivocal response from the Court, the universal direct effect of directives proved to be "a monist principle too far". Ironically, given the public law nature of the recalcitrant national courts, the ECJ rationalised any direct effect for directives on the basis of an "estoppel" principle that only the Member States could not be allowed to rely in their own courts upon national laws which they ought to have amended.[24] In the case of *Marshall* Miss Marshall had been "retired" by an Area Health Authority at the age of sixty-two, although a male in a similar position would not have been dismissed until he was sixty-five. She successfully relied upon the direct effect of Article 5 of the Equal Treatment Directive 1976.[25] Hence, in that case, the Court concluded that directives could only have "vertical direct effect" against emanations of the State and not "horizontal direct effect" against private parties.[26]

This reversal reflects a significant modification of the Court's drive towards monist solutions. Within the increasingly vital arena of directives, a monism with renewed dualist overtones has emerged.[27] The directive can override national law but only against the "contracting party", the Member State, an outcome which preserves elements of monism but which is much more in keeping with dualist traditions (and with the originally perceived role of a directive).

[23] *Minister of the Interior* v. *Cohn-Bendit* [1980] 1 CMLR 543 (French *Conseil d'Etat*); *Re VAT Directives* [1982] 1 CMLR 527 (*Bundesfinanzhof*).

[24] Case 148/78 *Pubblico Ministero* v. *Ratti* [1979] ECR 1629: "Consequently a Member State which has not adopted the implementing measures required by the directive in the prescribed periods may not rely, as against individuals, on its own failure to perform the obligations which the directive entails."

[25] She could not rely upon the Sex Discrimination Act 1975 because s. 6(4) excluded from the operation of the employment provisions of the Act "provisions relating to death or retirement".

[26] Case 152/84 *Marshall* v. *Southampton and South West Hampshire Area Health Authority (Teaching)* [1986] ECR 723: "wherever the provisions of a directive appear, as far as their subject-matter is concerned, to be unconditional and sufficiently precise, those provisions may be relied upon by an individual against the State where that State fails to implement the directive in national law by the end of the period prescribed or where it fails to implement the directly correctly.

With regard to the argument that a directive may not be relied upon against an individual, it must be emphasised that according to Article 189 of the EEC Treaty the binding nature of a directive, which constitutes the basis for the possibility of relying upon the directive before a national court, exists only in relation to 'each Member State to which it is addressed'. It follows that a directive may not of itself impose obligations on an individual and that a provision of a directive may not be relied upon as such against such a person."

[27] Strictly for the purpose of this chap., a Eurocentric distinction is drawn between a more dualist approach which endeavours to restrict the scope of external norms to liability on the part of the State, albeit in municipal law, and a more monist approach, which seeks to include liability of private parties within the scope of international obligations. This latter scenario will rarely be at issue in public international law, given the nature of the obligations, but is an issue of vital concern within the Community legal order. In this sense, a more monist approach would promote an integrationalist approach towards the relationship between Community and national law. A dualist approach would preserve national autonomy even in the face of inconsistency with Community principles.

A directive, by definition, brings about two sets of laws, the Community law in the directive and the national implementing measure. To some extent, the Court appears to be respecting the legitimate expectations of private parties in their national law at the expense of the uniform application of the directive.

Sustained pressure[28] has led to a reappraisal by the ECJ of this vertical/horizontal direct effect distinction which has nevertheless been dogmatically reiterated[29] on the basis that directives cannot, by their nature, create obligations upon private parties, a reassertion of this dualist approach towards the essentially monist device of direct effect, albeit in relation to the essentially dualist instrument of the directive. On the other hand, the Court has taken a broad view of what is an "emanation of the State" for the purpose of the direct effect of directives.[30] In Case C–188/89 *Foster* v. *British Gas*,[31] the Court was concerned with the pre-privatised British Gas. Any organisation could come within the scope of direct effect within the following terms:

> "unconditional and sufficiently precise provisions of a directive could be relied on against organisations or bodies which were subject to the authority or control of the State or had special powers beyond those which result from the normal rules applicable to relations between individuals."

So, within the fluctuating fortunes of more monist and more dualist approaches towards direct effect, the Court has tempered the dualist conclusion that direct effect of directives only applies to emanations of the State with yet another monist overtone, that the State must be widely interpreted. Nevertheless, our question upon the extent of monism within Community law cannot even yet be answered. The relationship between Community and national law has been given further binding aspects by the Court through the principles of indirect effect and State liability, in each case based upon the imperatives of Article 5 EC and involving elements of monism but also surviving elements of dualism.

---

[28] See, in particular, the Opinions of Van Gerven A.G. in Case C–271/91 *Marshall* v. *Southampton and South West Hampshire Area Health Authority (Teaching)* [1993] ECR I–4367, Jacobs A.G. in Case C–316/93 *Vaneetveld* v. *Le Foyer* [1994] ECR I–763 and of Lenz A.G. in Case C–91/92 *Faccini Dori* v. *Recreb Srl* [1994] ECR I–3325.

[29] Case C–91/92 *Faccini Dori* v. *Recreb Srl.* See T. Tridimas, Note on *Faccini Dori*, (1994) 19 ELR 621–36.

[30] Indeed one argument for the abandonment of the vertical/horizontal direct effect distinction is that this *Foster* definition is so wide as to include many organisations of a semi-public (or even privatised) nature and to undermine the rationale for restricting direct effect to the State "responsible" for the failure of implementation. See Joined Cases C–253–258/96 *Kampelmann* v. *Landschaftsverband Westfalen-Lippe* [1998] IRLR 333, in which the Court included within the "emanation of the State" formula "bodies which, irrespective of their legal form, have been given responsibility, by the public authorities and under their supervision, for providing a public service".

[31] [1990] ECR I–3133.

### Indirect Effect

First, the Court requires that the interpretation of national law should be in the light of relevant directives. This process, known as indirect effect, because the Community obligation is reaching the national legal system indirectly through interpretation of the national law, is less controversial than direct effect.[32] The purpose of a directive is to bring about implementing legislation and even a strictly dualist system such as the UK's is not totally averse to taking an international obligation into account when interpreting a UK statute which transformed the international obligation in UK law.

However, the Court has overlaid this largely dualist approach with more monist elements. Although the Court's case law was initially ambiguous,[33] it is now clear that all national legislation, whether or not specifically implementing a directive, must be reinterpreted in the light of the relevant provisions of the directive. So also the Court's test for indirect effect is one based upon reinterpretation, *as far as possible*, in conformity with the directive.[34] A vital consideration is the extent to which national legislation must be radically reinterpreted in the light of a directive. On the one hand, a prevalent view is that the reinterpretation cannot be *contra legem*,[35] based upon a notion that the citizen will have legitimate expectations in the validity of the national law and that these expectations would be frustrated if a radical reinterpretation occurred. Once again, we have complications brought about by the two levels of law which

[32] B. Fitzpatrick, "The Significance of EEC Directives in UK Sex Discrimination Law" (1989) 9 *OJLS* 336. The author first coined the phrase "indirect effect" in a review of the Sex Discrimination Act 1986, (1987) 50 *MLR* 934.

[33] Case 14/83 *von Colson and Kamann* v. *Land Nordrhein-Westfalen* and Case 79/83 *Harz* v. *Deutsche Tradax* [1984] ECR 1891. Von Colson and Kamann had been discriminated against on the grounds of their sex contrary to Art. 3 of the Equal Treatment Directive 1976 by a regional authority responsible for a prison. German law provided only very limited compensation in such circumstances. First the Court concluded that Art. 6 of the 1976 Directive required effective remedies but was not sufficiently precise to give a directly effective right to an effective remedy. Then it established an alternative approach: "[h]owever, the Member States' obligation arising from a directive to achieve the result envisaged by the directive and their duty under Article 5 of the Treaty to take all appropriate measures, whether general or particular, to ensure the fulfilment of that obligation, is binding on all authorities of the Member States including, for matters within their jurisdiction, the courts. It follows that, in applying the national law *and in particular the provisions of a national law specifically introduced in order to implement Directive* No. 76/207, national courts are required to interpret their national law in the light of the wording and the purpose of the directive in order to achieve the result referred to in the third paragraph of Article 189" (emphasis added).

[34] Case C–106/89 *Marleasing SA* v. *La Comercial Internacional de Alimentacion SA* [1990] ECR I–4135 in which a Spanish court referred to the ECJ the question whether the Spanish Civil Code, which had not been amended upon Spain's accession to the Community to take account of Directive 68/151, a company law directive, should be interpreted in conformity with the directive. The Court (6th Chamber) replied: "in applying national law, whether the provisions concerned pre-date or post-date the directive, the national court asked to interpret national law is bound to do so in every way possible in the light of the text and the aim of the directive to achieve the results envisaged by it". See C. Docksey and B. Fitzpatrick, "The Duty of National Courts to Interpret Provisions of National Law in Accordance with Community Law" (1991) 20 *ILJ* 113.

[35] See Van Gerven A.G. in *Marshall (No. 2)*, n. 28 above, at 4386.

directives, by definition, create. On the other hand, the ECJ has also more recently moved away from the view that Community law creates rights only through direct effect. Rather, the rights are created autonomously through Community measures and it is then a question of giving full effect to them.[36] On this basis, it can be argued that Community norms take precedence over national norms in every situation. Since it is the national law which is contrary to the Community law, it is arguable that radical reinterpretation of the national law in the light of the superior Community law should be the common response.[37] A further heightening of the significance of indirect effect can be detected in the later case of *Wagner Miret*,[38] once again concerning non-implementation, this time in Spain, of the Insolvency Directive 1980. Here the Court developed a presumption that any national law within the sphere of the provisions of a directive was intended to implement the relevant directive, thereby intensifying pressures for re-interpretation.

Hence, we can see, even within the realms of the dualist task interpreting "transforming" legislation, the Court has imposed monist conditions which, to some extent, shift the focus from the national law being interpreted to the Community directive upon which the national law is, or ought to be, based.

### State Liability

Secondly, the Court is developing a new jurisprudence to ensure enforcement of Community law in national law. The first indication of this new thinking could be seen in Case C–213/89 *R. v. Secretary of State for Transport, ex p. Factortame (No. 2)*.[39] Here, although the House asked a question concerning a Community obligation to create a *new* remedy in national law (an injunction against the Crown), the ECJ chose to treat the question as one of surmounting an obstacle to the utilisation of an *existing* remedy and hence converted the question into one of direct effect. However, in *Francovich* v. *Italian State* and *Bonifaci* v. *Italian State*, the Court was considering a failure by Italy to implement Directive 80/987 on the protection of employees in the event of the

---

[36] Cases C–6/90 and C–9/90 *Francovich* v. *Italian State* and *Bonifaci* v. *Italian State* [1991] ECR I–5357: "It must be recalled . . . that the EEC Treaty has created its own legal order, integrated into the legal systems of the Member States and which is binding on their courts whose subjects are not only the Member States, but equally their nationals, and that, although it creates obligations on individuals, Community law also creates rights which form part of their legal heritage; these rights arise not only when explicit reference is made to them by the Treaty, but also by reason of the obligations which the Treaty clearly imposes as much on individuals as on member States and on Community institutions. It should equally be recalled that, just as it follows from established case law, it falls to the national courts, entrusted to apply, within the framework of their jurisdiction, the provisions of Community law, to ensure the full effect of those legal norms and to protect the rights which they confer on individuals". See M. Ross, "Beyond Francovich" (1993) 56 *MLR* 55.

[37] It is significant that the Court adopted this individual rights approach in *Dori* (note 29 above) to the provisions of a directive which it had decided did not themselves create direct effect.

[38] Case C–334/92 *Wagner Miret* v. *Fondo de garantia salarial* [1993] ECR I–691.

[39] [1990] ECR I–2433.

insolvency of their employer which resulted in Francovich and Bonifaci failing to receive a payment from a guarantee fund which ought to have been established in accordance with the provisions of the directive. The Court, once again invoking Article 5 EC, concluded that Community law empowered an individual, who had suffered a loss as a consequence of the non-implementation by a Member State of its Community obligations, to sue the Member State in damages for recovery of that loss, irrespective of any existing cause of action in national law. The Court stated:

> "the full effectiveness of Community provisions would be jeopardised and the protection of the rights they recognise would be weakened if individuals did not have the possibility to obtain compensation when their rights are infringed by a breach of Community law attributable to a Member State. . . . It follows that the principle of the liability of the state for damage caused to individuals by breaches of Community law for which it is responsible is inherent in the scheme of the Treaty."

Here, we once again find the ambivalent relationship between monism and dualism which we have come to expect within the Community legal system. On the one hand, State liability is a strongly monist cause of action in that Community law norms are intruding directly into the national systems which must accommodate them, if need be, through the conception of a new cause of action in national law. On the other, within the parameters which have been set in this chapter, it can also be seen as a dualist concept, in that the focus is upon *State* liability rather than that of private parties and indeed an emphasis upon State liability is capable of deflecting attention from the potential liability of private parties through direct and indirect effect.

Nevertheless, questions of State responsibility and the potentially enormous financial consequences are matters of some sensitivity, particularly before a Court more aware of State perspectives than in the past. Hence, it is hardly surprising that there has been a withdrawal by the Court from some of the wider implications of its *Francovich* ruling. In Joined Cases C–46/93 and C–48/93 *Brasserie du Pêcheur SA* v. *Federal Republic of Germany*; *R*. v. *Secretary of State for Transport, ex p. Factortame Ltd and Others*,[40] the Court ruled that State liability could apply to breaches by a Member State of Articles 30 and 59 EC, in *Brasserie du Pêcheur*, composition rules of German beer and, in *Factortame*, nationality, residence and domicile requirements on fishing companies through the Merchant Shipping Act 1988. Nonetheless, the Court concluded that where the Member State has a broad discretion how to act, only *sufficiently serious* breaches of Community law justify an action in damages against the State. Neverthless, total non-implementation of a Community obligation, for example in a directive, would be treated as an automatically manifest breach.[41] Hence, ironically because of its dualist aspects, this essentially monist cause of

---

[40] [1996] ECR I–1029.
[41] Joined Cases C–178/94, C–179/94, C–188/94, C–189/94 and C–190/94 *Erich Dillenkofer and others* v. *Federal Republic of Germany* [1996] ECR I–4845.

action has been seriously diluted by the Court and its function as a "cement" in the system of Community law enforcement, "bridging the gaps" left by deficiencies in direct and indirect effect, has been compromised.

### The ECJ—An Appraisal

The final picture is a patchwork of influences and outcomes. The original structure of the Community legal system is much less monist than might have been expected by a common law commentator. Certainly, the regulation appears to be a monist instrument but the focus of the relationship between Community and national law appears to be the laborious process of bringing an Article 169 action against the Member State. Only since Maastricht has this thoroughly dualist device been augmented by a power to fine recalcitrant Member States which disregard ECJ rulings under Article 169. Hence, on a sliding scale of one (purely dualist) to ten (monism amounting to full-blown federal relationship), the Community legal system, as originally envisaged, comes in at about three.

Clearly the advent of direct effect of Treaty articles was the high-water mark of a more monist approach in the Court. This development, in itself, can bring the Community legal system up two places to position five on our scale. More recent developments, although by and large intensifying the monist (and in EU terms, federalist) momentum of Community integration, are not without their equivocations.

The dramatic conclusion that directives might also have direct effect might have sent our assessment shooting up towards eight or nine but its restriction to direct effect against the State is a more cautious reassertion of dualist values, leaving us back at about six. Both indirect effect and State liability enhance the supremacy of Community law over national law. Radical indirect effect would achieve most of, if not more than, what horizontal direct effect could provide, but a reassertion of national values of interpretation could set that prospect back. So also with State liability, while autonomous causes of action in national law are clearly of a monist nature, the focus of the action is upon State liability rather than the universal application of Community law to both public and private parties. Indeed, the existence of State liability may inhibit the prospects of horizontal direct effect and even of radical indirect effect, thereby retarding, to some extent, the progress already made towards a monist, and hence quasi-federal, system of Community law enforcement. A "strict liability" approach towards State liability would doubtless trigger a higher score on our spectrum, perhaps up to eight or nine, but the limitations placed upon State liability by the Court have once again brought the final assessment back downwards.

Hence, the House of Lords cannot be said to be sailing into a "sea of monist Community law". The system deserves perhaps a mark of seven out of ten, no mean challenge for the highest court in such a strictly dualist system as that of the United Kingdom, but not a system of such unbending monism as to confound their Lordships' more traditional instincts.

THE PRESENT: THE EFFECTIVENESS OF COMMUNITY LAW IN UK LAW

In considering the response of the House of Lords to this extensive case law of the ECJ, we should first look at the broad question of Community law supremacy in the context of direct effect, and then of indirect effect, and of State liability. In this context, we might also bear in mind that the House has for over a century been the supreme arbiter upon the law of the UK. Not only has it had to come to terms with the principles of a fundamentally civilian legal system, it has also had to reconcile itself with a diminution of its role in favour of the overriding authority of the ECJ.

## The Legislative Context

The European Communities Act 1972, section 2(1), in convoluted language, introduces "directly effective" Community law into the UK legal system:

> "All such rights, powers, liabilities, obligations and restrictions from time to time created or arising by or under the Treaties, and all such remedies and procedures from time to time provided for by or under the Treaties, as in accordance with the Treaties are without further enactment to be given legal effect or used in the United Kingdom[,] shall be recognised and available in law, and be enforced, allowed and followed accordingly."[42]

This sub-section is meant to provide that directly effective laws, which require no further enactment, are to be enforced in UK law. Section 2(2) allows for delegated legislation by Order in Council or by regulations to implement Community obligations into UK law. Buried at the heart of section 2(4) is an attempt to ensure that Community law shall be given precedence over UK law, even if passed after 1972:

> "The provision that may be made under subsection (2) above includes, subject to Schedule 2 of this Act, any such provision (of any such extent) as might be made by Act of Parliament, and *any enactment passed or to be passed*, other than one contained in this Act, *shall be construed and have effect subject to the foregoing provisions of this section*; but, except as may be provided by any Act passed after this Act, Schedule 2 shall have effect in connection with the powers conferred by this and the following sections of this Act to make Orders in Council and regulations" (emphasis added).

---

[42] A comma has been added in brackets to give some sense to this extraordinarily worded provision.

Finally, section 3(1) of the Act seeks to require UK courts to abide by ECJ rulings:

> "For the purposes of all legal proceedings any question as to the meaning or effect of any of the Treaties, or as to the validity, meaning or effect of any Community instrument, shall be treated as a question of law and, if not referred to the European Court, be for determination as such in accordance with the principles laid down by and any relevant decision of the European Court."

It can therefore be argued that Parliament was aware of the 1960's case law of the ECJ on Community law supremacy, which we have already considered, and also that it was requiring all UK courts, including the House of Lords, to abide by ECJ rulings.

In rather stereotyped fashion, we could set out responses of the traditional UK constitutional lawyer and the more Eurocentric constitutional lawyer as follows:

|  | *traditional approach* | *European approach* |
|---|---|---|
| s. 2(1) | delegated power to EC Institutions | limitation of sovereignty in favour of directly effective EC law |
| s. 2(4) | later Acts should be interpreted in conformity with EC law but later Act still impliedly repeals ECA | recognition of supremacy of EC law over later UK legislation |
| s. 3(1) | respect ECJ rulings in interpretation but neither Parliament nor ECJ can limit legislative supremacy | acknowledgement of case law of ECJ upon EC law supremacy |

Hence, we find here an ambivalence towards the "monism" of Community law, as much precipitated by the political realities of the House of Commons in 1972 as by an inherent caution towards the implications of Community membership.

### The Direct Effect of Treaty Articles

A constant theme of the UK case law upon EC constitutional questions has been the question of the compatibility of UK equal opportunities legislation, the Equal Pay Act 1970 and the Sex Discrimination Act 1975,[43] with Article 119 EC,[44] which is directly effective both vertically and horizontally, and the Equal

---

[43] In fact the implementation of the 1970 Act was delayed to allow employers time to modify their payment structures and it was eventually enacted as a Schedule to the 1975 Act.

[44] Art. 119 EC at present states: "[e]ach Member State shall during the first stage ensure and subsequently maintain the application of the principle that men and women should receive equal pay for equal work".

Treatment in Working Conditions Directive 1976, which, of course, only has vertical direct effect. The first opportunity for the House of Lords to consider the direct effect of Treaty provisions came in relation to an Article 119 case, *Garland* v. *British Rail Engineering Ltd.*[45] In response to an ECJ ruling that Mrs Garland had a directly effective right to travel facilities for herself and her family, the House of Lords chose to follow an indirect effect route in order to protect her Community right.[46] Lord Diplock's approach was to disregard the direct effect of Article 119 and rely instead upon a relatively radical form of re-interpretation of the 1975 Act.[47] He stated:

> "it is a principle of construction of United Kingdom statutes, now too well established to call for citation of authority, that the words of a statute passed after the Treaty has been signed and dealing with the subject matter of the international obligations of the United Kingdom, are to be construed, if they are reasonably capable of bearing such a meaning, as intended to carry out the obligation, and not to be inconsistent with it."[48]

Hence, we find a quite broad application of the fundamentally dualist approach of reinterpretation in order to satisfy the monist demands of direct effect but without the adoption of a more monist approach.

Such a pragmatic approach could not cope with controversies which enveloped the Merchant Shipping Act 1988, and regulations passed under it, which sought to restrict the ownership of fishing boats fishing for the UK's Community fishing quota to those which had British nationality and domicile (normally living in the UK). In *R.* v *Secretary of State for Transport, ex p. Factortame Ltd and Others*,[49] a Spanish fishing company sought an injunction to stop the UK authorities enforcing the Act against it, on the ground that the 1988 Act contravened a series of directly effective Treaty Articles. In *Factortame*, Lord Bridge concluded, after citing section 2(1) and (4) of the European Communities Act 1972:

> "This has precisely the same effect as if a section were incorporated in Part II of the Act of 1988 which in terms enacted that the provisions with respect to registration of

---

[45] [1983] 2 AC 751. It is interesting to note that it took a period of 10 years' membership of the Community before the House of Lords was called upon to rule on a constitutional aspect of the Community/national law relationship. It was perhaps appropriate that a stark confrontation over such constitutional questions was avoided in the early years of membership. Compare Lord Denning in *Felixstowe Dock and Railway Company* v. *British Transport Docks Board* [1976] CMLR 655 (CA): "[i]t seems to me that once the Bill is passed by Parliament and becomes a Statute that will dispose of all discussion of the Treaty. These courts will have to abide by the Statute without regard to the Treaty at all".

[46] Her case was brought under the Sex Discrimination Act 1975 rather than the Equal Pay Act 1970 because her claim concerned a non-contractual benefit which did not come within the scope of the equality clause implied into her contract of employment by the 1970 Act.

[47] As with others after her, Mrs Garland's case was apparently excluded from the operation of the 1975 Act through the "provisions relating to death and retirement" exception in s. 6(4) of the Act.

[48] It was therefore possible to treat Mrs Garland's case as being one concerning a continuation of employment benefits *after* retirement rather than a case *about* retirement itself.

[49] [1990] 2 AC 85 (HL).

British fishing vessels were to be without prejudice to the directly enforceable Community rights of nationals of any member state of the EEC."

*Factortame* reflects the virtually total adoption by the House of a monist approach towards Community law supremacy, much in keeping with the absolute nature of the ECJ's case law on the subject, thereby untying the "Gordian knot" of legislative ambivalence which had beset the enactment of the European Communities Act 1972. One issue was, at least technically, "left to another day", namely the issue of what might be called "express repudiation". In *Macarthys* v. *Smith*,[50] the Court of Appeal took a much more conciliatory approach to the reconciliation of Community and national law than that exhibited in *Felixstowe Dock*.[50a] Smith established before the ECJ that she had a directly effective right under Article 119 to be receive equal pay to a man employed before her. While examining the Equal Pay Act 1970, Lord Denning then concluded:

> "In construing our statute, we are entitled to look to the Treaty as an aid to its construction, and even more, not only as an aid but as an overriding force. If on close examination it should appear that our legislation is deficient—or is inconsistent with Community law—by some oversight of our draftsmen—then it is our bounden duty to give priority to Community law. Such is the result of section 2(1) and (4) of the European Communities Act 1972.
>
> I pause here, however, to make one observation on a constitutional point. Thus far I have assumed that our Parliament, whenever it passes legislation, intends to fulfil its obligations under the Treaty. If the time should come when our Parliament deliberately passes an Act—with the intention of repudiating the Treaty or any provision in it—or intentionally of acting inconsistently with it—and says so in express terms—then I should have thought that it would be the duty of our courts to follow the statute of our Parliament. I do not envisage such a situation."

*Macarthys* represents a bold assertion of monist values coupled with an awkward residual dualism, refusing, even within the realms of a Eurocentric approach, to let slip the last traces of traditional constitutional theory. It is not entirely clear whether *Factortame* is a final assertion of a European approach that Parliament cannot legislate contrary to Community law or is merely a restatement of the "express repudiation" approach, whereby, if Parliament were to pass an Act "with the intention of repudiating the Treaty or any provision of it", Lord Bridge's implied section would not withstand such an express repudiation. In the context of the *Factortame* saga, we would have to envisage a precarious coalition of MPs successfully, at least in terms of parliamentary procedure, extricating the UK from the Community's common fisheries policy. Only in such circumstances would any role for a residual dualism be tested. When *Factortame (No. 2)*[51] returned to House after the ECJ reference Lord Bridge was, if anything, more categorical:

[50]   [1979] ICR 785 (CA).
[50a]   See note 45 above.
[51]   [1991] 1 AC 603 (HL).

"Under the terms of the 1972 Act it has always been clear that it was the duty of a United Kingdom court, when delivering final judgment, to override any rule of national law found to be in conflict with any directly enforceable rule of Community law."

Hence, on this central question of the direct effect of Treaty Articles, the House of Lords has dramatically cast off its dualist roots and embraced most, if not all, of the ECJ's monism.

## The Direct Effect of Directives

The contentious question before the House concerning the direct effect of directives has not been upon the concept of direct effect itself but rather upon the scope of vertical direct effect. We saw earlier that the Court has sought to add monist overtones to the more dualist distinction between vertical and horizontal direct effect by broadening the range of organisations which satisfy the "emanation of the State" definition. When *Foster* v. *British Gas*,[52] another *Marshall* case based upon discriminatory retiring ages, returned to the House of Lords, its application might have brought into focus a latent anxiety that a wide definition of the State would encompass organisations which might not traditionally be considered to be State bodies. While the ECJ appeared to set out three disjunctive criteria whereby an emanation of the State could be satisfied, their Lordships chose to focus upon the narrower ground upon which the ECJ had finally ruled in *Foster*.[53] The ECJ appeared almost to be saying that if an organisation was not strictly private, then it must be quasi-public. The House restricted itself to consideration of the operative part of the Court's judgment, but, in doing so, rejected any attempt to give the ECJ ruling a narrow interpretation. The outcome, in the terms of this chapter, was that while the House remained silent upon the monist overtones which the Court had put upon the vertical/horizontal direct effect distinction, it nevertheless faithfully applied the ECJ's ruling.

## Indirect Effect

Given its dualist traditions, it is perhaps surprising that the House has had greater difficulty with indirect than with direct effect. This may be because national courts, once reconciled with Community law supremacy, can accept

---

[52] [1991] 2 AC 306.

[53] [1990] ECR I–3133. The Court had concluded in *Foster* that vertical direct effect should, in any event, apply to "a body, whatever its legal form, which has been made responsible, pursuant to a measure adopted by the state, for providing a public service under the control of the state and has for that purpose special powers beyond those which result from the normal rules applicable in relations between individuals".

the incisive role of direct effect more easily than the more insidious role of indirect effect in bringing about reinterpretation of the very national law with which the national courts are more familiar. It may also be the case in the UK courts that, in their dualist tradition, they have no point of comparison with direct effect, whilst they can compare their approach to the indirect effect of Community law with their approach to the similar effect of international obligations.

It was once again in the field of equal opportunities that the controversy arose, indeed, as with *Foster* v. *British Gas*, at the cutting edge of the vertical/horizontal direct effect distinction. The ECJ, on reference from the Court of Appeal, had concluded that discriminatory retiring ages contravened Article 5 of the Equal Treatment Directive 1976, which was directly effective, albeit only vertically.[54] While Mrs Foster had sought to establish that her employer was within the scope of "emanation of the State", Mrs Duke was in no position to do so, having been dismissed by GEC Reliance. In *Duke* v. *GEC Reliance Systems Ltd*,[55] the House of Lords refused on two grounds to "re-interpret" section 6(4) of the Sex Discrimination Act 1975 in favour of a private sector woman discriminated against in similar circumstances to Miss Marshall. The first was that indirect effect applied only to *implementing* legislation[56] and hence could not apply to the 1975 UK Act which *predated* the 1976 directive. The second was that a UK court was not bound to "distort" the meaning of the statute in order to bring it into conformity with the terms of the directive. To this effect, Lord Templeman stated:

> "On hearing this appeal, your Lordships have had the advantage, not available to Lord Diplock,[57] of full argument which has satisfied me that the Sex Discrimination Act 1975 was not intended to give effect to the Equal Treatment Directive as subsequently construed in the *Marshall* case and that the words of section 6(4) are not reasonably capable of being limited to the meaning ascribed to them by the appellant. Section 2(4) of the European Communities Act 1972 does not in my opinion enable or constrain a British court to distort the meaning of a British statute in order to enforce against an individual a Community directive which has no direct effect between individuals."

Here we find a strong reassertion of dualist values. First, reinterpretation would only be considered in relation to an "enacted" international obligation. Secondly, the primacy of the UK statute could not be questioned. Some ambiguities might be reconciled but the traditional approach towards statutory interpretation would be largely preserved.

This traditionalist approach in *Duke* was dramatically reversed in yet another equal opportunities case, *Pickstone* v. *Freemans plc*,[58] concerning Article 119

---

[54] See Case 152/84 *Marshall* v. *Southampton and South West Hampshire Area Health Authority (Teaching)* [1986] ECR 723.

[55] [1988] AC 618 (HL).

[56] This was a narrow reading of Case 14/83 *von Colson*, n. 33 above.

[57] In *Garland* v. *British Rail Engineering Ltd* [1983] 2 AC 751.

[58] [1989] AC 66.

EC and the Equal Pay Directive 1975[59] on equal pay irrespective of sex. Here the applicant was seeking to compare herself with a man doing a different job but one which she claimed to be of equal value with hers. A technicality of the 1970 Act, as amended by the Equal Pay (Amendment) Regulations 1983, meant that she could make such a comparison only if there was no male doing the same or broadly similar work. Lord Templeman avoided the technicality by implying into section 1(3) of the Act a series of words, "as between the woman and man with whom she claims equality", which clearly distorted the natural meaning of the Act. At first glance, this radical application of indirect effect is more in keeping with a monist than dualist approach. However, there remained a strong dualist basis for this dramatic reversal of traditional principles of statutory interpretation.[60] Having taken what was then the extraordinary step of overtly examining *Hansard*, Lord Templeman was able to conclude:

> "Thus it is clear that the construction which I have placed upon the regulations corresponds to the intentions of the Government in introducing the regulations. . . . In *Duke* v. *GEC Reliance Systems Ltd* this House declined to distort the construction of an Act of Parliament which was not drafted to give effect to a directive and which was not capable of complying with the directive as subsequently construed by the European Court of Justice. In the present case I can see no difficulty in construing the regulations of 1983 in a way which gives effect to the declared intention of the Government of the United Kingdom responsible for drafting the regulations and is consistent with the objects of the EEC Treaty, the provisions of the Equal Pay Directive and the rulings of the European Court of Justice."

This dualist rationale for a monist solution to inconsistencies between Community and UK law was repeated in *Litster* v. *Forth Dry Dock and Engineering Co Ltd*,[61] concerning Directive 77/187 on the safeguarding of employees' rights in the event of transfers of undertakings. Once again the House was considering regulations passed under section 2(2) of the European Communities Act, the Transfer of Undertakings (Protection of Employees) Regulations 1981, and, once again, the House added words to the legislation[62] in order to bring it into conformity with ECJ interpretations of the 1977 Directive. As Lord Keith stated:

> "In these circumstances it is the duty of the court to give to regulation 5 a construction which accords with the decisions of the European Court upon the corresponding provisions of the directive to which the regulation was intended by Parliament to give effect."

---

[59] Directive 1975/117.

[60] It might also be mentioned that the House was technically interpreting regulations passed under s. 2(2) of the European Communities Act 1982 to amend the 1970 Act. This avoided the complication perceived by Lord Templeman in *Duke* that s. 2(4), which makes specific reference to the "foregoing provisions of this section", could apply only to directly effective Community law, as introduced into UK law by s. 2(1) of the Act.

[61] [1989] ICR 341.

[62] Lord Oliver suggested implying into regulation 5(1) "or would have been so employed if he had not been unfairly dismissed in the circumstances described in regulation 8(1)".

It is interesting to note the fate of the seminal ECJ judgment in *von Colson* during the course of Lord Templeman's speeches in these three cases. In *Duke*, *von Colson* is "distinguished" as applying only to implementing legislation and, in any event, as not interfering with UK principles of statutory interpretation. In *Pickstone*, it is mentioned in passing as a further justification for the implementation of parliamentary will while, in *Litster*, it becomes the basis of a Community principle of purposive interpretation being applied by a British court. It is also interesting to note the corresponding diminution in the significance of the legitimate expectations of those reading the UK legislation. In *Duke*, "distortion" of the statute was impossible in order to protect Community rights. By *Litster*, a convoluted implication into the legislation was permissible, indicating more significance for Parliament's purported intentions than for the citizens' "legitimate expectations".

At this point, a particularly Northern Irish dimension enters the saga. Mrs Finnegan was a Northern Irish Mrs Duke.[63] What might have distinguished her case from Mrs Duke's was, first, that the Northern Irish "equal treatment" legislation, the Sex Discrimination (NI) Order 1976,[64] post-dated the Equal Treatment Directive 1976 and, secondly, that the House had by then applied a radical approach to indirect effect in *Pickstone* and *Litster*. However, the strength of the dualist aspects of *Pickstone* and *Litster* became apparent in *Finnegan*. Lord Bridge trenchantly restated the apparently vital distinction between implementing and non-implementing legislation:

> "it would appear to me to be wholly artificial to treat the Order of 1976 enacting identical provisions for Northern Ireland, because it was made after the directive, as having been made with the purpose of implementing Community law in the same sense as the regulations which fell to be construed in the *Pickstone* and *Litster* cases."

It does say something about the unpredictability of Community law, a factor borne in mind by Lord Templeman in *Duke*, that this distinctly dualist approach to indirect effect was to be undermined by a reference to the ECJ from a Spanish court concerned with the compatibility of provisions in the Spanish civil code with a Community company law directive. As indicated earlier, the Court, perhaps not totally unaware of the House's case law on indirect effect, concluded in *Marleasing*[65] that the indirect effect principle applied to all national legislation whether post-dating, or pre-dating, the relevant directive.

Having rather scathingly rejected either a reference to the ECJ in *Finnegan*, or the invocation of the Practice Direction to overrule *Duke*, the House quietly accepted the *Marleasing* judgment in *Webb v. EMO Air Cargo*,[66] a case once again in the field of equal opportunities law, but this time concerning the com-

---

[63] *Finnegan v. Clowney Youth Training Programme Ltd* [1990] 2 AC 407 (HL (NI)).

[64] The Order was enacted at a time at which Northern Ireland suffered from what might be called "backwater implementation".

[65] Case C–106/89 *Marleasing SA v. La Comercial Internacional de Alimentacion SA* [1990] ECR I–4135.

[66] [1993] ICR 175 (HL).

patibility of the Sex Discrimination Act 1975 with Article 5 of the Equal Treatment Directive 1976 in the context of a woman dismissed because she was pregnant. Lord Keith stated that the UK court was required to:

> "construe domestic legislation in any field covered by a Community directive so as to accord with the interpretation of the directive as laid down by the ECJ if that can be done without distorting the meaning of the domestic legislation [*per* Lord Templeman in *Duke*]. This is so whether the domestic legislation came after or, as in this case, preceded the directive [citing *Marleasing*]."[67]

The attempt by the House to limit indirect effect to within more dualist parameters of implementing legislation appears to have failed. The vital battleground upon indirect effect, both at the Community and UK levels, concerns the scope for radical reinterpretation. It has already been suggested that an orthodoxy is emerging which prevents a reinterpretation which is *contra legem*. On the other hand, the assertion of the autonomy of Community rights leads towards a view that the supremacy of Community norms can be guaranteed through indirect effect only if a radical approach is adopted. This controversy is heightened in the UK by the potential re-emergence of the "implementing legislation" criterion in the guise of a difference of approach towards re-interpretation depending upon the nature of the UK legislation.

In *Marleasing*, the Court indicated that re-interpretation must occur within the limits of national discretion. Given the House's reluctance, borne perhaps out of its dualist traditions, to countenance radical indirect effect in some circumstances, we are nevertheless left with the paradoxical situation that national discretion in the UK courts encompasses radical reinterpretation of implementing legislation,[68] but national discretion in relation to non-implementing legislation encompasses merely the resolution of ambiguities. The inconsistency is accentuated by the fact that the radical approach cannot be justified as a rule of internal UK constitutional law. A UK court would not contemplate such radical reinterpretation outside the scope of legislation implementing a Community measure. One is driven to the view that legitimate expectations of citizens in national law hold greater weight than Community rights but may be overridden by a criterion of legislative intent, albeit in implementing Community norms. But given the superiority of the Community norms over the national norms, it is difficult to see why legitimate expectations can be overridden by the imperatives of the national legislator but not those of the Community legislator.

Therefore it is possible to argue that the implications of *Marleasing* are even more far-reaching that the House acknowledged in *Webb*. Albeit driven by a dualist concern to satisfy legislative intent, the radical approach to indirect

---

[67] The House eventually found an interpretation of the 1975 Act which was perceived to conform to the Court's ruling in *Webb* (see [1995] ICR 1021).

[68] A possible distinguishing factor between *Pickstone* and *Litster* and other cases of implementing legislation is that they were both concerned with the interpretation of secondary legislation passed under s. 2(2) of the European Communities Act, but this is a point not considered of any consequence in those judgments.

effect in *Pickstone* and *Litster* could arguably be within the discretion of UK courts on a general basis and therefore should be applicable to *all* statutory interpretation, a solution significantly more monist than that which the House is prepared is countenance at present.

## State Liability

We have already established that the *Francovich* action for damages is more monist in the sense that it reinforces yet again the supremacy of Community law over national law and yet also has a dualist dimension in that the focus of the action is the State rather than private parties, against whom liability should be invocable in order to achieve grades eight and nine on our dualism/monism spectrum.

The House has made only passing reference to *Francovich* in its case law to date. In *Kirklees Metropolitan Borough Council* v. *Wickes Building Supplies Ltd*,[69] the House was considering an undertaking in damages demanded of the Council in one of the Sunday trading cases. The House extricated the Council from this obligation partly with reference to State liability, on the basis that it was the State which should provide damages for breaches of Community law and not a local authority. It remains to be seen whether the Court of Justice takes a wide approach towards the standard of liability in State liability cases, but it would appear that the House in *Kirklees* was not unwilling to apply a generous approach to *Francovich* liability. However, Lord Goff's thinking in *Kirklees* does exhibit some of the more dualist thinking upon which cases such as *Duke* were decided, namely that a party should not be subjected to "unexpected" liability:

> "It would be wrong that the council, because it has performed its statutory duty under national law to enforce s. 47, was to find itself under a liability in damages as a result of performing that duty."

However, it is in *Factortame* and *Ex p. Equal Opportunities Commission*[70] that the House has willingly embraced the ECJ's case law, both in letter and in spirit, which is emerging in relation to State liability. Despite its repackaging as a direct effect question by the Court, what the House of Lords asked about, and what it really received, through the Article 177 reference to the Court in *Factortame (No. 2)*,[71] was a new remedy against administrative action which is contrary to Community law. Leading from earlier comments from Lord Bridge's speech, he went on to state:

---

[69] [1993] AC 227 (HL).
[70] R. v. *Secretary of State for Employment, ex p. EOC* [1995] 1 AC 1 (HL). See also Chap. 10 below.
[71] [1991] 1 AC 603 (HL).

"Thus there is nothing in any way novel in according supremacy to rules of Community law in those areas to which they apply and to insist that, in the protection of rights under Community law, national courts must not be inhibited by rules of national law from granting interim relief in appropriate cases is no more than a logical recognition of that supremacy."

In some ways, the ruling in *Ex p. EOC* is even further across our dualism/monism spectrum than *Factortame (No. 2)*. While the interim relief in *Factortame (No. 2)* was more dramatic than the declaration granted in *Ex p. EOC*, the basis of the House's decision in *Ex p. EOC* was further divorced from traditional UK judicial thinking than any of the other cases considered in this chapter. The case concerned the validity of primary legislation rather than administrative action based upon it.[72] It concerned essentially private law legislation which provided not merely rights for individuals but also obligations upon private parties.[73] There was no issue concerning the direct effect of the 1976 Directive.[74] The legislation in question was not, in any sense, nor did it purport to be, equivalent to, implementing legislation.[75] None of this deterred their Lordships from taking the ratio of *Factortame (No. 2)* and applying it to the issuing of a declaration upon the incompatibility of primary legislation with a Community directive.[76] It was sufficient for Lord Keith to state that it was "not suggested in *Factortame* that judicial review was not available for the purpose of obtaining an adjudication upon the validity of legislation". Upon this rather slender basis is the ultimate exercise in a monist approach founded. It is at this point that the contrast between cases concerning compatibility of UK law with Community law and with international law, even the European Convention of Human Rights, is at its most acute.

## The House of Lords—An Appraisal

In some ways, the case law of the House mirrors that of the ECJ. Where we gave five out of ten to the Court for the direct effect of Treaty obligations, the House of Lords deserves no less for consistent adoption of a monist approach towards

---

[72] The case concerned judicial review, on grounds of indirect sex discrimination, of the requirement, under s. 64(1) of the Act, that employees working at least 16 hours a week gained protection from unfair dismissal after two years' employment while employees working between 8 and 16 hours a week had to wait for 5 years before protection was accorded to them. The EOC had felt obliged to attack a "decision" of the Secretary of State not to reduce the qualifying number of hours on the cautious assumption that the primary legislation itself could not be directly challenged.

[73] Hence a *Factortame* injunction would not have been adequate.

[74] The legislation applies equally to public and private employers.

[75] The Employment Protection (Consolidation) Act 1978, providing unfair dismissal protection, in no way "implements" the 1976 Directive, which does require, in Art. 5(2)(a), that "any laws, regulations and administrative provisions contrary to the principle of equal treatment shall be abolished".

[76] Their Lordships could have relied upon *obiter* comments in Cases C–143/88 and C–92/89 *Zuckerfabrik Süderdithmarschen AG* v. *Hauptzollamt Itzehoe* [1991] ECR I–415 but appear not to have done so.

this question, culminating in *Factortame (No. 2)*. On the direct effect of directives, a quite generous application of vertical direct effect deserves six where the ECJ was also given six. On indirect effect, the *Webb* judgment on non-implementing legislation retrieves a more monist approach, albeit still subject to controversy over reticence towards a radical approach to indirect effect. On State liability, the House has submerged itself in a monist determination to give effect to superior Community norms even at the expense of the previously perceived sanctity of primary legislation. Without indulging too assiduously in "judge watching", it may be the case that the arrival in the House of Lord Slynn after a long career as both an Advocate General and then a judge at the Court is some guarantee that the spirit as well as the letter of ECJ rulings will continue to be respected within the House. Particularly in the light of *Factortame (No. 2)* and *Ex p. EOC*, it would be churlish to award their Lordships anything else than their brethren at Luxembourg, namely a point seven on our spectrum. Indeed, in the light of *Ex p. EOC*,[77] and wishing to be generous to those who have emerged from the dark mists of dualism, a final "mark" of 7.5 seems to be appropriate.

Given the enormous burdens of Diceyean insularity from which their Lordships have had to escape, it is a tribute to their adaptability and pragmatism that they can be accredited with a status "at least as monist as the ECJ", if not "more monist than the ECJ". But then, as we have seen, the system of Community law enforcement in national law is not as monist as a reading of *van Gend en Loos* would have us believe. Instead we have a quasi-monist House of Lords sailing quite comfortably upon a sea of quasi-monist Community law. It might also be said that, despite a wavering, perhaps unintentional, in *Duke* and *Finnegan*, from ECJ orthodoxy, the House has meticulously followed both the letter and the spirit of ECJ rulings on these constitutional questions and hence deserves at least nine out of ten for judicial solidarity.

THE FUTURE: MARKET INTEGRATION AND EUROPEAN CITIZENSHIP

These complimentary conclusions mask some more fundamental questions. The shorthand of monism and dualism utilised in this chapter provides a façade behind which vital questions of European Union policy must be addressed. Since 1957, we have seen the ascendancy, even within the Court's case law, of a market integration imperative.[78] Our survey of the Court's case law suggests that all is not yet well with the system of Community law enforcement which it has evolved. For example, it might still be quite possible for an individual to have inflicted upon her a breach of her Community rights by a non-governmental body on the basis of a national law perceived to be beyond reinterpretation but enacted in circumstances which may not justify a State liability action. The per-

---

[77] Where the House might even be seen to be a little ahead of the Court.
[78] See in particular Case 106/77 *Simmenthal*, n. 19 above

sistence with the vertical/horizontal direct effect distinction, the possible limitations upon indirect effect of a *contra legem* approach and the development of a "sufficiently serious breach" basis for State liability all conspire to undermine the universal application of minimum Community standards across the European Union, jeopardising the attainment of comprehensive market integration.

More recently, since the Treaty on European Union, we have an acknowledgement of our European citizenship.[79] Coupled with the assertion by the ECJ of the autonomy of Community rights, this realisation of European citizenship is tarnished by the incompleteness of the Community legal system's capacity to protect our Community rights. Some of the more dualist aspects of the case law of the House which we have surveyed do accentuate these anxieties. It may be marginally more difficult to convince a UK court that an applicant is litigating against an emanation of the State. So also it may be that a UK court will be more dismissive of interpretations of UK law which are consistent with supposedly superior Community rights but apparently distortive of the UK statute. On the whole, it is for the ECJ to fill the continuing gaps in the Community legal system and then for the House of Lords, and lower UK courts, to ensure that the respect for superior Community rights, exhibited in *Factortame (No. 2)* and *Ex p. EOC,* continues to motivate the response of the once dualist UK legal system to whatever further progress the ECJ makes towards a comprehensive system of Community law enforcement in national law. Indeed, to the extent that the Court appears more cautious in the 1990s of offending national judicial sensitivities, it can hardly be said that the national judges arguably most in need of convincing, namely the common law judges in the highest court of the UK, have exhibited any serious resistance to whatever principles and decisions the Court has enunciated. We are left to wonder whether other more stridently dualist aspects of traditional doctrine can survive the liberating influence of Community membership?

---

[79] Art. 8(1) EC.

# 10

# The House of Lords as a Constitutional Court—The Implications of EX PARTE EOC

PATRICIA MAXWELL

## INTRODUCTION

In the case of *R. v. Secretary of State for Employment, ex p. the Equal Opportunities Commission*[1] the House of Lords considered applications for judicial review brought by the EOC. The House took the view that the provisions of the Employment Protection (Consolidation) Act 1978 ("the EPCA"), which effectively excluded many part-time workers from the right to claim unfair dismissal or redundancy payments, were unlawful, being incompatible with European Community law. Although the substantive point of employment law is important, the decision is likely to have a more long-lasting effect in constitutional and administrative law, and in particular upon the judicial review procedure. It is this effect which is discussed in this chapter. The role of the House of Lords as a constitutional court will be further enhanced when the proposal to incorporate the European Convention for the Protection of Human Rights and Fundamental Freedoms[2] into the domestic law of the United Kingdom takes effect.

*The Times* of 5 March 1994[3] began a leading article with the following sentence: "Britain may now have, for the first time in its history, a constitutional court." The event which prompted such a comment was the decision in *Ex p. EOC*, the previous day. The article went on to suggest that what had happened, and had gone almost unnoticed by the British public, was a substantial revision of the traditional constitutional balance between Parliament and the judiciary. In decidedly concerned tones the leader explained how the House of Lords had ruled that sections of a British statute were incompatible with European law and had "struck down" an Act of Parliament as being "unconstitutional". Dicey,

---

[1] [1994] 2 WLR 409, hereafter referred to as *Ex p. EOC*.
[2] This is proposed in the Human Rights Bill, which at the time of writing had passed all stages in the House of Commons and was about to be debated in the Lords.
[3] At 19.

whose views on the supremacy of Parliament had "nourished generations of lawyers and lawmakers", would not be amused. In the opinion of the leader writer, the decision went far beyond the *Factortame* litigation of 1990–92,[4] where the Divisional Court had suspended the operation of a statute while waiting for the European Court of Justice (ECJ) to rule on the substantive question. In *Ex p. EOC* the Law Lords themselves had decided to measure the validity of the legislation by reference to its social and economic impact. In this, they were acting as nothing short of a constitutional court, along the lines of the American model. Concern was expressed that the case might open the floodgates to allow pressure groups of all descriptions, from the Friends of the Earth to the Cats Protection League, to subject Acts of Parliament to "trial by judicial review".

Despite the alarmist nature of the article it did raise serious and legitimate concerns about the shift in constitutional power away from Parliament, and about the *locus standi* of pressure groups. The purpose of this chapter is to examine some of these issues, particularly in the light of the proposals to give the courts new powers in cases which raise the possibility of a conflict between domestic law and the principles of the European Convention. It starts by looking briefly at the facts and the substantive issues raised by the case, and then turns in more detail to the wider constitutional questions.

## The Facts of the Case

The employment rights of individual workers, at the time of the decision in *Ex. p. EOC* were to be found, in the main, in the Employment Protection (Consolidation) Act 1978 (EPCA)[5]. Amongst the most important of the rights conferred by the EPCA were the right not to be unfairly dismissed and the right to receive a statutory redundancy payment.[6] These rights were not acquired automatically by every employee, however, but had to be earned by satisfying qualifying conditions which were prescribed.[7] Generally, the provisions distinguished between full-time and part-time employees, since there was a requirement for a two-year period of continuous employment for those who worked more than sixteen hours a week, but a five-year period for those who worked between eight and sixteen hours a week. Those who worked fewer than eight hours would never qualify.

On the face of things, these provisions did not appear to discriminate on grounds of sex, as they applied equally to men and to women. There is no question of *direct* discrimination, defined in the Sex Discrimination Act 1975[8] as less favourable treatment on the ground of a person's sex. On the other hand, there

---

[4] *Factortame Ltd* v. *Secretary of State for Transport (No. 2)* [1991] 1 All ER 70 (HL).
[5] The rights are now to be found in the Employment Rights Act 1996.
[6] Respectively, ss. 54 and 81 of the 1978 Act.
[7] The relevant conditions were laid down in Sch. 13 to the EPCA.
[8] S. 1(1)(a).

was a possibility that the provisions could be *indirectly* discriminatory under the Act,[9] if the qualifying thresholds affected more women than men, and they could not be objectively justified.

It was common ground in the case that the great majority of those working more than sixteen hours a week were men, while the majority of those working fewer than sixteen hours were women. The stastistics were compelling, some eighty seven per cent of part-time workers being female.[10] Historically, part-time workers have been considerably disadvantaged in the labour market. Frequently they are appointed on basic grades, denied access to overtime rates and bonus payments, to paid holidays, sickness pay or annual increments. They may not be eligible for training opportunities, for promotion or for occupational pension schemes.[11] The number of part-time workers has increased dramatically throughout the post-war years. In 1951 they accounted for a mere 4 per cent of the workforce: by 1990 the proportion had risen to twenty-five per cent. Over the last two decades the growth in part-time employment has risen at twelve times the rate of full-time employment growth.[12] Given these increasing numbers, and their unfavourable position in the labour market, the Equal Opportunities Commission (the EOC) was concerned to see that the law itself did not add to the disadvantage of part-time workers.

Feeling that it was necessary to elicit some sort of "decision" susceptible to judicial review, the EOC wrote to the Secretary of State for Employment, asking him to reconsider the allegedly discriminatory provisions. The Secretary of State duly replied by letter, expressing his opinion that the 1978 Act was in conformity with European law. Within the three-month time limit required by Order 53 of the Rules of the Supreme Court, the EOC sought judicial review. Subsequently Mrs Patricia Day, a cleaner who worked eleven hours a week with a Health Authority, was joined as a named individual applicant. She had failed to qualify for a statutory redundancy payment, even though she had worked for the same employer for almost five years.

The remedies sought were originally a series of declarations, though the application was amended before the Divisional Court to include a request for an order of mandamus to compel the Secretary of State to amend the EPCA. The request for mandamus was later abandoned before the Court of Appeal. In the Divisional Court all applications were refused. On appeal the applications were again refused, though on different grounds. In the House of Lords Mrs Day's application was refused, while the EOC's applications succeeded.

[9] S. 1(1)(b).

[10] The figures were taken from the Employment Department's own questionnaire-based Labour Force Survey. This does not use the same definition of full-time work as is used in the EPCA. Instead it uses a system of self-classification. Not all those classified as part-time by the LFS in fact suffer discrimination under the EPCA. According to the *Employment Gazette* 1994, 102 (1), over forty per cent of female part-time workers work fewer than sixteen hours.

[11] For a full account see C. Hakim, "Employment Rights: A Comparison of Part-time and Full-time Employees" (1989) 18 *Ind.LJ* 69.

[12] See O. Robinson, "Part-time Employment in the Economies of Ireland" (1993) *Review of Employment Topics*, vol. 1, p. 143.

## The Substantive Issues

It was common ground that the majority of part-time workers were indeed women, and that the onus was on the Secretary of State to put forward an objective justification for the measures, which was unrelated to the difference in sex. According to the authority of *Bilka-Kaufhaus GmbH* v. *Weber von Hartz*[13] and *Rinner-Kuhn* v. *FVW Spezial-Gebäudereinigung GmbH and Co. KG*[14] the Secretary of State would have to show the provisions met a necessary aim of social policy, and that they were suitable and requisite for achieving that aim. It was also accepted (on the authority of *Rinner-Kuhn*) that whether or not an objective justification had been made out was a matter for the national court.

The bulk of the substantive part of the case concerned the issue of justification. In essence the argument put forward by the Secretary of State was that the aim of the thresholds was to increase the amount of part-time work available. If employers had to make redundancy payments and pay unfair dismissal compensation to part-time staff they would employ fewer part-timers and take on more full-time staff. This would reduce flexibility for employers and would also work against women, many of whom wanted part-time work, to combine with their roles as carers. This was accepted in the Divisional Court, where Nolan L.J. held that:

> "the mere fact that many part-time employees prefer such work would not of course justify discrimination in pay and conditions on the ground of sex. However, the preference for part-time work becomes significant in the light of the evidence that employment opportunities in part-time work would be reduced by the imposition of additional burdens on potential employers."

There was general agreement in all three courts that this increase in part-time work was a legitimate and beneficial social policy aim. There was disagreement, however, on the question whether the thresholds in the 1978 Act were "suitable and requisite" means for achieving that aim. The evidence put forward by the Secretary of State consisted largely of an affidavit sworn by an official in the Department of Employment, which set out the views of the Department but contained little factual evidence to support those views. The CBI and the Institute of Directors agreed that improving conditions for part-timers would damage their job opportunities.

This evidence was accepted at face value by the Divisional Court (Nolan L.J., Judge J.) and expressly by Hirst L.J. in the Court of Appeal. It was rejected by Dillon L.J. in the Court of Appeal, and in the Lords by Lords Keith, Lowry and Browne-Wilkinson. The view which ultimately prevailed, therefore, was that there was no factual evidence led by the Secretary of State to show that the existence of the thresholds had led to any increase in the availability of part-time

---

[13] [1986] IRLR 317.
[14] [1989] IRLR 493.

work, or that their removal would lead to a reduction in the number of part-time jobs available. The evidence of the EOC was preferred. They relied on evidence which had been presented to the House of Commons Employment Committee and to the House of Lords Select Committee, and on research carried out by the Department of Employment.[15] This indicated that fewer than one per cent of employers gave as their reason for employing part-timers the fact that they had fewer rights.

A number of substantive issues were left unresolved by the decision. Most of these have been rendered academic, at least in the context of part-time workers' rights, by the amending legislation introduced as a direct result of the case. This took the form of the Employment Protection (Part-Time Employees) Regulations 1995 (made on 6 February 1995). There are separate regulations for Northern Ireland. These new regulations were made under section 2(2) of the European Communities Act and remove all hours thresholds in respect of the main employment protection rights.[16] The issues which were not resolved by the case itself were, firstly, did the ruling cover both the sixteen-hour threshold and the eight-hour threshold, or just the former; and secondly, was compensation for unfair dismissal "pay" within the meaning of Article 119, and therefore a directly enforceable Community right against private as well as public sector employers? In *Barber* v. *Guardian Royal Exchange*[17] the ECJ had ruled that redundancy payments fell within Article 119, but there is as yet no ECJ ruling on unfair dismissal compensation.[18] In *Ex. p. EOC* Dillon and Hirst LJ.J. felt that it was "pay" and Lord Keith hinted that he might agree. It is undoubtedly payment from the employer based on the previous employment relationship, and the analogy with statutory redundancy pay is strong. The issue is important in relation to the question of when the time limits for complaints for part-time workers will run and may prove significant in contexts other than the present one. Some of these are discussed below.

## The Constitutional and Procedural Issues

These can be considered under four broad headings, recognising that these are not entirely discrete issues and that there is a degree of overlap and some interconnection between them. The four areas are: the "decision" issue, the forum or jurisdiction issue, *locus standi* and the question of remedies.

---

[15]  D. Wood and P. Smith, "Employers' Labour Use Strategies: First Report on the 1987 Survey", (1988) Research Paper No. 63 (London, Department of Employment, 1988).

[16]  The definition of a "normal working week" in Sch. 13 to EPCA was amended to include any week in which a contract of employment subsisted, irrespective of the number of hours worked.

[17]  Case C–262/88 [1991] 1 QB 344.

[18]  The issue is raised directly by *R.* v. *Secretary of State for Employment, ex p. Seymour-Smith and Perez*; [1997] 2 All ER 273 (HL); [1995] IRLR 464 (CA); [1994] IRLR 448 (QBD). The House of Lords has referred the question whether unfair dismissal compensation constitutes "pay" to the ECJ. This case, which concerns the question whether the two-year qualifying period for unfair dismissal discriminates indirectly against women, is discussed in detail later in this chapter.

## *The "Decision" Issue*

In the Divisional Court and the Court of Appeal the question whether the Secretary of State had actually made a "decision" capable of being judicially reviewed was treated as an important issue. It would seem that the EOC itself took the view that such a "decision" was indeed necessary, and for that reason wrote to the Secretary of State in the first place, and then took great care to commence the proceedings within three months of his reply.

For the record, the Divisional Court took the view that the letters of the Secretary of State were "decisions" and susceptible of judicial review, while the majority of the Court of Appeal felt that they were not, being no more than deliberately solicited expressions of his views as to the scope of Community law, and in themselves not affecting the rights or obligations of any person. Thus they did not constitute either a "decision" or a view susceptible to judicial review.

As has been pointed out by Gordon,[19] this approach is flawed. Whether or not a "decision" has been reached is a question going to remedy, rather than susceptibility to judicial review. In particular the prerogative order of certiorari will only lie where there is something amounting to a decision or a determination capable of being quashed.[20] The absence of one form of relief does not of itself affect the wider issue of whether or not the court's supervisory jurisdiction may be invoked.

Although this point was not articulated in the Lords, it was recognised there that it was immaterial whether or not the Secretary of State had arrived at a "decision". However Lord Keith did express the view (and this may be significant in other cases) that the letter did not constitute a "decision".[21] He went on to say:

> "The real object of the EOC's attack is these provisions themselves. The question is whether judicial review is available for the purpose of securing a declaration that certain United Kingdom primary legislation is incompatible with European Community law."

Reviewing the series of *Factortame* cases,[22] he continued:

> "At no stage in the course of the litigation, which included two visits to this House, was it suggested that judicial review was not available for the purpose of obtaining an adjudication upon the validity of the legislation as it affected the applicants.
>
> The *Factortame* case is thus a precedent in favour of the EOC's recourse to judicial review for the purpose of challenging as incompatible with EC law the relevant provisions of the Act of 1978."

This is an important aspect of the case, confirming as it does the availability of judicial review proceedings to challenge primary legislation which is incom-

---

[19] R. Gordon, [1994] *PL* 217.
[20] See Parker J. in *R. v. St Lawrence's Hospital Statutory Visitors, ex p. Pritchard* [1953] 1 WLR 1158 at 1166.
[21] [1994] 2 WLR 409 at 418.
[22] Supra n. 4.

patible with European law, and supporting the litigation strategy of the EOC. It has implications for the question of time limits, which was undoubtedly one of the concerns of the EOC which led it to seek a "decision" in the first place. It now seems that the three month time limit under Order 53 will not come into play in a case involving a direct challenge to the validity of primary legislation. It must not be forgotten, however, that judicial review proceedings involve a large element of judicial discretion, and the issue of undue delay was not addressed *per se* in any of the speeches in the Lords. In the case noted earlier, *R. v. Secretary of State for Employment, ex p. Seymour-Smith and Perez*,[23] a challenge to secondary legislation was defeated in the Divisional Court on the grounds (*inter alia*) that the application for certiorari should have been made within three months of the making of the Order in question.

## The Forum or Jurisdiction Issue

The issue here was whether the Divisional Court is the (or an) appropriate forum for the resolution of these proceedings. The position of Mrs Day must be considered separately from that of the EOC. As we have seen, Mrs Day, a part-time public-sector worker who was made redundant and who did not meet the threshold requirements, was joined as an individual applicant. At the same time she commenced proceedings in the Industrial Tribunal, and these had been adjourned pending the result in the present case. In the view of Dillon L.J. in the Court of Appeal, Mrs Day's former employer, being a health authority, was to be treated in Community law as an "emanation of the State", and so was not entitled to set up against Mrs Day, as a defence, any failure of the State to amend its legislation so as to comply with Article 119 and the Equal Pay Directive. Any offending provisions of the national statute could be disapplied by the Industrial Tribunal. It was conceded by the Secretary of State that if the threshold provisions were found not to be objectively justified, then Mrs Day could recover her redundancy payment from her former employer in the Industrial Tribunal.

In other words, her claim was essentially a private law claim, and the Industrial Tribunal, having ample jurisdiction to hear her claim, was the appropriate forum. The court will always be reluctant to grant judicial review where there is an alternative remedy. Dillon L.J.'s view was supported by the other members of the Court of Appeal, and unanimously by the House of Lords.[24]

What is not clear is the situation of private sector workers who cannot rely directly upon a Directive. Their only recourse in a case of non-implementation may be to sue the government in a *Francovich* action.[25] Does this amount to an "alternative remedy"? The question has come up in *Ex p. Seymour-Smith*,

---

[23] Supra n. 18, hereafter referred to as *Ex p. Seymour-Smith*.

[24] Similar arguments, discussed *infra*, were accepted by the House of Lords in *Ex p. Seymour-Smith*.

[25] *Francovich* v. *Italian State* Case 6/90 [1992] IRLR 84.

where the House of Lords has suggested that it might be regarded as such by approving the statement of Lord Keith in *Ex parte EOC*:[26].

> "If there is any individual who believes that he or she has a good claim to compensation under the *Francovich* principle, it is the Attorney General who would be the defendant in any proceedings directed to enforcing it, and the issues raised would not necessarily be identical with any of those which arise in the present appeal."[27]

The arguments applied to Mrs Day are clearly wholly inappropriate in relation to the EOC, which has no standing whatsoever to bring proceedings in its own name before an Industrial Tribunal.

The Divisional Court expressed forcefully the idea that what the case was really all about was the non-implementation of Directives. It was an attempt to enforce obligations which are Treaty obligations, and which, if they exist at all, exist only in international law. Even the European Communities Act did not entitle the "courts of this country to enforce obligations of that kind". The court said:[28]

> "Domestic legislation remains a matter for Parliament, not for the courts. How could it be right for us to tell the Secretary of State that he must introduce legislation amending the Act of 1978 when so far as we can see it would equally be open to him as a Member of Parliament to introduce legislation amending or repealing the Act of 1972. It would be wrong and unconstitutional . . . for the courts to make a declaration that such was his duty."

This view was supported by Kennedy L.J. in the Court of Appeal. He too felt that it was not for the domestic courts to pronounce upon whether the United Kingdom is or is not in breach of "international obligations", but merely to apply directly effective Community law in preference to domestic law, where there was a conflict. He said:

> "I do not accept that it is possible to use the procedure of judicial review as a form of fast track to give Community Directives full and immediate effect in English law . . . if that route is available then there really is very little left of the Community law concept of direct effect. Even where there is no direct effect the rights will be enforceable."[29]

The majority in the Court of Appeal took the view that it was for the European Commission, rather than the EOC, to bring proceedings against the government or a minister for failure to meet European obligations, under the procedure in Article 169 of the European Treaty. Even though that procedure was slow and cumbersome it was available, and, again, the court should be reluctant to grant judicial review where an alternative procedure existed. Nor was the Court of Appeal prepared to consider a reference to the ECJ.

---

[26] At 182, para. 27, approved per Lord Hoffmann [1997] IRLR 319 at paras. 21–22.

[27] If the ECJ in *Seymour-Smith* rules that it is the Equal Treatment Directive rather than Art. 119 which applies to the qualifying period, then the applicants may bring cases against the State under *Francovich*. However, the time limit for commencing such a writ action is no more than six years from the date of dismissal, and the applicants will find themselves out of time.

[28] [1992] ICR 341 at 358.

[29] At p. 494.

Thus we see the lower courts expressing the traditional view of the respective roles of Parliament and the courts, and demonstrating a marked reluctance to implement European law in preference to a conflicting British statute. A similar stance was adopted, by a differently constituted House of Lords, in the later case of *Ex p. Seymour-Smith*. Counsel for the applicants (Robin Allen QC) argued in that case that Directives could confer rights on individuals against the State as legislator. On the basis that the State should not legislate incompatibly with a Directive, the applicants were entitled to have relief against the State, clearing the Order which had introduced the two-year qualifying period for unfair dismissal out of their way, and leaving them free to sue their employers. Lord Hoffmann, delivering the judgment of the House, adhered to the more traditional view:[30]

> "But the individual has no right to a mandamus against the State in his national court, requiring that the Directive be implemented.[31] . . . In the last resort it is for the Commission to take proceedings under Article 169. The "right" asserted by Mr. Allen would be something quite different from the rights against the State applied in *Marshall*. The effect would be to give the Directive, by an easy two-stage process, the very effect which the jurisprudence of the Court says it cannot have, namely to impose obligations upon an individual. Furthermore, these obligations would be imposed arbitrarily and retrospectively, depending upon whether and when some interested person brought proceedings in public law to assert his "right" against the State to have incompatible domestic legislation set aside. This seems to me inconsistent with the principle of legal certainty which is one of the fundamental doctrines of European Law."

Certainly, until the United Kingdom's entry into the European Community a prerogative remedy could be sought only in respect of unlawful administrative or executive acts or omissions. The idea of a challenge to the legality of a legislative act was unthinkable, given the basic constitutional principle of parliamentary sovereignty. The principle of the supremacy of European law over all domestic law, including primary legislation, is now binding on the British courts by virtue of Article 5 of the European Treaty and section 2 of the European Communities Act 1972. Where a British statute is inconsistent with Community law and cannot be interpreted to comply with that law, it is, on the authority of the ECJ in *Simmenthal*,[32] automatically "inapplicable". The reluctance of the courts to acknowledge this is alarming indeed, and suggests that even yet some senior members of the British judiciary have not fully understood the effect of the United Kingdom's membership of the European Union.

It is fortunate that, on this crucial issue, a much more robust attitude was taken in the Lords in *Ex p. EOC*. Four members of the House expressed the view that the Divisional Court was the appropriate forum and had jurisdiction to declare that primary legislation was incompatible with Community law. This was probably the single most significant aspect of the case, and the issue which

---

[30] At para. 13
[31] In fact there was no application for mandamus in the instant case.
[32] *Simmenthal SpA* v. *Amministrazione delle Finanze dello Stato* [1978] ECR 1453.

most concerned the author of the leader in *The Times*. Again the precedent used was *Factortame*. This had been relied upon in argument before the Court of Appeal but was not referred to in the judgments. In the Lords, Lord Keith said:

> "A declaration . . . is capable of being granted consistently with the precedent afforded by *Factortame*. This does not involve, as contended for the Secretary of State, any attempt by the EOC to enforce the international treaty obligations of the United Kingdom. The EOC is concerned simply to obtain a ruling which reflects the primacy of European Community law enshrined in section 2 of the Act of 1972 and determines whether the relevant United Kingdom law is compatible with the Equal Pay Directive and the Equal Treatment Directive."[33]

### *The* Locus Standi *Issue*

We turn now to the question whether the EOC had "sufficient interest" under Order 53 to bring the proceedings. This is clearly closely related to the forum issue; indeed in some judgments the two are indistinguishable. This was the only issue to be decided in favour of the EOC by both the Court of Appeal and the House of Lords, though in each court there were dissenting opinions (Kennedy L.J. and Lord Jauncey).

This was not the first time that the EOC had used an application for judicial review to secure compliance with the Sex Discrimination Act. That had first happened in 1987, when the EOC successfully challenged the provision of single-sex grammar school places by Birmingham City Council.[34] One year later the EOC for Northern Ireland brought judicial review proceedings to challenge the Department of Education's use of quotas in the "11-plus" selection procedures in Northern Ireland.[35] In 1990 the EOC used judicial review to obtain a ruling on whether the provisions of the Social Security Act 1975 were contrary to European equality principles—the ECJ ruled that they were not.[36] That same year the EOC sought judicial review of the Queen's Regulations for the Army and the RAF, which permitted the dismissal of pregnant servicewomen.[37] The EOC argued that these provisions conflicted with the Equal Treatment Directive and should be disapplied, so as to allow aggrieved applicants access to the industrial tribunals. The Defence Secretary put up the white flag at the outset of the hearing and appropriate declaratory relief was granted. The important point is that in none of these four cases was any objection taken to the standing of the EOC to bring judicial review proceedings. There was a complete change of stance in the present case.

The House of Lords ruled that the applicant had sufficient interest. This result was achieved by analysing the EOC's statutory remit under Part VI of the 1975 Act. Lord Jauncey, dissenting, used an identical method to reach the opposite conclusion. The majority of their Lordships adopted a liberal approach to

[33] [1994] 2 WLR 409 at 419.
[34] *R. v. Birmingham City Council, ex p. EOC* [1989] AC 1155 (HL).
[35] *In re the EOC and Others (No. 2)* [1988] NI 178.
[36] *R. v. Secretary of State for Social Security, ex p. EOC* [1992] ICR 782.
[37] *R. v. Secretary of State for Defence, ex p. EOC* (unreported, 20 Dec. 1991).

the issue of standing. Lord Keith focused on the wide duties of the EOC under section 53(1) of the Act, in particular the duty "to work towards the elimination of discrimination", and the duty "to promote equality of opportunity between men and women generally". The present proceedings, he felt, clearly fell within the scope of these statutory duties. It is arguable that the point could have been more fully reasoned, but the decision is preferable on policy grounds to the restrictive interpretation suggested by Lord Jauncey. His interpretation focused upon the particular relationship envisaged by Part VI of the 1975 Act between the Secretary of State and the EOC. The role of the EOC was to advise the Secretary of State; the Act made the EOC answerable to him or her. In an implicit application of the maxim *expressio unius est exclusio alterius*, he suggested that if Parliament had intended that the EOC should have the power "to challenge the decisions of the Secretary of State and impose its will upon him" it was "quite remarkable" that the Act, which set out in detail the powers and duties of the EOC, should have remained silent on this particular matter.

This is clearly another important aspect of the case and does much to undermine the premise that only an individual can have standing to monitor directly effective rights. This was the basis upon which Turner J. in *Wychavon DC v. Secretary of State for the Environment*[38] held that a district council (not being an individual for the purposes of Community law) could not rely on the provisions of an EC Directive, not implemented by UK legislation, in the national courts.

The decision seems to be very much in line with the recent decisions of the House on the issues of whether and which pressure groups have "sufficient interest" under Order 53. It seems true to say that in recent cases the courts have adopted an expansionist view of *locus standi* in respect of pressure groups. Some examples of these pressure groups include:

—Greenpeace, which was held to have sufficient interest to seek judicial review of a decision of the Nuclear Inspectorate in respect of the discharge of radioactive waste from Sellafield.[39]
—The Child Poverty Action Group, which was declared by the Court of Appeal to have standing in a case against the Secretary of State for Social Services.[40]
—The World Development Movement Ltd ("a non-partisan pressure group"!), which successfully challenged decisions of the Foreign Secretary in relation to aid to fund the Pergau Dam project.[41]
—The Royal Society for the Protection of Birds, which found that no exception was taken to its challenge to the Government's implementation of the Birds Directive.[42]

[38] Unreported, *The Times*, 7 Jan. 1994.
[39] *R. v. Inspectorate of Pollution, ex p. Greenpeace* [1994] 4 All ER 329.
[40] *R. v. Secretary of State for Social Services, ex p. CPAG* [1990] 2 QB 540.
[41] *R. v. Secretary of State for Foreign and Commonwealth Affairs, ex p. World Development Movement Ltd* [1995] 1 WLR 385.
[42] *R. v. Secretary of State for the Environment, ex p. RSPB*, (unreported) *The Times*, 10 Febr. 1995.

—Trades unions such as the Fire Brigades Union, which successfully challenged the proposed Criminal Injuries Compensation Scheme.[43]

Indeed the only exception to this line of decisions seems to have been the denial of standing to the Rose Theatre Trust Co. in 1990.[44]

The cases in general seem to suggest that if there is a sufficiently important issue raised and a strong public interest element to the case, then standing will be granted. The EOC case is probably just part of that pattern, but it has served to demonstrate clearly that judicial review of statutes which do not conform to the provisions of directly effective Community law will be permitted. Given the statutory remit of the EOC, something approaching a class action along American lines may have been established for such cases. However, this does leave the rather curious result that individuals whose rights are directly affected by Government action may not have *locus standi* (generally there is an alternative forum open to them) while a pressure group or other agency will have standing.[45]

### The Available Remedy

Community law is currently addressing key issues about the need for effective remedies. Is a declaration an adequate remedy, or does Community law require mandatory relief? We have noted already that in *Ex p. EOC* the application for mandamus, compelling the Secretary of State to amend the legislation, was abandoned before the Court of Appeal. Thus, on appeal to the Lords, the House did not address directly the question of its availability. Lord Keith, speaking for a House which was unanimous on this point, held that there was no need to declare that the United Kingdom government or the Secretary of State were in *breach* of their Community law obligations. A declaration that the provisions of the EPCA were *incompatible* with Article 119 and the two Council Directives 75/117 and 76/207 would suffice for the purposes of the EOC, and could be granted quite consistently with the precedent afforded by *Factortame*. This suggests that our courts will not be prepared to grant prerogative orders in actions based on statutory infringements of EC law, but that the reason for this is the fact that it will not be necessary to do so in order to guarantee effective protection for individuals' Community rights.

However, the conventional wisdom that government ministers would inevitably implement the terms of a declaration was momentarily challenged after *Ex p. EOC*. An article in the Sunday Telegraph of 17 April 1994 suggested

---

[43]   R. v. *Secretary of State for Home Affairs, ex p. Fire Brigades Union* [1995] 1 All ER 888.

[44]   R. v. *Secretary of State for the Environment, ex p. Rose Theatre Trust* [1990] 1 QB 504, and see further the discussion by A. P. Le Sueur, in B. Hadfield (ed.), *Judicial Review: A Thematic Approach* (Dublin, Gill and Macmillan, 1995), at 238–9.

[45]   In *Ex p. Seymour-Smith* their Lordships only reluctantly conceded standing to the two individual applicants, emphasising that theirs was a special case, and the case having been allowed to go so far, it would be wrong to tell the women that they must start all over again, at the Industrial Tribunal.

that the Employment Secretary was considering the possibility of circumventing the Lords' decision by introducing primary legislation which declared that the thresholds in the 1978 Act were objectively justified. In the event this did not happen, and the decision was implemented in the regulations noted earlier.

This question of the appropriate form of relief was considered subsequently by the Court of Appeal in *Ex p. Seymour-Smith*. In this case two women who worked in the private sector challenged the provisions of an Order of 1985[46] which increased the period of continuous employment required for an employee to complain of unfair dismissal from one year to two years. Both women had worked for more than one year, but less than two, at the time of their dismissals. Their complaints of unfair dismissal were consequently dismissed by industrial tribunals, because they lacked the requisite service. The women applied for judicial review in the High Court, and sought orders of certiorari to quash the 1985 Order. They claimed that the proportion of women who could comply with the two year qualifying period was considerably smaller than the proportion of men, so as to amount *prima facie* to indirect discrimination against women. They argued that the qualifying period in question, unless it could be objectively justified, was contrary to the EC Equal Treatment Directive. The Divisional Court[47] rejected the applications, ruling that even if the case were to succeed on its merits, an order of certiorari would not be appropriate. It then went on to hold that the applicants had failed to establish indirect discrimination, in that the proportion of qualifying women was not "considerably smaller".

On appeal, the appellants were given leave to amend their applications to include a contention that the right to compensation for unfair dismissal constitutes "pay" for the purposes of Article 119 of the EEC Treaty, and that by making and maintaining in force the 1985 Order the United Kingdom was in breach of its obligations under Article 119. The Court of Appeal chose to side-step this issue. While acknowledging that there is now a considerable body of judicial opinion, if not authority, that compensation for unfair dismissal does constitute "pay" under Article 119, the court was not convinced that the matter was *acte claire*. The court decided on balance not to make a reference to the ECJ for a preliminary ruling, because it seemed probable that there would be an appeal (on other issues) to the Lords, who might either decide the question themselves or alternatively decide to refer to the ECJ. The Court of Appeal went on to find that the women had demonstrated that the two-year qualifying period was discriminatory (*contra* the Divisional Court) and that the Employment Secretary had not made out a defence of justification. On the question of the appropriate form of relief to be granted in their claim based on the Equal Treatment Directive, the Court of Appeal was satisfied that it would be quite inappropriate to quash the 1985 Order, and that the only form of relief available was a declaration.

Neill L.J., delivering the judgment of the court, advanced a number of reasons

---

[46]  The Unfair Dismissal (Variation of Qualifying Period) Order 1985.
[47]  [1994] IRLR 448.

for this.[48] He argued that it was purely a matter of chance that the increase in qualifying period in 1985 was contained in secondary rather than primary legislation. The court would have had no power to quash primary legislation, merely to declare its provisions incompatible with European law. It will be remembered that this issue was not fully argued in *Ex p. EOC,* the Lords being content to assume that an order of mandamus was not available. Secondly, it was suggested by Neill L.J.[49] that to grant certiorari would require countless previous cases to be reopened, resulting in financial hardship and being detrimental to good administration.[50] The point was not argued in the Lords.

Before we leave the matter of remedies it is worth noting that in *Ex p. EOC* Lord Browne-Wilkinson discussed why the House could make a declaration in an application for judicial review, even though in the circumstances of the case no prerogative order was available to strike down the legislation in question. He emphasised that Order 53 rule 1(2) does *not* say that a declaration is to be made only in lieu of a prerogative order.

### The Importance of *Ex Parte EOC*

I must confess to some sympathy with the opinion expressed in *The Times* leader, that the House of Lords in *Ex p. EOC* assumed a role very close to that of a constitutional court. The case does demonstrate an incremental shift in the balance of power between the executive and the judiciary. The judgments in the lower courts can be seen to reflect more traditional thinking about the constitutional issues, whereas the House of Lords has shown itself prepared to adopt a more radical and robust approach, and has grasped the nettle even more firmly than it did in *Factortame.* The unwillingness of the Court of Appeal to make a reference to the ECJ on the issue of unfair dismissal compensation as "pay" is perhaps another example of the reluctance and uncertainty of the lower courts in this area. The Lords have abandoned the fiction that the courts are concerned only to ascertain and implement the intention of Parliament. The fact that they did not even pay lip sevice to the assumed limitations of their office perhaps inevitably produced disquiet of the kind expressed in *The Times.* The case demonstrates the increasing willingness of the judiciary to review executive decision-making once believed to be outside the courts' control, not least in the European arena.

This role is likely to achieve a higher profile when the proposal to incorporate the ECHR into domestic law takes effect. The government proposes that people

---

[48] See para. 65, where Neill L.J. advances five reasons.

[49] For a full discussion of the issues see J. Steiner, *Enforcing EC Law* (London, Blackstone, 1995) chap. 6.

[50] This may yet be the case, given that, if the 1985 Order is ultimately found to be incompatable with the Equal Treatment Directive, there may be many *Francovich*-type claims against the United Kingdom for failing to implement the Directive.

and organisations should be able to argue that Convention rights have been infringed by a public authority, in the ordinary courts, at any level.[51] This would allow Convention rights to be applied from the outset of a case.[52]

It seems that under the Bill courts may strike down or set aside incompatible secondary legislation;[53] or make a declaration of incompatibility (by higher courts only)[54], which will almost certainly prompt Parliament to change the law in question. The government has thus stopped short of giving to the courts the power to set aside primary legislation on grounds of incompatibility with the Convention.

This is clearly quite different from European (Community) law, where directly effective European law takes precedence over domestic law. It is a requirement of membership of the E.U. that Member States give priority to such law in their own legal systems, whereas there is no such requirement in the European Convention. In spite of (or could it be because of) the experience of the House of Lords as a constitutional court in the European law arena, the present executive is not yet prepared to extend further the powers of a fully fledged constitutional court to the judiciary. Perhaps Dicey can rest easy after all!

---

[51] Clause 3 of the Human Rights Bill 1998.
[52] See the White Paper "Rights Brought Home: The Human Rights Bill" (Cm. 3872, 1997) at para 2.4. The emphasis is on the accessability of the Convention to ordinary people.
[53] Clause 3.
[54] See clauses 4 and 5.

# 11

# *The Impact of* Pepper *v.* Hart

KENNY MULLAN

## INTRODUCTION

The purpose of this chapter is to examine the impact of the decision of the House of Lords in *Pepper* v. *Hart*.[1] In that case the long-established rule that courts were not permitted to refer to parliamentary materials when construing legislation was abrogated and certain tests for the admissibility of *Hansard* as an aid to statutory interpretation were established. The immediate significance of the case has been examined in a number of articles.[2] It is the application of the tests by the House of Lords in cases subsequent to *Pepper* v. *Hart* which will be the primary focus of this chapter.

The number of House of Lords' cases in which the ruling has been applied is small in comparison with the number of cases in lower courts and tribunals. However a number of the House of Lords' cases were decided immediately after the ruling in *Pepper* v. *Hart*. The initial approach of the House was to apply the new ruling in a liberal and permissive manner—an approach which was followed by lower courts and tribunals. The House, principally through Lord Browne-Wilkinson who gave the main speech in *Pepper* v. *Hart*, then sought to reassert its authority by reaffirming that the new ruling was meant to be implemented in a strict manner within the clear limits set out in the case itself. This recent approach of the House of Lords demonstrates that judges are taking a contradictory attitude towards the use of parliamentary materials, using them for certain defined purposes within the imposed limits as well as for other purposes outside those limits.

## WHAT WAS THE RULING IN *PEPPER* V. *HART*?

The facts and the decision in the case are well-known to lawyers and to some non-lawyers. However it is useful to remind ourselves of the specificity of the

---

[1] [1993] 1 All ER 42.

[2] See, e.g., D. Miers, "Taxing Perks and Interpreting Statutes: *Pepper* v. *Hart*" (1993) 56 *MLR* 695; B. Davenport, "Perfection—But at What Cost?" (1993) 109 *LQR* 149; D. Oliver, "*Pepper* v. *Hart*: A Suitable Case for Reference to *Hansard?*" [1993] *PL* 5; M. Styles, "The Rule of Parliament: Statutory Interpretation after *Pepper* v. *Hart*" [1994] *OJLS* 151.

facts and of the precise nature of the test for the admission of parliamentary materials which was established. Five speeches were given, by the Lord Chancellor (Lord Mackay), Lord Bridge of Harwich, Lord Griffiths, Lord Oliver of Aylmerton and Lord Browne-Wilkinson. The opinions of the Lord Chancellor and Lord Browne-Wilkinson are referred to most often, the former because Lord Mackay dissented on the main issue and the latter because his ruling is seen as the most definitive.

Lord Mackay indicated that his major difficulty with the case was the submission of Mr Anthony Lester Q.C., for the appellants, that reference to parliamentary material should be allowed with the permission of the court and where the court was satisfied that the reference is warranted:

> "(a) to confirm the meaning of a provision as conveyed by the text, its object and purpose, (b) to determine a meaning where the provision is ambiguous or obscure or (c) to determine the meaning where the ordinary meaning is manifestly absurd or unreasonable."[3]

The Lord Chancellor believed that virtually every case involving the interpretation of statutes could fall under one of these heads, thereby adding considerably to the level, practice and cost of litigation—a practical objection of substance by which he was willing to stand. The greater significance which the quotation from Lord Mackay's speech has since assumed lies in the fact that he was the only judge to allude to the possibility of using parliamentary material to *confirm* the already-established construction of an ambiguous legislative provision. The other speeches concentrate on the proposed use of parliamentary material to *determine* the meaning of obscure or ambiguous legislation. We shall see below that it appears that the House of Lords is now prepared to use *Hansard* in both ways, even though the latter use is not permitted by the decision of the House as a whole and the supposed basis for that use may even have been included in the judgment of the Lord Chancellor by error.[4]

Lord Browne-Wilkinson gave the leading judgment of the majority, and it is his summary of the circumstances in which the exclusionary rule could be relaxed which is most often quoted as representing the *ratio* of the case:

> "the exclusionary rule should be relaxed so as to permit reference to parliamentary materials where: (a) legislation is ambiguous or obscure, or leads to an absurdity; (b) the material relied on consists of one or more statements by a minister or other promoter of the Bill together if necessary with such other parliamentary material as is necessary to understand such statements and their effect; (c) the statements relied on are clear. Further than this, I would not at present go."[5]

---

[3] [1993] 1 All ER 42 at 47.

[4] Lord Lester has indicated that while he had initially argued for recourse to parliamentary materials to confirm the meaning of legislative provisions, this argument was abandoned in submissions before the Appellate Committee. Apparently the Lord Chancellor was unaware of this change of position at the time of preparation of his speech. See further A. Lester, "*Pepper* v. *Hart* Revisited" [1994] *Stat.LR* 10 at 21.

[5] [1993] 1 All ER 42 at 69.

It is submitted that the words of Lord Browne-Wilkinson are clear and that the conditions which he formulates are specific. Each condition follows in sequence from its predecessor, so that there can be no reference to parliamentary materials unless the legislative provisions are ambiguous, obscure or lead to an absurdity. That condition must be satisfied *before* there can be any reference to the parliamentary material. We shall see below, however, that some judges are reviewing parliamentary materials in order to decide whether the legislative provisions are ambiguous, obscure or absurd in the first place, or in order to confirm a particular construction.

Lord Browne-Wilkinson gave an indication of what he meant by "ambiguity" or "obscurity". He said the Finance Act 1976 was ambiguous or obscure because the statutory words were, on their face, capable of bearing one of two different, and opposing, meanings. That is a definition of ambiguity or obscurity which has been readily accepted as definitive in a large number of cases over a period of centuries.[6] Lord Browne-Wilkinson's ruling does not establish a novel test. We shall see, however, that the definition of ambiguity or obscurity has since been extended by the House of Lords beyond the relatively simplistic and logical approach taken by Lord Browne-Wilkinson.

Lord Browne-Wilkinson limited the range of admissible parliamentary material to:

> "one or more statements by a minister or other promoter of the Bill together if necessary with such other parliamentary material as is necessary to understand such statements and their effect".[7]

He makes it clear that the reason for limiting the range is to avoid unnecessary searches through parliamentary materials in the hope of uncovering the "crock of gold", that is, a clear indication of Parliament's intentions.[8]

In the case itself, Lord Browne-Wilkinson set the pattern for a liberal interpretation of the range of admissible materials by referring, in some detail, to a press release which had been issued simultaneously with the statement of a minister and the contents of which confirmed that minister's particular intentions. This pattern has been maintained by subsequent House of Lords decisions as well as by those in other courts and tribunals. His Lordship gave some further guidance on the matter by stating that parliamentary material should be admitted only where:

> "such material clearly discloses the mischief aimed at or the legislative intention lying behind the ambiguous or obscure words."[9]

Later in his speech he added a further qualification suggesting that clarity also includes the requirement that the statement of the minister represents the inten-

---

[6] The analysis of any textbook on statutory interpretation will confirm this. See, e.g., J. Bell and G. Engle, *Cross on Statutory Interpretation* (2nd edn., London, Butterworths, 1997).

[7] [1993] 1 All ER 42 at 69.

[8] *Ibid.*, at 65.

[9] *Ibid.*, at 64.

tion of Parliament as a whole. In the case before him he was satisfied that the minister's statement did represent the collective intention, in that the matter was not raised again, certain amendments were withdrawn and no further amendment was made affecting the correctness of the statement.[10] In subsequent cases before the House of Lords, this requirement has not been elaborated upon.

One or two other aspects of the speech of Lord Browne-Wilkinson are worth noting at this stage. On the particular facts of the case he found that section 63 of the Finance Act 1975 was ambiguous and that if the relevant parliamentary materials on the point were reviewed he would favour a particular construction. If the parliamentary materials were not reviewed he would favour an opposing, literal construction of the provision. However he arrived at this finding in his speech *after* having reviewed at length the parliamentary materials on the provision and *before* making the final decision on whether a reference is permissible at all. This illustrates the difficulty, discussed again below, of the potential influence of cited and sighted parliamentary materials on the decision to permit its admission. As Lord Browne-Wilkinson freely admitted: "[h]aving once looked at what was said in Parliament, it is difficult to put it out of mind".[11]

In considering the issue of the potential increase in the volume and cost of litigation which might be brought about by a relaxation of the exclusionary rule, Lord Browne-Wilkinson indicated that any attempt to introduce materials which do not satisfy the tests which he had outlined ought to be met by orders for costs against the party who has improperly introduced the materials.[12] This warning about costs has been repeated in a Practice Direction on the citation of *Hansard* which was issued with the concurrence of the Lord Chancellor, the Lord Chief Justice, the Master of the Rolls, the President of the Family Division and the Vice-Chancellor on 20 December 1994.[13] The Direction compels any party intending to refer to an extract from *Hansard* in support of an argument to serve copies of the extract on the court and all other parties to the action. Failure to comply may lead to an order for costs. We shall see below, however, that despite the fact that there are cases where Lord Browne-Wilkinson's tests have not been satisfied—in that the legislation was not ambiguous nor the minister's statement unclear—the warning as to orders for costs has so far gone unheeded.

THE CASES

A LEXIS search of the phrase "Pepper w/5 Hart", undertaken on 23 June 1998, revealed a list of 219 cases in which the decision in *Pepper* v. *Hart* was either cited in argument or referred to in judgments. The cases emanate from a wide

---

[10] [1993] 1 All ER 42 at at 71.
[11] *Ibid.*
[12] *Ibid.*, at 67.
[13] [1995] 1 WLR 192.

variety of courts and tribunals and concern a broad diversity of legislation. Twelve of the cases are from the House of Lords; forty-seven are decisions of the Civil Division of the Court of Appeal; fourteen are decisions of the Criminal Division of the Court of Appeal; one is a decision of the Northern Ireland Court of Appeal; thirty-one are decisions of the Chancery Division of the High Court; sixty-one are decisions of the Queen's Bench Division of the High Court; two are decisions of the Family Division of the High Court; one is a decision of the Privy Council; thirteen are decisions of the Employment Appeal Tribunal; four are decisions of the Scottish Court of Session; ten are decisions of the VAT Tribunal; eighteen are decisions of the Special Commissioners; one is a decision of the Registered Designs Appeal Tribunal;[14] two are decisions of the Lands Tribunal; one is a decision of an Industrial Tribunal; one is a decision of the Supreme Court of Hong Kong, High Court.

The most troublesome type of legislation appears to have been that relating to taxation; it was involved in over fifty of the cases. Of course it was also the subject-matter of *Pepper v. Hart* itself. One of the cases did not involve any legislation at all. In *(WF Trustees) Limited* v. *Evpo Safety Systems Ltd*,[15] Mr J. Sumpton Q.C., sitting as a Deputy High Court Judge, was considering the details of a difficult contract case when he had this to say:

> "[The parole evidence rule] has been relaxed in relation to the construction of a statute. But there is a considerable difference between reading Parliamentary debates which are transcribed and published daily and reading the exchanges of parties in contracts which are private to themselves."[16]

This is certainly a novel way of referring to the ruling in *Pepper* v. *Hart*, but it is illustrative of the enthusiasm with which judges have taken the case on board.

In a small number of cases appearing on the list no reference at all seems to be made to *Pepper* v. *Hart*. Two of these cases are House of Lords' decisions.[17] The probable reason for these minor aberrations is that the decision in *Pepper* v. *Hart* was referred to or cited in lower court decisions in the same case. Two other cases[18] did not concern the primary aspect of the ruling in *Pepper* v. *Hart*, relating to the relaxation of the exclusionary rule, but rather dealt with that part of the case which analysed the constitutional relationship between the courts and Parliament and the applicability of the Bill of Rights 1688.[19] These decisions will be of more interest to constitutional lawyers.

[14] One case involving Ford Motor Company's application in relation to certain intellectual property rights was appealed from the Registered Designs Appeal Tribunal to the House of Lords and thus appears four times on the list of cases. It is interesting to note that by the time the case had reached the House of Lords any discussion of the admissibility of *Hansard* had been abandoned.

[15] *The Times*, 24 May 1993.

[16] LEXIS transcript.

[17] *Imperial Chemicals Industries plc* v. *Colmer (Inspector of Taxes)* [1996] 2 All ER 23 and *Robert Gordon's College* v. *Customs and Excise Commissioners* [1996] 1 WLR 201.

[18] *Prebble* v. *Television New Zealand* [1994] 3 All ER 407 and *Allason* v. *Haines and another, The Times*, 25 July 1995.

[19] [1993] 1 All ER 42, at 50 *per* Lord Griffiths, at *per* per Lord Oliver, and at 67–9 and 73–4, *per* Lord Browne-Wilkinson.

THE APPLICATION OF *PEPPER* V. *HART* IN SUBSEQUENT HOUSE OF LORDS CASES

Within two weeks of having given its historic decision in *Pepper* v. *Hart*, the House of Lords was already having to deal with the implications. In *Warwickshire County Council* v. *Johnson*,[20] the House was asked to consider the construction of the Consumer Protection Act 1987.

The appellant, Neil Johnson, was employed as the branch manager of a retail electrical goods shop. With the authority of the owners of the shop, he had placed a notice outside the shop indicating that the shop would "beat" the price of any television or video recorder by twenty pounds. While the notice was displayed a customer saw a television advertised for sale elsewhere in the area for a particular price and, having taken the appellant to see it, sought to purchase an identical set from his shop at twenty pounds less. Although the appellant had a television in stock, he refused to sell it. The customer reported the matter to Warwickshire County Council's Trading Standards Department, which brought an action against the appellant under section 20(1) of the Consumer Protection Act 1987. That section reads as follows:

> "a person shall be guilty of an offence if, in the course of any business of his, he gives . . . to any consumers an indication which is misleading as to the price at which goods, services . . . are available."

The justices who initially heard the action dismissed it on the basis that the notice was not misleading, but they were clear that the appellant had been acting "in the course of a business of his". The Divisional Court (Stuart-Smith L.J. and Popplewell J.) allowed the Council's appeal on the basis that the notice was misleading and that in failing to honour it the appellant was acting "in the course of a business of his". The Court interpreted that phrase as meaning "in the course of his business, trade or profession". The Divisional Court then certified two points of law for consideration by the House of Lords as follows:

1. Whether for the purposes of section 20(1) of the Consumer Protection Act 1987 a statement, which in itself is not misleading on the face of it, can be rendered misleading by virtue of the fact that, even in the absence of evidence to show a general practice or intention to dishonour the offer contained therein, on one occasion the person making the statement declined to enter into a contract within the terms of the statement.
2. Whether for the purpose of section 20(2)(a) of the Consumer Protection Act 1987 an employed branch manager who fails to comply with a price indication, so that the same is to be regarded as misleading, does so "in the course of any business of his".

The appellant added a third issue in his printed case to the House of Lords on the basis that the House, in the interim, had given judgment in the case of *Pepper*

---

[20] *Ibid.*, 299.

v. *Hart*. The appellant invited the House to look at what was said in the House of Lords at the report stage of the passage of the Consumer Protection Bill by the minister concerned, Lord Beaverbrook. The appellant contended that if the House considered the legislation to be ambiguous then the ambiguity should be resolved in favour of the appellant on the basis of what had been said by the minister as to the clear intention of the legislative provisions.

The case was heard by a five-member Committee of whom two (Lord Griffiths and Lord Ackner) had also sat in *Pepper* v. *Hart*. Lord Roskill gave the only speech, with which the other Lords concurred. His speech is a curious mixture of the traditional approach to statutory interpretation coupled with the new-found freedom to relax the exclusionary rule. On the applicability of the ruling in *Pepper* v. *Hart*, he states:

> "It has thus become proper in the strictly limited circumstances defined by Lord Browne-Wilkinson in his speech . . . to have regard to what was said in Parliament in the course of the passage of the Bill . . . But before considering this matter further I shall first consider the two questions of construction."[21]

He gives no indication whether counsel for the appellant had cited the relevant parliamentary material in his submissions and thus whether he had already had sight of it. More importantly, he does not indicate, at this stage in his speech, whether the "strictly limited circumstances" to which he referred did in fact exist in the present case. He goes on to consider the issue further in his speech, but before he does so is impelled to consider the "two questions of construction" which were originally stated for the House's construction.

His approach to these two questions is to construe the legislative provisions by traditional methods of interpretation. The first question could be dealt with simply. The customer was misled by the notice which was deceptive because the appellant failed, in accordance with its terms, to beat any price: "[t]o hold otherwise would be seriously to restrict the efficacy of this part of the consumer protection legislation".[22] No mention yet of *Hansard* or any other relevant material. On the basis of traditional rules of construction he is able to answer the first question affirmatively.

A similar approach is taken to the second question, although it proved to be more difficult. His Lordship is clear that it must be answered by reference to the statute and what might be deduced from its language in the relevant sections. Finding that the language of the sections was obscure, Lord Roskill examines a number of academic commentaries on the legislation. While it had seemed curious to these commentators that the person who was actually responsible for the act in question might be immune from prosecution, he is driven to the conclusion that the phrase "in the course of any business of his" must mean any business of which the defendant is either the owner or in which he has a controlling interest.

---

[21] *Ibid*., at 302.
[22] *Ibid*.

So Lord Roskill feels able to dispose of the two substantive questions of construction without recourse to *Hansard* and by applying traditional methods of statutory interpretation. He considers the words on their face and arrives at a construction which he believes is indicative of Parliament's intentions.

However he then moves on to a consideration of the applicability of the argument concerning the admissibility of the parliamentary material. His basis for so doing is probably the inclusion of this issue in the submissions made by counsel. It is clear that a number of other courts are following this pattern of giving judgment on the admissibility of parliamentary material by applying, either explicitly or implicitly, the maxim *de bene esse*. *De bene esse* could be translated as meaning "for what it is worth". In the context of court procedure, it often refers to the practice of taking evidence out of order in the event of that evidence being lost at a future date before the substantive issue can be tried. The evidence so obtained is only to be used if the witness is not available to be examined in the normal way. As such the initial examination is a provisional one to be taken on its particular merits as and when required. The use of the principle in this manner has been incorporated into the Rules of the Supreme Court, Order 39.

The principle may also be used by the courts to take submissions from counsel at an appropriate time on issues which are to be decided at a future date. This could mean that a judge could listen to arguments on a particular issue and consider their merits at a future date. It is very arguable that this represents the normal practice of the superior courts and that judges are adept at hearing initial submissions on issues without allowing those submissions to influence their subsequent judgments.

The difficulty with allowing initial submissions on the admissibility of parliamentary materials which refer to texts or which actually contain citations from them is that they could, directly or indirectly, influence the eventual decision on admissibility. No doubt the judges will argue that they are equally adroit at hearing, seeing and reading parliamentary material without allowing what they hear, see or read to influence their decision on its admissibility. Lord Roskill is clear that the relevant parliamentary material is admissible under the ruling in *Pepper* v. *Hart* in the present case but gives no indication as to the precise basis for the finding that Lord Browne-Wilkinson's tests are satisfied:

> "As already stated it is now, within the limitations already mentioned, permissible to have regard to statements by a minister in Parliament in order to ascertain the true intention of ambiguous legislation the interpretation of which has become a matter of controversy."[23]

As he then turns immediately to a consideration of the parliamentary material, it is presumed that he has found that the relevant provisions of the Consumer Protection Act 1987 fall into the category of legislation classified above.

The parliamentary material which Lord Roskill considers consists of a statement of a minister, Lord Beaverbrook, in reply to an amendment moved by a

[23] *Ibid.*, at 304.

fellow member of the House of Lords, Lord Morton of Shuna. When the reply was heard, Lord Morton withdrew his amendment and, as Lord Roskill notes, the matter was never referred to again. Having reviewed the parliamentary material, Lord Roskill makes the following comment on its relevance:

> "In my view the answers given by the minister are consistent with the construction I have felt obliged to put upon the legislation. Although the minister said that the government would look into the matter again there are no further references to this issue at any later stage of the progress of the Bill through Parliament. The adoption of the contrary construction would be to reach a conclusion contrary to the plain intention of Parliament simply because the draftsman has used language which on one view has failed to give effect to that intention."[24]

Two issues arise from this finding. First, as stated above, the use of parliamentary material to *confirm* the already-established construction of an ambiguous legislative provision is probably not permitted under a strict interpretation of the speeches in *Pepper* v. *Hart*. Yet the use of parliamentary material in this way has been adopted by a variety of lower courts and tribunals. For example, in *Petch* v. *Gurney (Inspector of Taxes)*,[25] Millett L.J. gives a classic judgment in this category:

> "In my judgment this is not a case in which it would be appropriate to invoke the principle in *Pepper* v. *Hart* for the absence of any power to extend the time laid down by what is now s 56(4) of the 1970 Act is too plain for argument. But as it happens examination of the extracts from Hansard confirms the impression which is conveyed by the words I have quoted."[26]

Secondly, the statement by Lord Roskill that the matter had not been raised again in Parliament during the passage of the Bill confirms Lord Browne-Wilkinson's observations in *Pepper* v. *Hart* that a minister's statement will represent the collective intention if the matter is not raised again.

This initial application of the ruling in *Pepper* v. *Hart* by the House of Lords set a pattern which was to be followed in subsequent House of Lords cases as well as in other tribunals and courts. In *Chief Adjudication Officer and another* v. *Foster*,[27] decided some two months after *Pepper* v. *Hart*, the House of Lords considered the interpretation of the Social Security Acts of 1975 and 1986. The appellant was a severely disabled woman who lived at home with her parents. She received a severe disablement allowance under the Social Security Act 1975 and income support under the Social Security Act 1986, calculated in accordance with regulation 17(1) of the Income Support (General) Regulations 1987. The amount payable by way of income support included a severe disability premium because she was in receipt of attendance allowance under paragraph 13(2) of Schedule 2 to the 1987 regulations and had no non-dependants aged eighteen or

[24] *Ibid.*, at 305.
[25] [1994] 3 All ER 731.
[26] *Ibid.*, at 736.
[27] [1993] AC 754.

over residing with her within sub-paragraph (2)(a)(ii). On 8 October 1989, following an amendment of the definition of "non-dependant" in the regulations, her parents were no longer classed as non-dependants.

An adjudication officer ruled that she was no longer qualified for the premium. His decision was affirmed by a social security appeal tribunal. On appeal, a Social Security Commissioner allowed her appeal, holding that paragraph 13(2)(a)(ii) and (iii) was *ultra vires* because the Secretary of State's power to make regulations under section 22(4) of the 1986 Act applied when there were "circumstances in which persons [were] to be treated as being or as not being severely disabled". The Commissioner held that regulations made under this provision were limited to specifying circumstances directly related to the degree of physical or mental disability and could not prescribe other circumstances which might affect the extent of the disabled person's needs. On appeal by the chief adjudication officer and the Secretary of State, the Court of Appeal allowed the appeal, holding that the Commissioner had no jurisdiction to question the validity of a regulation made by the Secretary of State and that in any event paragraph 13(2)(a)(ii) and (iii) was *intra vires*. The case was appealed further to the House of Lords

Again a five-member Committee considered the case. The only speech was given by Lord Bridge. His Lordship began by outlining his construction of the relevant legislative provisions before considering the admissibility and relevance of the parliamentary materials relating to those provisions. He was able to conclude that the Commissioner had jurisdiction to determine any challenge to the validity of a provision in regulations made by the Secretary of State on the ground that it was beyond the scope of the enabling power whenever it was necessary to do so in order to determine whether a decision under appeal was erroneous in point of law. In addition he found the particular provision (paragraph 13(2)(a)(I)) to be *intra vires*.

Having reached that conclusion independently of the parliamentary material, Lord Bridge felt compelled to consider its admissibility and relevance. He indicated that, at the end of the oral arguments in the case, he had formed the opinion that the appellant must fail on the *vires* issue. Since the oral argument the decision in *Pepper* v. *Hart* had been delivered, resulting in the respondents' further submission that the House ought to look at the parliamentary material relevant to the present legislation. The House received further written submissions on the issue from both parties.

Lord Bridge then gave a fairly detailed account of aspects of the legislation's passage through Parliament. For the most part the quotations are taken from the ministers involved with the passage of the Bill, but account is also taken of the speech of a member who was moving a government amendment.[28] At the conclusion of this analysis Lord Bridge states:

---

[28] [1993] AC 754 at 770G.

"This account of the circumstances in which s 22(3) and (4) came to be enacted and the statements made by the government spokesman moving the relevant amendment in both Houses seem to me to provide precisely the kind of material which was considered in *Pepper* v. *Hart* to be available as an aid to statutory construction. Section 22(4) is undoubtedly ambiguous, as the difference of opinion in the courts below clearly shows. But it was made perfectly clear to both Houses that it was intended to use the regulation-making power. . . . Thus the parliamentary material unequivocally endorses the conclusion I had reached as a matter of construction independently of that material."[29]

A number of issues arise from this. First, does the statement of a member of either House of Parliament come within the range of admissible materials under Lord Browne-Wilkinson's tests? Clearly that person may not be a minister. Is he or she a promoter of the Bill or does the statement come within the residual category of materials necessary to understand the statements of ministers and their effect? Secondly, Lord Bridge makes no clear statement that *he* finds the legislation ambiguous or obscure. Rather the ambiguity or obscurity lies in the difference of opinion in a lower court. Thirdly, the parliamentary material appears again to be being used to *confirm* rather than to *determine* the construction of the statute. The danger remains that the sight of the material may have had an influence over the initial construction. Finally, Lord Bridge's basis for considering the material at all appears to be the fact that the issue was brought to him via the submissions of counsel and he felt compelled to deal with them despite the fact that he could arrive at a certain construction independently of that consideration.

Lord Bridge's regard for the ruling in *Pepper* v. *Hart* does not cease at this point in his speech. He enthused that this is the third case in which the admission of parliamentary material had been decisive in resolving a statutory ambiguity. He said this illustrated the potential value of the relaxation of the exclusionary rule in avoiding unnecessary litigation. The other two cases to which he referred were *Warwickshire CC* v. *Johnson*,[30] dealt with above, and *Stubbings* v. *Webb*.[31]

The decision in *Stubbings* v. *Webb* was actually given between those in *Johnson* and *Foster*. The case concerned the interpretation of the Limitation Act 1980. The respondent issued a writ on 18 August 1987, when she was over 30 years old, claiming damages against the appellants (her stepfather and stepbrother) for mental illness and psychological disturbance allegedly caused by the former's sexual and physical abuse of her as a child between the ages of two and fourteen and the latter's rape of her when she was twelve. The respondent's case was that, although she knew that she had been raped and persistently sexually abused by the appellants, she did not appreciate that she had suffered sufficiently serious injury to justify starting proceedings for damages until

[29] [1993] AC 754 at 772B.
[30] [1993] AC 754.
[31] [1993] AC 498.

September 1984 when she realised that there might be a causal link between her psychiatric problems in adult life and her sexual abuse as a child. Under section 28 of the Limitation Act 1980 the primary limitation period of three years prescribed by section 11 of the Act in respect of any personal injuries action which could have been brought by the respondent was extended in her case to January 1978, that is, three years after the date on which she attained her majority, but it then expired.

The respondent's claim was initially dismissed by the master, but on appeal the judge held that the respondent was entitled to pursue her action as of right under section 14 as she had sued within three years of the date of acquiring the knowledge that her injury was attributable to acts of the appellants which were alleged to constitute a breach of duty. The Court of Appeal dismissed an appeal by the appellants, who then appealed to the House of Lords. Their main contention was that section 11(1) of the 1980 Act did not apply to the respondent's action. The relevant parts of that section read as follows:

> "This section applies to any action for damages for negligence, nuisance or breach of duty . . . where the damages claimed . . . consist of or include damages in respect of personal injuries."

The argument was that the respondent's action was in tort, namely trespass to the person, for which section 2 of the 1980 Act prescribed a limitation period of six years from the date on which the cause of action accrued and that the provisions for the extension or non-application of the primary limitation period in personal injury actions did not apply to claims in damages for intentional trespass to the person.

Again there was a five-member Committee to hear the appeal and again only one speech was delivered, this time by Lord Griffiths. The beginning of his speech consists of an extensive analysis of the legislative and other history of the law on limitation since 1939. During that review his Lordship refers to the report of the Tucker Committee on the Limitation of Actions,[32] the contents of the Law Reform (Limitation of Actions) Act 1954, judicial interpretation of that Act, academic comment on the Limitation Act 1963, an analysis of the Limitation Act 1975, the relationship between the 1980 Act and its precedents and an analysis of the parliamentary material relevant to the passage of the 1954 Bill through Parliament.

On the question of the admissibility of this parliamentary material, Lord Griffiths is brief and to the point:

> "we now have an advantage denied to Bingham L.J. because we are now permitted to look at Hansard and when we do it becomes clear that Parliament had enacted s 2(1) of the 1954 Act with the deliberate intention of giving effect to the Tucker Committee's advice that the three-year period should apply."[33]

---

[32] *Report of the Committee on the Limitation of Actions* (London, HMSO, Cmd 7740).
[33] [1993] AC 498 at 507A.

Again a number of specific issues arise. There is no reference at all to *Pepper* v. *Hart*. There is no specific reason given for the applicability of Lord Browne-Wilkinson's tests. There is no express indication that his Lordship considers the legislation to be ambiguous or obscure or that the statement of the promoter of the Bill—who in this instance was a private member—was clear. Lord Griffiths also quotes from Lord Tucker himself who, having chaired the committee whose recommendations the Bill was proposing to introduce, commented during the second reading of the Bill upon the proceedings of the Committee. Is this part of the material necessary to understand the statement of the minister or other promoter?

Lord Griffiths had made it clear at the beginning of his speech that he favoured a construction of the legislation which barred the respondent's right of action. During the latter part of his speech he indicates that the parliamentary material *confirmed* his already-established view: "[e]ven without reference to Hansard I should not myself have construed 'breach of duty' as including a deliberate assault".[33a] The most significant aspect of this judgment lies in the fact that the House of Lords was prepared to consider references to parliamentary material without giving any obvious reason for so doing. Within two weeks of a tightly-drawn, limiting ruling, the Lords appear to have favoured a liberal interpretation of the decision—an interpretation which is being followed by the lower courts and tribunals.

*Stubbings* v. *Webb* does not appear on the LEXIS list of cases refrred to earlier because *Pepper* v. *Hart* itself was not mentioned in the case even though the relaxation of the exclusionary rule was. This discovery persuaded the author to conduct a more sophisticated LEXIS search.

In *Attorney-General* v. *Associated Newspapers Ltd and Others*[34] the House of Lords was asked to consider the Contempt of Court Act 1981. The appellants, the publishers and editor of a national newspaper and a journalist employed on the paper, published an article in the paper referring to statements, opinions and arguments made by some members of the jury as they discussed their verdicts in a well-publicised fraud trial. The appellants had not obtained the information directly from the jurors concerned but from transcripts of interviews with the jurors conducted supposedly for the purpose of *bona fide* research by persons who had placed an advertisement in another newspaper offering a reward to jurors who had taken part in a trial if they contacted a box number. The Attorney-General brought proceedings for contempt under section 8(1) of the Contempt of Court Act 1981 against the appellants for publishing the information. This sub-section reads:

> "Subject to subsection (2) below, it is a contempt of court to obtain, disclose or solicit any particulars of statements made, opinions expressed, arguments advanced or votes cast by members of a jury in the course of their deliberations in any legal proceedings."

[33a] [1993] AC 498 at 508A.
[34] [1994] 2 AC 238.

The appellants contended that the prohibition was against disclosure of deliberations by jurors themselves and did not apply to publication of information about the jury's deliberations which had been obtained indirectly from another source. The Divisional Court held that the appellants were in contempt and imposed fines.

The appeal was heard before a five-member Committee of whom Lord Lowry gave the only speech. His Lordship applied a traditional approach to find, *inter alia*, that the significant word in the legislation—"disclose"—was not ambiguous. However, as the appellants' counsel had advanced the argument that recourse ought to be had to relevant parliamentary materials, Lord Lowry felt that he ought to say something about it. Having considered certain aspects of the legislative history of the Act, including a statement in the House of Commons by the Attorney-General, he stated:

> "I deliberately refrain from discussing the question whether it would have been appropriate for your Lordships to apply *Pepper* v. *Hart* to the facts of this case."[35]

This conclusion is qualified by his Lordship's finding that the legislative history was "complicated and controversial". However it is clear that the parliamentary materials were considered before the decision not to deliberate on the admissibility under *Pepper* v. *Hart* and no clear and obvious reason is given for not admitting the materials.

A similar approach was taken by the House in *Scher and others* v. *Policyholders Protection Board and Others (No. 2)*.[36] The House had been asked to consider aspects of the Policyholders Protection Act 1975 and the Insurance Companies Act 1982. The plaintiffs were lawyers, doctors and accountants practising in the United States and Canada who had taken out professional liability policies with four insurance companies which were authorised under the Insurance Companies Act 1982 to carry on insurance business in the United Kingdom. The plaintiffs were either individuals in private practice or individual partners and professional corporation partners of a legal partnership and shareholders in the corporation partners. In 1990 the insurers became insolvent, petitioned for their winding-up and stopped paying claims under the policies taken out by the plaintiffs. The question arose in the liquidation whether the Policyholders Protection Board was under a duty to indemnify the plaintiffs in consequence of the insurers' failure to meet the plaintiffs' claims.

The Board was established pursuant to the Policyholders Protection Act 1975 for the purpose of assisting or protecting policyholders who had been or might be prejudiced as the result of the inability of authorised insurance companies carrying on business in the United Kingdom to meet liabilities under policies issued by them. The plaintiffs sought declarations that the Board was liable to indemnify them in respect of the insurers' failure to meet their claims, contend-

---

[35] [1994] 2 AC 238 at 261H.
[36] [1993] 4 All ER 840.

ing that the insurers were carrying on insurance business in the United Kingdom. The defendants contended that paying claims in the United States and Canada could not constitute carrying on insurance business in the United Kingdom.

The case was dealt with at length in the Court of Appeal and the House of Lords, where the Appellate Committee received submissions and gave judgment on the construction of the legislation on two occasions. In the first case,[37] the ruling in *Pepper* v. *Hart* was argued by counsel but was not referred to in the judgments. By the time the case was heard for the second time, Lord Mustill was prepared to consider the matter further. He indicated that the House had:

> "consented to receive, in accordance with *Pepper (Inspector of Taxes)* v. *Hart* extracts from the parliamentary records of debates during the committee and report stages of the passage of the Policyholders Protection Bill through the House of Lords."[38]

Implicit in the judgment is the question of the interpretation of provisions of that legislation, but no distinct reason, under the conditions imposed by the ruling in *Pepper* v. *Hart*, is given for having considered the parliamentary material. Lord Mustill goes on to indicate that the examination of the parliamentary material confirmed the construction which he was already prepared to put on the legislation:

> "I should record that so far as they went these extracts supported the view that the general nature of the problem had been recognised, and that Parliament, unable to devise a more precise solution, had chosen to treat it in the very broad manner suggested above."[39]

As indicated above, there now appears to be a series of cases where the courts, including the House of Lords, are prepared to consider submissions, hear arguments or view the contents of parliamentary material without obviously linking that consideration to the ruling in *Pepper* v. *Hart*. The case of *Stubbings* v. *Webb* is one such example. Another is the case of *Steele, Ford & Newton* v. *Crown Prosecution Service and another*.[40] Here the House of Lords was considering aspects of the Supreme Court Act 1981. Orders had been made at trials in the Crown Court that four firms of solicitors should personally pay costs thrown away as a result of their conduct of the defences of their clients. The solicitors successfully appealed to the Court of Appeal, and the Lord Chancellor's Department in turn appealed to the House of Lords.

A five-member Committee heard the appeal and one speech was given by Lord Bridge. After considering in detail a variety of pieces of legislation relevant to the issue, Lord Bridge, in considering why a certain provision had been inserted into the Supreme Court Act 1981, states: "I was at first puzzled by this

[37] [1993] 3 All ER 384.
[38] [1993] 4 All ER 840 at 852a.
[39] *Ibid.*
[40] [1993] 2 WLR 934.

. . . Happily our new freedom to refer to Hansard solves the mystery."[41] He refers to an amendment to the Bill at the instance of the Law Society and quotes from the speech of the Solicitor-General in moving the amendment. It is implicit in his speech that he is attempting to discover the intention of Parliament in enacting a particular provision. It is not clear that the provision is ambiguous or obscure or could lead to an absurdity. It merely puzzles the judge that it was included. That the provision is not ambiguous or obscure or leads to an absurdity is evidenced by Lord Bridge's conclusion that even without the explanation offered by the parliamentary material he would have favoured a particular construction.

This review of the application of the ruling in *Pepper* v. *Hart* has shown that the early decisions of the House of Lords do not appear to favour a strict interpretation of Lord Browne-Wilkinson's tests. A strict interpretation would mean that the three conditions outlined by his Lordship must be applied in a sequential fashion. The first task for the court would be to decide whether the legislation in question is ambiguous, obscure or leads to an absurdity. This would be determined *without* argument about, or recourse to, parliamentary material. Should the court determine that the legislation is not ambiguous or obscure and does not lead to an absurdity, that should be the end of the matter and there should be no further reference to *Hansard*. Should the court determine that the legislation *is* ambiguous, obscure or leads to an absurdity then reference to *Hansard* to determine the second (the material consists of a statement by a minister or other promoter of the Bill) and third (the clarity of the statement) of Lord Browne-Wilkinson's conditions should be permitted. At this stage counsel could present argument on the existence and content of such material.

Initially, the House of Lords did not support such an approach. The application of the tests was not strict. Rather the House seemed to be prepared to consider parliamentary material without giving a clear indication that it had found the legislation to be ambiguous, obscure or absurd. Occasionally the decision on ambiguity, obscurity or absurdity was based not on a finding by the House itself, but on the difference of opinion in the courts below as to how interpret the provision. Often the House considered parliamentary material *de bene esse*, compelling itself to have regard to it because arguments on it had appeared in counsel's submissions. The result was that it often had sight of parliamentary material prior to a decision on its admissibility and the material looked at included not just statements of ministers. Rarely did a consideration of the parliamentary material dispose of the issue of construction. More often than not the House used the statements in *Hansard* to confirm a construction of legislation which had already been established by traditional methods. Use of parliamentary material for this purpose is *not* justified by *Pepper* v. *Hart* itself. The House nevertheless appeared to feel that it could have recourse to *Hansard* without giving a clear exposition of the basis for doing so.

[41] *Ibid.* at 944.

## HAS THIS APPROACH BEEN MIRRORED IN THE DECISIONS OF OTHER COURTS AND TRIBUNALS?

An analysis of a large number of cases shows that the trends established by the House of Lords in its initial application of the ruling in *Pepper* v. *Hart* have indeed been reflected in the lower courts and tribunals. There are instances where those courts do appear to be taking a strict line. In *R.* v. *Singleton*,[42] for instance, the Court of Appeal applied the ruling in the most precise manner. Counsel had argued that this was a case in which recourse to parliamentary material was warranted but Farquharson L.J. answered the point very succinctly:

> "It is necessary prior to that evidence being admitted by the court, to establish that the provision which it is sought to explain is one that contains an ambiguity. In our opinion no such ambiguity is disclosed by subsection (1) of s 9."[43]

There is no evidence that the court had sight of the relevant parliamentary material before arriving at its decision to exclude it. A similarly concise approach was taken in *R.* v. *Stipendiary Magistrates, ex p. Director of the Serious Fraud Office*.[44] Butler-Sloss L.J. was clear that there was no ambiguity, obscurity or absurdity warranting recourse to *Hansard*. She arrived at that conclusion by examining a previous case in which the possibility of examining *Hansard* to assist in the construction of the same legislative provision had received short shrift from Steyn L.J. (as he then was).[45]

In *R.* v. *Moore*[46] the Court of Appeal gave no indication that counsel had submitted argument on the applicability of *Pepper* v. *Hart* (which does not necessarily mean that it was not presented) and Sedley J., giving the judgment of the Court, stated:

> "there is no ambiguity of language or obscurity of literal meaning . . . taken on its own as would entitle the court to seek out the meaning by other means."[47]

In *R.* v. *Dorset County Council, ex p. Rolls and another*,[48] Laws J. himself raised the possibility of whether the legislation was obscure, ambiguous or could lead to an absurdity such as to justify recourse to the relevant parliamentary material. Remarkably it was he who then received short shrift from counsel, who did not want an adjournment and could see potential listing difficulties!

---

[42] *The Times*, 22 June 1994.
[43] LEXIS transcript.
[44] *Independent*, 24 June 1994.
[45] *Re Arrows Ltd (No. 4)* [1993] 3 All ER 861.
[46] 159 JP 101.
[47] LEXIS transcript.
[48] 26 HLR 381.

In *Re Ford Motor Company Ltd*,[49] the superintending examiner acting for the Registrar considered that the relevant legislative provision was sufficiently ambiguous or obscure to justify recourse to the relevant parliamentary material. He made it clear that the possibility of access to *Hansard* had not been raised in submission by counsel. He did, however, state that he had considered it appropriate to "consider whether any relevant parliamentary statement conflict (*sic*) with the decision I have reached".[50] This suggests that he had seen the relevant material prior to arriving at his decision that the legislative provision was ambiguous.

What are the difficulties with the remaining cases? The courts have either had the parliamentary materials cited to them in argument or have had sight of them by other means. In some cases the judges have applied the maxim *de bene esse* to allow the submissions on the parliamentary material to be heard, in other cases the judges are not explicit that they are hearing submissions *de bene esse* but this appears to have been their intention, and in a number of cases the courts have given no reason at all for hearing submissions on the use of parliamentary material.

An example of the last approach occurred when *Re Ford Motor Company Ltd* reached the Court of Appeal.[51] McGowan L.J., in agreeing with the decision of the lower tribunal, stated:

> "In so doing I have not been influenced by the statements of Government ministers in piloting the 1988 Act through the Houses of Parliament, although we looked at many passages in those statements *de bene esse*. I have not considered it appropriate to have regard to those statements because, in accordance with the words of Lord Browne-Wilkinson . . . I do not consider the legislation to be ambiguous or obscure or that the literal meaning of it leads to an absurdity."[52]

Obviously "regard" in this context means "judicial consideration", because the learned judge had already looked at the statements.

In *R. v. Secretary of State for the Home Department, ex p. Okello*,[53] Laws J. indicated that he was having regard to the material out of deference to counsel's argument. Likewise, in *Hassall and another v. Secretary of State for Social Security*[54] Henry L.J. stated that the court would allow the admission of parliamentary material because the question had been contended before the court by counsel. And in *Griffin (Inspector of Taxes) v. Craig-Harvey*,[55] Vinelott J., after having decided that the legislation was not ambiguous or obscure, indicated that, because the parliamentary material had been adduced, he should say something about it.

---

[49] LEXIS transcript.
[50] LEXIS transcript.
[51] LEXIS transcript.
[52] LEXIS transcript.
[53] [1994] Imm.AR 261.
[54] *The Times*, 26 Dec. 1994.
[55] [1994] STC 54.

In a large number of the cases examined, the courts followed the initial lead of the House of Lords and were willing to consider submissions, hear arguments or consider the contents of parliamentary material without giving an obvious reason for doing so or, alternatively, after having considered the parliamentary material, the courts refrained from answering the question of their admissibility under the *Pepper* v. *Hart* principle.

Let us look at some examples of this approach. In *Massmould Holdings Ltd* v. *Payne*,[56] Vinelott J. indicated that he had reached his own conclusion on the construction of the relevant provisions of the Finance Act 1972 but agreed to read the applicable parliamentary material on those provisions. He stated that, *if they were admissible*, he was not persuaded that they assisted counsel's submissions on the construction point. He gave no indication whether they would be admissible under the ruling in *Pepper* v. *Hart*.

In *Connolly* v. *Secretary of State for Northern Ireland*,[57] MacDermott L.J. indicated that it was permissible under the principle in *Pepper* v. *Hart* to look at a ministerial statement as an aid to statutory interpretation if the legislation was ambiguous or obscure. He then went on to consider the relevant passage from the parliamentary material. Implicit in his decision to do this is his finding that the legislation was ambiguous or obscure, but this is not clearly stated to be the reason for the referral to *Hansard*.[58]

In *R.* v. *Jefferson*,[59] Auld J., in a startling admission that the material should not be before the court, stated:

> "We are fortified in our conclusion by preparatory material for the 1986 Act, to which, *if there had been any ambiguity*, we would be entitled to have regard."[60]

Having seen the parliamentary material in advance, the lower courts have often gone on to decide that the legislation was not ambiguous or obscure so as to invoke the principle in *Pepper* v. *Hart*. The difficulty lies in deciding whether or not the decision on ambiguity, obscurity or absurdity was influenced by the earlier access to the parliamentary material on the issue. In some of these cases the courts declined to comment further on the matter, but in some the courts went on to make comments about what they had read or seen. In a number of the cases the courts, in a somewhat self-congratulatory manner, indicated that the parliamentary material confirmed their initial construction of the legislation. For example, in *Petch* v. *Gurney (Inspector of Taxes)*,[61] Millett L.J. gave a classic judgment in this category:

---

[56] [1993] STC 62.

[57] LEXIS transcript.

[58] It is interesting to note that the judge refers to a ministerial statement on the predecessor to the legislation actually in contention. The legislation in contention was an Order in Council about which there was, presumably, no ministerial statement. The preceding legislation was an Act of the Stormont Parliament.

[59] [1994] 1 All ER 270.

[60] *Ibid.*, at 281, emphasis added.

[61] [1994] 3 All ER 731.

"In my judgment this is not a case in which it would be appropriate to invoke the principle in *Pepper* v. *Hart* for the absence of any power to extend the time laid down by what is now s.56(4) of the 1970 Act is too plain for argument. But as it happens examination of the extracts from Hansard confirms the impression which is conveyed by the words I have quoted that what was under consideration was the power."[62]

In certain cases the courts have indicated that there was no assistance to be derived from the parliamentary provisions. Again this points to the obvious danger that the construction has been influenced by what was seen or read in the parliamentary material.

In two of the cases where the courts had access to the parliamentary material apparently *de bene esse*, they eventually refused recourse to *Hansard* under the third of Lord Browne-Wilkinson's conditions, that is, that the statement of the minister was not clear.[63] The two cases are worthy of note for other reasons too. In the *Hawthorne* case, there is the most extensive recourse to the material in *Hansard* in any of the cases examined. The material included statements by ordinary Members of Parliament. In the *Van Dyck* decision, the case was relisted after the original judgment had been given so that submissions on the applicability of *Pepper* v. *Hart* might be heard. Again the analysis of the parliamentary material is fairly extensive. The eventual judgment is given in two chapters.

In one of the cases the court decided that there could not be recourse to *Hansard* on the basis that the material relied on did not form part of the matrix of the statute.[64] They included the recommendations of the Keith Committee and the response by the Board of the Inland Revenue. These could not be considered to be evidence of the intentions of Parliament.

In one or two cases the reasons given for eventually disallowing recourse to *Hansard* under the principles in *Pepper* v. *Hart* could not be easily explained. In *Mendip District Council* v. *Glastonbury Festivals Ltd*,[65] the court allowed recourse to *Hansard* in relation to one piece of legislation without giving any reason for so doing and then indicated that no useful assistance could be gained from the material found. In relation to the second piece of legislation, which post-dated the commission of the criminal offences which were the subject of the case, the judge indicated that he doubted: "whether it is permissible to endeavour to construe an earlier statute, that in question, by reference to a later statute".[66] In *R.* v. *Newham London Borough Council, ex p. Barking*[67] we have probably seen the most illogical application of the ruling in *Pepper* v. *Hart* from a legal point of view. In this case, Potts J. was invited by counsel to look, under

---

[62] *Ibid.*, at 736.
[63] *R.* v. *London Borough of Wandsworth, ex p. Hawthorne*, CO/2122/93, LEXIS transcript; *Van Dyck and another* v. *Secretary of State for the Environment and Another* [1993] 1 PLR 124.
[64] *Joint (Inspector of Taxes)* v. *Bracken (Chancery)* [1994] STC 300.
[65] [1993] Crim.LR 701.
[66] LEXIS transcript.
[67] LEXIS transcript.

the principle in *Pepper* v. *Hart*, at certain parliamentary material which, it was believed, supported a certain construction of the legislation. After referring to all the conditions laid down by Lord Browne-Wilkinson, the judge indicates: "[i]n order to decide the point I looked at the Parliamentary material".[68] He is of the belief that the fact that he then discovers that the statement of the minister is not clear is sufficient to make it impermissible to have regard to the material in construing the statute.

In a number of the cases where the courts originally considered the parliamentary material, recourse to *Hansard was* permitted under the principles in *Pepper* v. *Hart*. For example, in *Botross* v. *London Borough of Hammersmith and Fulham*,[69] the court considered that the assistance which could be gained from the parliamentary material fell within the limits of *Pepper* v. *Hart*. Having considered the material the court was reassured to discover that its construction of the legislation was confirmed by the statement of the government minister in accepting the amendment.

In *Sunderland Polytechnic* v. *Evans*,[70] the Employment Appeal Tribunal decided that on the basis of the submissions which had been made before it, the construction of the legislation was obscure. However in order to satisfy itself that the approach which it was taking, based on an earlier judgment,[71] was correct, it would look at the parliamentary material. Once regarded, that material did confirm that the earlier precedent was wrong and that the tribunal ought to move away from it.

It is equally clear that there are a range of cases where the courts are prepared to have recourse to *Hansard* without giving an explicit reason under the ruling in *Pepper* v. *Hart* and indeed without referring to that judgment at all.

MELLUISH *(INSPECTOR OF TAXES)* V. BMI *(NO. 3)* LTD—
LORD-BROWNE-WILKINSON REVIEWS *PEPPER* V. *HART*

In *Melluish (Inspector of Taxes)* v. *BMI (No. 3) Ltd*,[72] Lord Browne-Wilkinson gave his first critique of the use of his prior ruling in *Pepper* v. *Hart*. His Lordship's comments about the admissibility of parliamentary materials in *Melluish* are critical and are reflective of a concern that the ruling, which was initially formulated in terms of strict limitation, has since been applied in too liberal and permissive a manner.

*Melluish*, like *Pepper* v. *Hart*, is a case concerned with the interpretation of finance legislation. In particular the appeal raised the question of the capital

---

[68] LEXIS transcript.
[69] *The Times,* 7 Nov. 1994.
[70] [1993] IRLR 196.
[71] *Home Office* v. *Ayres* [1992] IRLR 59.
[72] [1995] 4 All ER 453.

allowances which could be claimed by taxpayers who carried on the business of purchasing plant and machinery and leasing it to relevant users. The particular difficulty in the case arose from the fact that the plant purchased by the appellant taxpayer companies, such as central heating, lifts, boilers and ventilation, was incorporated into the structure of the buildings owned by the lessees of the plant. As a result they became fixtures. Ordinarily they would then become the property of the owner of the land. In order to claim capital allowance under the Finance Acts of 1971 and 1985, the appellant taxpayer companies had to show that the plant, which had at all material times been affixed to the land, nevertheless "belonged" to the companies..

In his speech dismissing the appeals, Lord Browne-Wilkinson addressed the submissions of counsel for the Crown that his Lordship should have regard to statements made by ministers in the course of the progress through Parliament of the Finance Bill in 1985. Applying the test to the present facts, his Lordship accepted that some of the language in the Finance Act 1985 was ambiguous or obscure. However the remaining tests for the admissibility of the parliamentary material were not satisfied:

> "The parliamentary materials sought to be introduced by the revenue in the present case were not directed to the specific statutory provision under consideration or to the problem raised by the litigation but to another provision and another problem. The Revenue sought to derive from the ministerial statements on that other provision and other problem guidance on the point your Lordships have to consider . . . In my view this is an improper use of the relaxed rule introduced by *Pepper* v. *Hart* which, if properly used, can be a valuable aid to construction when Parliament has directly considered the point in issue and passed the legislation on the basis of the ministerial statement. It provides no assistance to a court and is capable of giving rise to much expense and delay if attempts are made to widen the category of materials that can be looked at."[73]

His Lordship was further of the view that judges should be astute to check such misuse of the new rule by making appropriate orders as to costs wasted. In the present case, if the costs issue had been pertinent, he would have suggested disallowing some part of the costs of the Revenue for introducing such materials.

The significance of the critical remarks of Lord Browne-Wilkinson is twofold. Specifically, his remarks concerning costs reflect his view in *Pepper* v. *Hart* that, on the basis of a potential increase in the volume and cost of litigation which might be brought about by a relaxation of the exclusionary rule, any attempt to introduce material which does not satisfy the tests which he outlined ought to be met by orders for costs against the party who has improperly introduced the material. Secondly, and more importantly, his remarks about the inappropriate use of the relaxed rule are indicative of a belief that the three conditions for the introduction of parliamentary material were meant to be applied in a strict man-

---

[73] *Ibid.*, at 468f.

ner and that deviance from such an approach should be penalised by the impo-
sition of orders as to costs. The comments are also reflective of a concern that
the current practice is permissive and indulgent, allowing for the submission of
parliamentary material outside the confines of the rule.

## TO WHAT EXTENT HAS THE HOUSE OF LORDS HEEDED
## LORD BROWNE-WILKINSON'S SECOND WARNING?

*Secretary of State for Social Security and another* v. *Remilien*[74] is the most
recent decision of the House of Lords to consider the ruling in *Pepper* v. *Hart*
and it gives a good indication of the current attitude of the House towards the
ruling.

The appellants were single mothers and nationals of member states of the
European Community living in England and claiming income support. They
received letters from the Home Office informing each of them that the Secretary
of State was not satisfied that they were lawfully resident in the United Kingdom
under European Community law in view of the fact that they were present in a
non-economic capacity and had become a burden on public funds; they should
make arrangements to leave. An Adjudication Officer of the Department of
Social Security subsequently decided that the appellants were no longer entitled
to income support since they were persons who, for the purposes of regulation
21(3)(h) of the Income Support (General) Regulations 1987, had been required
by the Secretary of State to leave the United Kingdom. The Adjudication Officer
terminated payment of income support pursuant to paragraph 17 of Schedule 7
to the 1987 Regulations.

The Adjudication Officer's decision against one of the appellants was
quashed on her application for judicial review. A Social Security Appeal
Tribunal had already upheld the Adjudication Officer's decision in relation to
the other appellant. She then appealed to a Social Security Commissioner and
was successful. The Chief Adjudication Officer appealed to the Court of Appeal
against both decisions. The Court of Appeal, by a majority, allowed the appeals,
on the ground that the letters from the Home Office constituted a requirement
to leave the United Kingdom which ended the appellants' entitlement to income
support.

A five-member Committee allowed the appeals, by a majority.[75] Lord
Hoffmann gave the only speech for the majority. On first reading, his references
to the applicability of the ruling in *Pepper* v. *Hart* appear to show that he was
prepared to be strict in limiting its application. As noted above, the main issue
for consideration was the meaning of the phrase "required by the Secretary of
State to leave the United Kingdom". Counsel for the Secretary of State and the

---

[74] [1998] 1 All ER 129.
[75] Lord Slynn dissented on the substantive issues. His speech contains no reference to the decision in *Pepper* v. *Hart*.

Chief Adjudication Officer had sought to rely on a statement made by the Parliamentary Under-Secretary of State for Social Security to the House of Commons Standing Committee on Statutory Instruments on the meaning and intention of the relevant regulation and had argued that the parliamentary material was admissible under the principle in *Pepper* v. *Hart*. Lord Hoffmann, (perhaps mindful that his draft speech would be read by Lord Browne-Wilkinson?), was clear on the point:

> "One of the conditions for admissibility under that principle is that the statement must be clear . . . I do not think that the minister's statement passes this test. Nor, probably, did the departmental brief upon which it is based . . . I find the statement to be of no assistance."[76]

What is interesting about Lord Hoffmann's speech is that, while the above passage contains the only reference to the applicability of *Pepper* v. *Hart*, there are other excerpts which refer to the relevant parliamentary material. It is clear from those excerpts that Lord Hoffmann did, in fact, find the statement to be of assistance.

An earlier submission by counsel for the Secretary of State and the Chief Adjudication Officer related to the fact that the regulation in question had been passed, in part, to give effect to the decision in *R.* v. *Secretary of State, ex p. Antonissen*.[77] In rejecting the substantive argument, Lord Hoffmann had the following to say:

> "one cannot exclude the possibility that the Secretary of State (or, more realistically, his advisers) were simply muddled about what *Ex p. Antonissen* had decided. There is some support for this view in the passage from the minutes of a statement made on 27 April 1993 by Mr Alistair Burt, Parliamentary Under-Secretary of State for Social Security to the House of Commons Second Standing Committee on Statutory Instruments etc, to which Mr Plender drew our attention."[78]

This is the very parliamentary statement which Lord Hoffmann had already rejected under the third of Lord Browne-Wilkinson's tests for admissibility of parliamentary material and from which he could "find . . . no assistance". No reason is given for this later reference to the parliamentary material, beyond the fact that counsel made reference to it in his submissions. It is arguable that the inclusion or rejection of the relevant parliamentary material made little difference to Lord Hoffmann's overall conclusions on the meaning of the legislative provisions in these appeals and that he was able to arrive at a suitable construction on other substantive and unrelated grounds.

What is clear, however, is that judges are gaining sight of parliamentary material, largely through the submissions of counsel. The approach to the applica-

---

[76] [1998] 1 All ER 129 at 147. Lord Hoffmann is obviously of the view that the first limb of Lord Browne-Wilkinson's test is satisfied, i.e. that the legislative provision which he is being asked to interpret is ambiguous, obscure or leads to an absurdity. The sequential nature of the three limbs of the test demands that conclusion.

[77] Case C–292/89 [1991] ECR I–745.

[78] [1998] 1 All ER 129 at 145.

bility and use of the material, once cited and sighted, appears to be contradictory. Once seen, the parliamentary material is difficult to put out of one's mind, and, as the speech of Lord Hoffmann demonstrates, it is easy to use the material for certain purposes and not others.[79]

## CONCLUSION

The ruling in *Pepper* v. *Hart* is one which was initially formulated in terms of strict limitations. "Beyond that I would not go" were the initial words of Lord Browne-Wilkinson, a warning which was repeated by a number of other senior judges. This research has indicated that the House of Lords' initial approach to the interpretation and application of the rule in *Pepper* v. *Hart* was to relax the rule further. Judges were ready to hear submissions on and view the contents of parliamentary material *before* they had made a decision to admit such material under the ruling in *Pepper* v. *Hart*. The courts were using the material to *confirm* the construction of the legislation which they had already discovered. The judges appeared to be willing to extend the meaning of "ambiguity" and "obscurity" and to broaden the range of admissible parliamentary material by arguing that it was necessary to understand the statements of ministers and their effect. Further it was also clear that judges were willing to refer to *Hansard* without giving a clear basis for their decision to do so and without indicating that the basis for that recourse was the decision in *Pepper* v. *Hart*. The initial example set by the House of Lords has been followed by the lower courts and tribunals.

In speaking about the possibility of this situation arising Lord Lester has stated:

> "We also argued for a strict and disciplined approach to the use of extrinsic aids to construction, firmly controlled by the courts. If this is not happening, it is to be hoped that the House of Lords will reaffirm the need to keep recourse to *Hansard* within the clear limits which they stated in *Pepper* v. *Hart*."[80]

The speech of Lord Browne-Wilkinson in *Melluish* shows that he is concerned about the manner in which his ruling has been interpreted and implemented. He has also issued a warning to legal advisers that the inappropriate use of parliamentary material will be met with appropriate orders as to costs. A stringent, restrained approach to the use of extrinsic aids is not happening. Lord Browne-Wilkinson has had to lead the call to reaffirm the need to keep resort to *Hansard* within the distinct limitations which he stated in *Pepper* v. *Hart*. Despite this, the recent approach of the House of Lords demonstrates that judges are taking

---

[79] Another recent House of Lords decision, in the case of *Inland Revenue Commissioners* v. *Willoughby* [1997] 1 WLR 1071, demonstrates the extent to which judges will freely refer to parliamentary materials. In this case, Lord Nolan muses on how an earlier Committee might have decided an appeal, eventually reversed by a subsequent Committee, had it had access to relevant parliamentary material. See further his comments at 1073.

[80] "*Pepper* v. *Hart* Revisited" (1994) *Stat.LR* 10 at 21.

a contradictory attitude towards the applicability and use of parliamentary material. It may be that Lord Browne-Wilkinson's triple locks for the admissibility of parliamentary material are slowly being unpicked by the judiciary and that *Hansard* has become, or is becoming, an open book for guidance on the meaning and purpose of legislative provisions.

# 12

# *Uneasy Cases*

## SIMON LEE

In the *Bland* case,[1] Lord Mustill confessed to "acute unease" about adopting a way "through the legal and ethical maze", fearing that the decision "may only emphasise the distortions of a legal structure which is already both morally and intellectually misshapen". That would have been stinging criticism if it had come from a dissenting judge or a critic but it might seem extraordinary for someone who was a party to a unanimous decision. It might cause "acute unease" in the wider public if they gathered that the Law Lords are that critical of the results of their own work. On the same page of his judgment in the law reports, Lord Mustill uses the adjective "acute" again to describe the moral dilemma in the *Bland* case: "[t]his appeal obviously raises acute problems of ethics, but this should not obscure the fact that it is also exceptionally difficult in point of law".

Although academic lawyers are wont to talk about "hard cases", and the wider public knows that they are alleged to make "bad law", the major ethical dilemmas faced by the courts could equally well be described as cases which make us, or the Law Lords, "uneasy". It is not simply that informed lawyers could reasonably disagree on what the result should be. It is that the judges themselves, and the wider community if they too are informed about the case, will feel a moral unease, whichever way the result goes. The *Bland* case is the classic example of this so far in the 1990s in British law, as was the *Gillick* case in the 1980s.[2] Elsewhere, the *X* case in Ireland[3] rocked the nation and brought worldwide interest in the Irish Constitution and legal system. Such "uneasy cases", however, do not have to be confined to medical law and ethics, nor to the media's equation of morality with life, death and sex. We can feel a moral unease, for example, about the way in which prisoners or asylum-seekers are treated by the state (although, admittedly, it is often the death penalty or a life sentence which excites media interest in the former and the alleged prospect of assassination which attracts the media to asylum-seekers) or the way in which the law deals with inequality and discrimination. Nonetheless, it is the sexual context of the *Brown* decision (where the Law Lords divided three to two in

---

[1] *Airedale NHS Trust* v. *Bland* [1993] 1 All ER 821.
[2] *Gillick* v. *West Norfolk and Wisbech Area Health Authority* [1985] 3 All ER 402.
[3] *Attorney-General* v. *X and Others* [1992] 1 IR 1

favour of the proposition that consent in sado-masochistic homosexual encounters is not a defence to charges of actual bodily harm)[4] and the life and death nature of *Bland* (where the Law Lords were unanimous in ruling that withdrawing feeding by a tube did not amount to a criminal act where the patient was in a persistent vegetative state) that make them the most famously uneasy cases of the 1990s thus far.

Public discourse about morality is enhanced in many democracies by the quality of reasoning in the highest courts as they tussle with such ethical dilemmas. The way in which the legal system requires a yes/no result, usually in the context of a specific dispute between two parties, appeals to the media as reducing the complexities of moral dilemmas to something like the sporting simplicity of a football game. Supporters can choose a team and root for its success. The rhythm of a case as it wends its way through an appellate system gives opportunities aplenty for comment. There are positive and negative aspects of such debates, but one at least expects the supreme courts to raise the standard of argument and it is the quality of argument, not the weight of popular opinion, which ought to determine the outcome of the "uneasy cases" in such a constitutional system.

In our society, however, the Law Lords would not pretend to be regularly at the forefront of public debates about morality. This is in marked contrast to the leading role played by the highest courts in jurisdictions which in other respects have something in common (especially the common law and a common language) such as in Australia, Canada, Ireland, New Zealand, South Africa, the USA.[5] Indeed, the Law Lords as the Appellate Committee of the House of Lords seem to face moral questions less frequently than they do *themselves* under another guise, when they sit (augmented occasionally by judges from the jurisdiction in question) as the Judicial Committee of the Privy Council.[6] By contrast with many other supreme courts, then, the Law Lords' lot is not usually a morally stimulating one.

Nonetheless, the Law Lords seem to be intrigued by moral argument, albeit in a self-deprecating way as if we should not expect too much from amateurs enjoying a hobby. They have two defence mechanisms lest anyone think that they over-estimate their own abilities or scope. They send out explicit messages to the effect that this should really be Parliament's responsibility and implicit messages that we need not be too uneasy when, in Parliament's absence, they have to take decisions because they will only be steering a moderate middle course.

This fascinates me, partly because I do not believe that the next generation of Law Lords will defer to Parliament as the right body to take the difficult moral decisions in a divided society and partly because I do not accept their (unarticu-

---

[4] *R. v. Brown* [1993] 2 All ER 75.

[5] Cf. Christopher J Peters, "Foolish Consistency: On Equality, Integrity and Justice in *Stare Decisis*" (1996) 105 *Yale LJ* 2031.

[6] See also Chap. 7 above.

lated) line of thinking which reduces moral dilemmas to two extreme views (broadly speaking, crudely utilitarian on the one hand and crudely religious on the other), leaving judges to glide through the middle as if in an enlightened, not-too-utilitarian and not-too-religious, but rather a right-on or at least rights-on, way.

The best efforts by Law Lords to grapple with moral dilemmas in the 1990s have been by Lord Mustill, with whom we began, and by Lord Browne-Wilkinson. Although their judgments are the most reflective of the Law Lords' opinions in *Bland*, they are still subject to these two manœuvres. Lord Mustill pointed out that:

> "The whole matter cries out for exploration in depth by Parliament and then for the establishment by legislation not only of a new set of ethically and intellectually consistent rules, distinct from the general criminal law, but also of a sound procedural framework within which the rules can be applied to individual cases."[6a]

Lord Browne-Wilkinson opined that:

> "Where a case raises wholly new moral and social issues, in my judgment it is not for the judges to seek to develop new, all-embracing, principles of law in a way which reflects the individual judges' moral stance when society as a whole is substantially divided on the relevant moral issues."[6b]

This immediately followed the sentence in which he noted that the Court of Appeal in the instant case:

> "reaching the conclusion that the withdrawal of food and Anthony Bland's subsequent death would be for his benefit, attaches importance to impalpable factors such as personal dignity and the way Anthony Bland would wish to be remembered but does not take into account spiritual values which, for example, a member of the Roman Catholic church would regard as relevant in assessing such benefit."[6c]

Although Lord Browne-Wilkinson is being generous to, and inclusive of, a particular viewpoint, there is a danger that this approach inadvertently marginalises the important contribution which could otherwise be made by religious groups. The first problem is an assumption which others might make, perhaps even subconsciously, that because the values are described as "spiritual", the viewpoint can be disregarded by those who do not share the faith in question. The second concern is that the "for example" might be lost and the assumption could be made that there is an "absolutist" position endorsed only by Catholics and perhaps orthodox Jews.

In fact, the Catholic and Anglican bishops were at one in their submission on *Bland* to the House of Lords Select Committee, "*Euthanasia—No!*" (June 1993).[7] We are told by the patient's father (described by Sir Stephen Brown P. in the case as a "splendid straightforward Yorkshireman"), as relayed in the first instance judgment, that Anthony Bland "was not religious but that he had

---

[6a] [1993] 1 All ER 821 at 889b.
[6b] *Ibid.*, at 879g.
[6c] *Ibid.*, at 879f.
[7] Reprinted as an appendix to this chap.

attended Sunday School in the Church of England". Let us suppose, counterfac-
tually, that Anthony Bland had been enthused by Sunday school, that he was a
communicant member of the Church of England and that the Law Lords wanted
to know his church's position. It would be remarkably similar to the position
which Lord Browne-Wilkinson ascribes to "the Roman Catholic church and
orthodox Jews". One could go further and say that the joint Anglican-Catholic
document could be justifiably described as representing almost all Christians
since the covering note explains that:

> "There has been no opportunity for the joint submission to be considered by the Free
> Church Federal Council. However, a number of people from the Free Churches with
> expertise in this field have been consulted. It is clear that the joint submission would
> also receive the support of the Free Churches."

The document is clear, easy to read and accessible to all, regardless of their
religious beliefs, of whatever variety, their agnosticism or their atheism. Which
is not to say that all will agree with it, of course, but the short text is reprinted
as an appendix to this chapter in order to show that such church documents are
relevant and not couched in abstruse theological rhetoric. The churches' analysis is more simply expressed, and yet I would argue that it is more profound,
than are the Law Lords' opinions. The document explicitly rejects the "false
contrast" between religious and secular values. It makes it clear that "[n]either
of our Churches insists that a dying or seriously ill person should be kept alive
by all possible means for as long as possible". This is not to say that it is
irrefutable by Law Lords or others, still less that it should have determined the
result in *Bland*, or indeed that it gives a clear indication of what the churches
believe that result should have been. My point is rather to illustrate that there is
nothing mystifying about such presentations of a moral viewpoint and that Law
Lords have nothing to fear and much to gain from taking them seriously.

This is particularly important because when it comes to jostling with
Parliament for the poisoned chalice of resolving moral dilemmas, the Law Lords
of the next couple of decades are likely to be more adventurous, as illustrated by
the enthusiasm with which Lord Hoffmann (as he now is) engaged with the
moral questions in the Court of Appeal in *Bland* and by the prolific and erudite
way in which Sir John Laws and Sir Stephen Sedley pepper the law journals with
their constitutional theorising.[8] These two must count as two of our most distinguished, and certainly most prolific, constitutional thinkers. They seem to
relish the prospect of British judges facing moral questions in our highest courts,
not surprisingly in the view of cynics who expect this to happen around the time
that Sirs John and Stephen arrive in the Appellate Committee. When they join
Lord Hoffmann there, few will doubt that the Law Lords will drop what I
described above as their first line of defence and be more than willing to by-pass,
override or supplement Parliament.

[8] John Laws, "Law and Democracy" [1995] *PL* 72; Stephen Sedley, "Human Rights: A Twenty-
first Century Agenda" [1995] *PL* 386.

The second point therefore becomes all the more important. The Law Lords should not rely implicitly on an assumption that moral discourse can be reduced to two lines of argument, one secular and the other religious. In particular, if they are going to address the moral questions seriously, they should hear (or at least read, through *amicus* briefs filed by interested and informed "third parties") arguments from and about the different positions.

This could be seen as a plea for professors of jurisprudence to have our day in court. Certainly, legal philosophers have contributed to *Bland* after the event and, not surprisingly, with contradictory views. It is natural, one might say, for the doyen of contemporary natural lawyers, John Finnis, to lambast all nine judges in Bland.[9] One of his criticisms is directed principally at Hoffmann L.J., whose judgment would generally be regarded as the most philosophically honed. Nonetheless, for Finnis the "philosophy" in the judgments is diabolical. To give just one example of Finnis' criticism of the judges, after quoting Hoffmann's dictum that Bland's "body is alive, but he has no life", Finnis concludes that:

> "This sort of dualism, which thinks of the body as if it were some kind of habitation for and instrument of the real person, is defended by few philosophers indeed (religious or otherwise). It renders inexplicable the unity in complexity which one experiences in everything one consciously does."

On the other hand, Neil MacCormick is more positive, and positivist, about the Law Lords in *Bland*:

> "one vital point of legal institutions is exactly that they exist (inter alia) to settle authoritatively for practical purposes what cannot be settled morally. Citizens of this country still disagree morally about the right way to treat PVS patients. . . . But . . . the judges have . . . pronounced on the issues raised, and the law is for the time being settled in quite clearly formulated terms on points that are unsettlable morally."[10]

More generally, MacCormick believes that:

> "law is institutional where morality is controversial and personal; law is authoritative, settling questions by acts of authority, where morality is discursive, always open to fresh argument on equal terms by any interested participant in the discourse; finally, law is heteronomous, binding us from without, where morality is autonomous, binding us by our own reflective judgment and will."

MacCormick uses *Bland* throughout his essay to illustrate the importance of a decisive ruling which can guide citizens in future dilemmas. He sees this as the essence of law's role in society. From this perspective, the Law Lords in Bland can be congratulated on providing a clear, authoritative ruling. For Finnis, in contrast, the Law Lords should be berated for coming to the wrong conclusion through poor reasoning.

---

[9] John Finnis, "*Bland*: Crossing the Rubicon?" (1993) 109 *LQR* 329.
[10] Neil MacCormick, "The Concept of Law in *The Concept of Law*" in Robert P. George (ed.), *The Autonomy of Law* (Oxford, OUP, 1996).

Much as I enjoyed John Finnis' swift case-note (July 1993) and Neil MacCormick's even quicker incorporation of *Bland* into his lecture (May 1993, although published some three years later), it is not with the intention of providing openings for professors of jurisprudence that I would argue for the systematic use of *amicus* briefs to address the moral questions *before* the Law Lords decide. Nor is my concern to be regarded as any criticism of the *amicus curiae* in the case, Anthony Lester Q.C. I have long since been an advocate of the involvement of just such a lawyer in these cases and I welcome the growing use of *amici curiae* in medical law and ethics more generally. Nor am I suggesting that the Law Lords were unaware of religious arguments—Lord Browne-Wilkinson, in a phrase mentioned above, says that "[t]*he evidence* shows that the Roman Catholic church and orthodox Jews are opposed" (emphasis added) so one assumes that some of the arguments were put to their Lordships.

What we do not yet get from the Law Lords, however, is any *engagement* with such arguments. Nor will we, so long as the twin lines can be run that it is really for Parliament to deal with the moral dilemmas and that meanwhile all we can expect from a Law Lord is to steer between the Scylla of crude utilitarianism and the Charybdis of crude religiosity. This is not simply a failing in the courts, for part of the blame for the latter point can also be directed at the churches themselves. In the United Kingdom, their hierarchies are comfortable with making submissions to *legislative* bodies (not that the legislature did much in this instance, the House of Lords Select Committee saying little more than that the courts were jolly good at dealing with this and should be left to it, notwithstanding the fact that the Committee was established in response to the Law Lords' point, mentioned above, that Parliament ought to address the issue). They should, however, be more willing to engage in dialogue with the *courts* as contentious cases proceed through the judicial system and the judges should respond in kind. This is illustrated, to give but one example, by the influential brief filed by the Catholic church before the Zimbabwe Supreme Court's rejection of the death penalty.[11] Instead, the tendency in the UK is for pressure groups to seize the initiative and to become identified in and by the media as if they represented churches or other faith communities.

In any event, it is at least some kind of progress towards more rounded decision-making on matters of law and morals that philosophers have recently begun to feature in English judicial opinions. In this context, the turning-point for English judgments on moral issues could prove to be Hoffmann L.J.'s exegesis in *Bland*, albeit in the Court of Appeal. He described the case as presenting a "terrible decision", but chose to answer the legal point very briefly so that he could instead focus on the ethical issues because "this case has caused a great deal of public concern". In an important passage, he explains that:

> "This is not an area in which any difference can be allowed to exist between what is legal and what is morally right. The decision of the court should be able to carry con-

[11] *Catholic Commission for Justice and Peace in Zimbabwe* v. *Attorney-General, Zimbabwe and Others* 1993 (4) SA 239.

viction with the ordinary person as being based not merely on legal precedent but also upon acceptable ethical values. . . . To argue from moral rather than purely legal principles is a somewhat unusual enterprise for a judge to undertake. It is not the function of judges to lay down systems of morals and nothing which I say is intended to do so. But it seemed to me that in such an unusual case as this, it would clarify my own thought and perhaps help others, if I tried to examine the underlying moral principles which have led me to the conclusion at which I have arrived. In doing so, I must acknowledge the assistance I have received from reading the manuscript of Professor Ronald Dworkin's forthcoming book, *Life's Dominion*, and from conversations with him and Professor Bernard Williams."[11a]

If this is "progress", however, some may be unenthusiastic. The idea of judges chatting (in the pub?) to pals who happen to be philosophers, or even conversing in senior common rooms or on the cocktail party circuit, or anywhere else except in open court, might seem to violate the principle that counsel should be privy to, and able to comment on, all the influences which are set before the judicial decision-maker. That principle has probably been honoured only in the breach hitherto, however, so what is unusual is more the judge's willingness to acknowledge publicly the kind of help which judges have previously sought privately and the fact that the charmed circle is not simply confined to lawyers. These are positive developments even if the judge is relying on philosophical insights not vouchsafed to the parties and from a narrow band of like-minded thinkers. The effort to address the moral questions is to be welcomed even if, like John Finnis, one finds the judgment philosophically defective.

What is lacking, however, is the failure to engage with arguments from somebody who took a radically different stance, such as John Finnis, or indeed the combined Anglican and Catholic bishops. There is a world of difference between the judge setting up his view of the relevant slogans and choosing between them, on the one hand, and the judge setting out the reasoned position of, say, various faith communities or philosophers and then explaining point by point where they err. If this were an essay on the Court of Appeal, a detailed analysis of this particular judgment ought to follow, but since this is part of an assessment of the Law Lords, our interest lies in a different direction.

In this context, the significance of Hoffmann L.J.'s judgment in *Bland* is at least fourfold. First, it gives us a glimpse of the future, as to how ethical issues will feature in judgments of the next generation of Law Lords. Secondly, it reveals that judges do consult philosophers and points, I would argue, towards the need for this to be more widespread, systematised and open. Thirdly, it shows that the most talented lawyer, even one with a philosophical bent, can give a movingly written account of the ethical issues which another legal philosopher will dismiss as nonsense. Fourthly, it shows by contrast the weakness of the Law Lords' efforts in *Bland*, where they dodge the issue.

Now *Bland* is not an isolated case of "moral unease". Lord Mustill, for example, has spotted the moral dimension to several decisions during the 1990s. He

[11a] [1993] 1 All ER 821 at 850h.

even begins one judgment in an asylum case with a sentence including the "high moral ground" although those who expect this to be occupied by Law Lords will be disappointed to learn that he is discussing those whom he later says the unsympathetic nowadays describe as "terrorists":

> "My Lords, during the nineteenth century those who used violence to challenge despotic regimes often occupied the high moral ground, and were welcomed in foreign countries as true patriots and democrats. Now, much has changed."[12]

In the leading case on the giving of reasons in public law, *Doody v. Home Secretary*,[13] Lord Mustill reduces the legal issues to the simple moral question: is it fair? In *R. v. Kingston*,[14] he deals with misunderstandings about the need for moral culpability in the criminal law:

> "The professional burglar is guilty in a moral as well as a legal sense; he intends to break into the house to steal, and most would confidently assert that this is wrong. But this will not always be so. In respect of some offences the mind of the defendant, and still less his moral judgment, may not be engaged at all. Such cases are not uncommon."

His dissenting judgment in the sado-masochism case of *R. v. Brown* also shows that he is prepared to assert when he thinks that the Law Lords are *not* being asked to make moral judgments:

> "it must be emphasised that the issue before the House is not whether the appellants' conduct is morally right but whether it is properly charged under the 1861 Act. When proposing that the conduct is not rightly so charged I do not invite your Lordships' House to indorse it as morally acceptable. Nor do I pronounce in favour of a libertarian doctrine specifically related to sexual matters. Nor in the least do I suggest that ethical pronouncements are meaningless, that there is no difference between right and wrong, that sadism is praiseworthy, or that new opinions on sexual morality are necessarily superior to the old, or anything else of the same kind."[15]

Reassuring though those comments will be to many, it might be thought that it is still a moral question which faced the Law Lords in *Brown*, although not the moral question which the majority thought. For it is a moral question whether the law should enforce, or reinforce, moral values of one sort or another. Indeed, it is also a moral question whether society should penalise conduct through the criminal law when there might have been reasonable doubt about its criminality at the time it was undertaken. Neither of these is the moral question whether the conduct in question was right or wrong, of course, so Lord Mustill's approach is right in so far as it goes.

The trouble is that it does not go far enough, and that is the central problem with the Law Lords in cases of moral unease, up to and including the 1990s. The Law Lords are increasingly prepared to acknowledge a moral dimension to their

---

[12]   *T v. Secretary of State for the Home Office* [1996] 2 All ER 865 at 867.
[13]   [1993] 3 All ER 92.
[14]   [1994] 3 All ER 353 at 360.
[15]   [1993] 2 All ER 75 at 115–16.

decision-making, which is to be welcomed. Whether they always spot *the* most pertinent moral dimension(s) is less clear, however, and they have yet to engage with the moral arguments in anything like the depths into which Hoffmann L.J. dived in the Court of Appeal, no doubt for fear of drowning. Even his efforts have been dismissed as if he were merely paddling in shallow waters.

Which brings us back to the starting-point of this chapter and the readiness with which judges call on Parliament to explore the issues which make for uneasy cases and depict themselves as steering a safe course pending such an inquiry. Having begun with Lord Mustill, it is appropriate to conclude with Lord Browne-Wilkinson, who also developed this theme in his address to the conference which gave rise to this collection.[16] Lord Browne-Wilkinson's judgment was obviously thoughtful, sympathetic and full of moral and legal unease, but that does not mean it is beyond criticism.

On our first point, it seemed to his Lordship "imperative that the moral, social and legal issues raised by this case should be considered by Parliament".[16a] Although the House of Lords in its legislative capacity (or, cynics would say, in its fobbing-off capacity) did indeed look at the matter, it did so to no effect. Some would say that it is entirely predictable that the Lords, including the Law Lords, and even more so the Commons, will as part of the legislature ignore, or merely pay lip-service to, calls from the Law Lords as the apex of the judiciary to review the law. Has the time come, therefore, to move on from the ritual incantation that it would be better for others to address the issue outside the confines and urgency of a particular uneasy case? Does the failure of Parliament to respond meaningfully suggest that the judges have to be more adventurous in grappling with the issues in a deeper way? On our second point, Lord Browne-Wilkinson ended his judgment by apparently conceding that it would:

> "appear to some to be almost irrational. How can it be lawful to allow a patient to die slowly, though painlessly, over a period of weeks from lack of food but unlawful to produce his immediate death by a lethal injection, thereby saving his family from yet another ordeal to add to the tragedy that has already struck them? I find it difficult to find a moral answer to that question. But it is undoubtedly the law."[16b]

What connects these two points is, of course, Lord Browne-Wilkinson's theory of adjudication in what I would call uneasy cases. To his credit, he has at least set it out clearly:

> "Where a case raises wholly new moral and social issues, in my judgment it is not for the judges to seek to develop new, all-embracing, principles of law in a way which reflects the individual judges' moral stance when society as a whole is substantially divided on the relevant moral issues."[16c]

---

[16] This was a Colloquium in Belfast organised by the University of Ulster in May 1995. Lord Browne-Wilkinson's remarks were not presented in the form of a written paper.
[16a] [1993] 1 All ER 821 at 879j.
[16b] *Ibid.,* at 884f.
[16c] *Ibid.,* at 879g.

There is much in this with which I would agree but it does not follow that the judge should rest content, or even rest uneasy, with an answer which makes no moral sense even to the judge. What I like about this formulation is that it recognises moral and social dimensions, what I would call questions of evaluating policy considerations, that it recognises divisions and that it is the formulation of a position as to the judges' role in our democracy in the 1990s (in contrast to some theories of adjudication which seem to freeze the role as if every judge in every context should act like a US Supreme Court Justice in the 1950s). What I dislike, however, is the assumption that the question is whether or not the judges are asked to inveigle their own moral stances into the law. As I have indicated above, there are several layers of moral questions in a case like *Brown*. It is not the judges' personal views on the (im)morality of sado-masochism which we are seeking. What we should expect is that the Law Lords ought to seek out well-argued presentations of a range of moral positions and then sift through them, treating them with at least as much respect as they would arguments of precedent or statutory interpretation, weighing them, explaining why they accept or reject them or wish to recast them in some way.

Moral arguments are not the preserve of professors of jurisprudence or philosophers more generally. There is a role for theology, *pace* Professor Glanville Williams, who long ago sought to banish this discipline from the ambit of the law:

> "For the legislator (*a fortiori* the judge), it seems sufficient to say that theological speculations and controversies should have no place in the formation of rules of law, least of all the rules of the criminal law which are imposed upon believers and non-believers alike."[17]

The proposal was memorably described by Professor Basil Mitchell as being we "should be permitted to listen to Lady Wootton but not to the Archbishop of Canterbury (unless, perhaps, he forgets his theology)".[18] Professor Mitchell rejected this proposition, suspecting that "the critic likes theology to be doctrinaire enough to be discounted with impunity. We are more comfortable with stereotypes. We are happy to know that our theologians are doctrinaire and irrelevant, just as we are happy to know that our dons are remote and ineffectual."

The Law Lords, then, have rich veins of theological and philosophical arguments which they ought to tap as they face more and more cases of acute moral unease. What is encouraging in the 1990s is that the judges are beginning to acknowledge the breadth and depth of the moral issues which increasingly face them. What we need for the new millennium is a willingness to expand the horizons of argument before the courts so as to respond to these challenges. This would recognise that our democracy is changing as Parliament shows itself to be even less willing to come to terms with these dilemmas and the judges display an enthusiasm for greater involvement. The way forward is for the judges to be ever more explicit about how they see their roles and about exactly why they are

---

[17] See Glanville Williams, *The Sanctity of Life and the Criminal Law* (London, Faber, 1958).
[18] Basil Mitchell, *Law, Morality & Religion in a Secular Society* (Oxford, OUP, 1967).

accepting or rejecting countervailing arguments as to how they should evaluate the consequences of alternative decisions in these uneasy cases. This is the moral of *Bland*. It is that the Law Lords' task in uneasy cases is a moral one of evaluating competing arguments, not an amoral one of choosing a safe option in the absence of a wider-ranging enterprise undertaken by the legislature.

APPENDIX

A JOINT SUBMISSION FROM THE CHURCH OF ENGLAND HOUSE OF BISHOPS AND THE ROMAN CATHOLIC BISHOPS' CONFERENCE OF ENGLAND AND WALES TO THE HOUSE OF LORDS SELECT COMMITTEE ON MEDICAL ETHICS

## Foundations

1. The arguments presented in this submission grow out of our belief that God himself has given to humankind the gift of life. As such, it is to be revered and cherished.
2. Christian beliefs about the special nature and value of human life lie at the root of the Western Christian humanist tradition, which remains greatly influential in shaping the values held by many in our society. They are also shared in whole or in part by other faith communities.
3. All human beings are to be valued, irrespective of age, sex, race, religion, social status or their potential for achievement.
4. Those who become vulnerable through illness or disability deserve special care and protection. Adherence to this principle provides a fundamental test as to what constitutes a civilized society.
5. The whole of humankind is the recipient of God's gift of life. It is to be received with gratitude and used responsibly. Human beings each have their own distinct identities but these are formed by and take their place within complex networks of relationships. All decisions about individual lives bear upon others with whom we live in community.
6. For this reason, the law relating to euthanasia is not simply concerned either with private morality or with utilitarian approaches. On this issue there can be no moral or ethical pluralism. A positive choice has to be made by society in favour of protecting the interests of its vulnerable members even if this means limiting the freedom of others to determine their end.

## The sanctity of life and the right to personal autonomy

7. Attention is often drawn to the apparent conflict between the importance placed by Christians on the special character of human life as God-given and thus deserving of special protection, and the insistence by some on their right to determine when their lives should end.

8. This contrast can be falsely presented. Neither of our Churches insists that a dying or seriously ill person should be kept alive by all possible means for as long as possible. On the other hand we do not believe that the right to personal autonomy is absolute. It is valid only when it recognises other moral values, especially the respect due to human life as such, whether someone else's or one's own.

9. We do not accept that the right to personal autonomy requires any change in the law in order to allow euthanasia.

10. The exercise of personal autonomy necessarily has to be limited in order that human beings may live together in reasonable harmony. Such limitation may have to be defined by law. While at present people may exercise their right to refuse treatment (although this may be overridden in special but strictly limited circumstances), the law forbids a right to die at a time of their own choosing. The consequences which could flow from a change in the law on voluntary euthanasia would outweigh the benefits to be gained from more rigid adherence to the notion of personal autonomy. But in any case we believe (paragraph 6) that respect for the life of a vulnerable person is the overriding principle.

11. The right of personal autonomy cannot demand action on the part of another. Patients cannot and should not be able to demand that doctors collaborate in bringing about their deaths, which is intrinsically illegal or wrong.

12. It would be difficult to be sure that requests for euthanasia were truly voluntary and settled, even if safeguards were built into the legislation, and not the result either of depression or of undue pressure from other people. Circumstances may be envisaged in which a doctor managing scarce resources might, perhaps unwittingly, bring undue pressure to bear on a patient to request voluntary euthanasia. Similarly families anxious to relinquish the burden of caring (or to achieve financial gain) might exert influence. Experience suggests that legislative change can lead to significant changes in social attitudes, and that such changes can quickly extend into supporting actions which were not envisaged by the legislature.

## The distinction between killing and letting die

13. Because human life is a gift from God to be preserved and cherished, the deliberate taking of human life is prohibited except in self-defence or the legitimate defence of others. Therefore, both Churches are resolutely opposed to the legalisation of euthanasia even though it may be put forward as a means of relieving suffering, shortening the anguish of families or friends, or saving scarce resources.

14. There is a distinction between deliberate killing and the shortening of life through the administration of painkilling drugs. There is a proper and

fundamental ethical distinction which cannot be ignored between that which is intended and that which is foreseen but unintended. For example, the administration of morphine is intended to relieve pain. The consequent shortening of life is foreseen but unintended. If safer drugs were available, they would be used: pain would be controlled and life would not be shortened.

15. Doctors do not have an overriding obligation to prolong life by all available means. The Declaration on Euthanasia in 1980 by the Sacred Congregation for the Doctrine of the Faith proposes the notion that treatment for a dying patient should be "proportionate" to the therapeutic effect to be expected, and should not be disproportionately painful, intrusive, risky, or costly, in the circumstances. Treatment may therefore be withheld or withdrawn. This is an area requiring fine judgement. Such decisions should be made collaboratively and by more than one medically qualified person. They should be guided by the principle that a pattern of care should never be adopted with the intention, purpose or aim of terminating the life or bringing about the death of a patient. Death, if it ensues, will have resulted from the underlying condition which required medical intervention, not as a direct consequence of the decision to withhold or withdraw treatment. It is possible however to envisage cases where withholding or withdrawing treatment might be morally equivalent to murder.

16. The recent judgment in the House of Lords to permit the withdrawal of artificial nutrition and hydration from the PVS patient, Tony Bland, must not be used as an argument for the existing law to be changed. As with the general question of proportionate means, the complexity of the issue of artificial nutrition and hydration and the associated medical regimes means that there can be no blanket permission as regards PVS patients or those in a similar situation. At the very least, every person's needs and rights must be dealt with on a case to case basis.

### The extent of the doctor's duty of care

17. The preceding paragraphs have touched on limits to treatment. The value attaching to human life implies that the primary duties of doctors are to ensure that patients are as free from pain as possible, that they are given such information as they and their carers request and require to make choices about their future lives, and that they are supported through the personal challenges which face them. We believe that to accede to requests for voluntary euthanasia would result in a breakdown of trust between doctors and their patients. Medical treatment might come to be regarded by the vulnerable person as potentially life-threatening rather than something which confers benefit.

### The treatment of patients who cannot express their own wishes

18. Where formerly competent people have expressed their wishes about the way they would like to be treated, these should form an important consideration for doctors in determining how to proceed. Such wishes can only act as guidelines since medical conditions may exist for which they are inappropriate. If such wishes are unknown or inappropriate, or if a person has never been competent to express such wishes, then decisions about treatment should be worked out between doctors, families, carers and other health service personnel such as social workers or hospital chaplains.

### Advance directives

19. Advance directives may be useful as a means of enabling discussion between doctors and patients about future treatment. Where they exist, they can only be advisory. They should not contain requests for action which is outside the law, nor ask for the cessation of artificial nutrition and hydration. Care should be taken to establish that any advance directive was not made under duress. We would resist the legal enforcement of such directives since the medical conditions envisaged might be susceptible to new treatment, and medical judgements would have to be made about whether a person's condition was such as to require their advance directive to take effect.

### Care of terminally ill people

20. The hospice movement developed from the concern of Christians that people should be helped to die with dignity. This work has enriched not only the lives of terminally ill people but also their carers, volunteers and health professionals, who have found that caring for those who are dying can be a great source of blessing.
21. We are concerned that the lessons learned in hospices about pain control, and emotional and spiritual support should be applied throughout the health service to all dying people. This requires that medical personnel remain aware of how advice on pain control may be obtained, and that adequate resources are made available for the care of sick and elderly people.
22. We believe that deliberately to kill a dying person would be to reject them. Our duty is to be with them, to offer appropriate physical, emotional and spiritual help in their anxiety and depression, and to communicate through our presence and care that they are supported by their fellow human beings and the divine presence.

# Index